REHEATED

Liō

BRAND ©

Other Liō books by Mark Tatulli

Liō: Happiness Is a Squishy Cephalopod
Silent But Deadly
Liō's Astonishing Tales
There's Corpses Everywhere

A Delicious Liō Collection Ready to Devour

by Mark Tatulli

Andrews McMeel
Publishing, LLC
Kansas City • Sydney • London

Liō is distributed internationally by Universal Uclick.

Andrews McMeel Publishing, LLC
an Andrews McMeel Universal company
1130 Walnut Street, Kansas City, Missouri 64106

www.andrewsmcmeel.com

11 12 13 14 15 WKT 10 9 8 7 6 5 4 3 2 1

ISBN: 978-1-4494-0794-0

Library of Congress Control Number: 2011921394

To Donna
x o x o

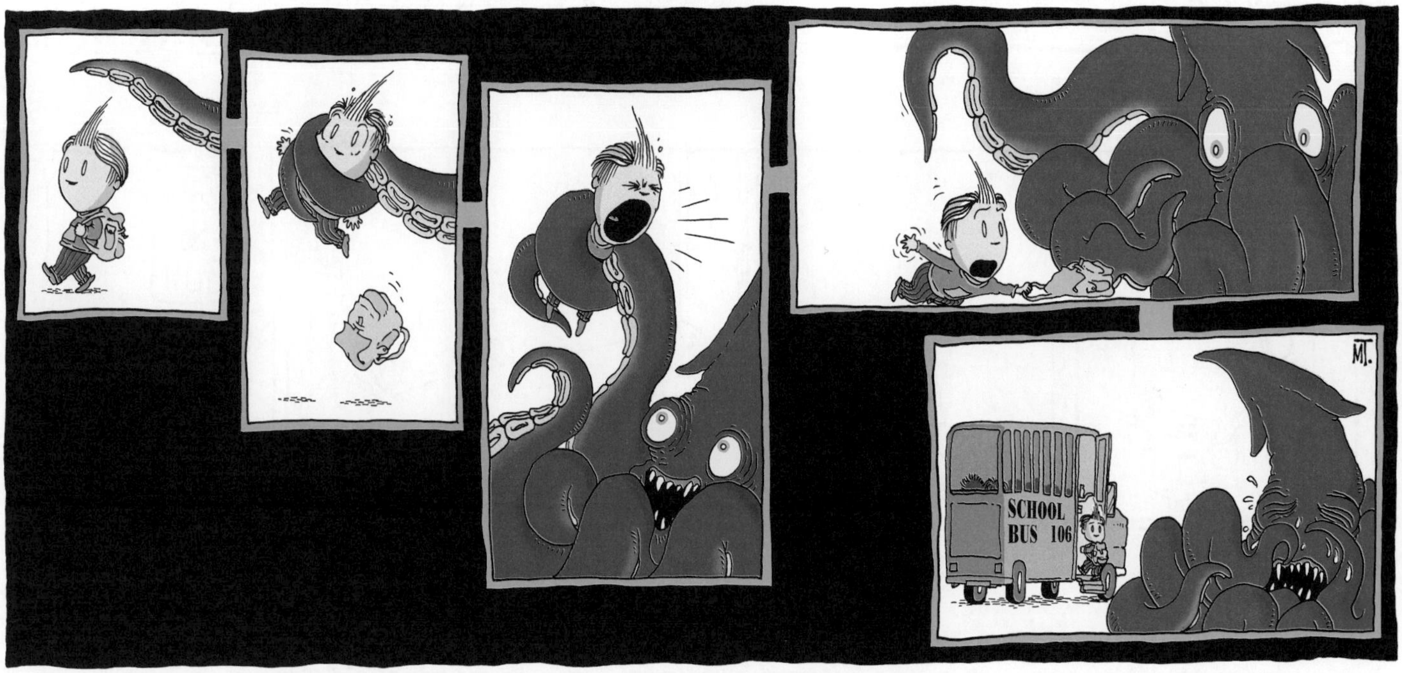
SCHOOL
BUS 106

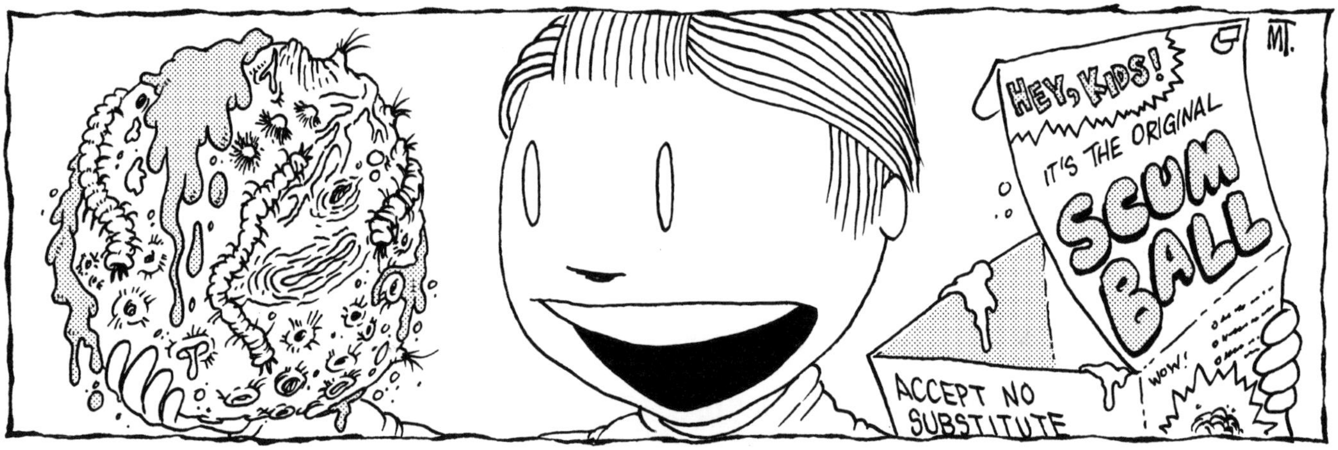
HEY, KIDS!
IT'S THE ORIGINAL
SCUM BALL
WOW!
ACCEPT NO SUBSTITUTE
MT.

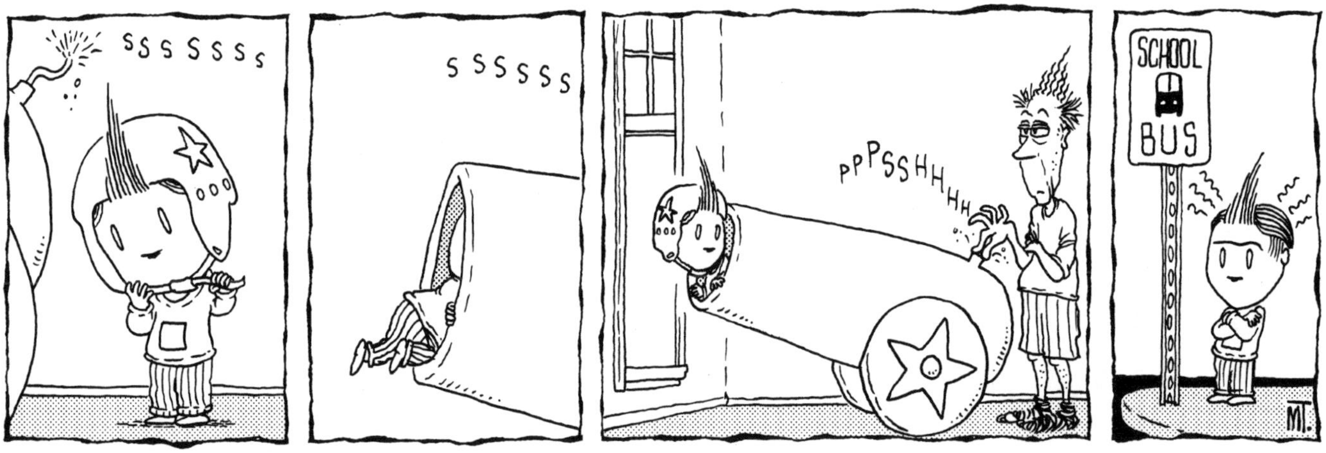
SSSSSSS
SSSSSS
PPPSSHHHHH
SCHOOL
BUS
MT.

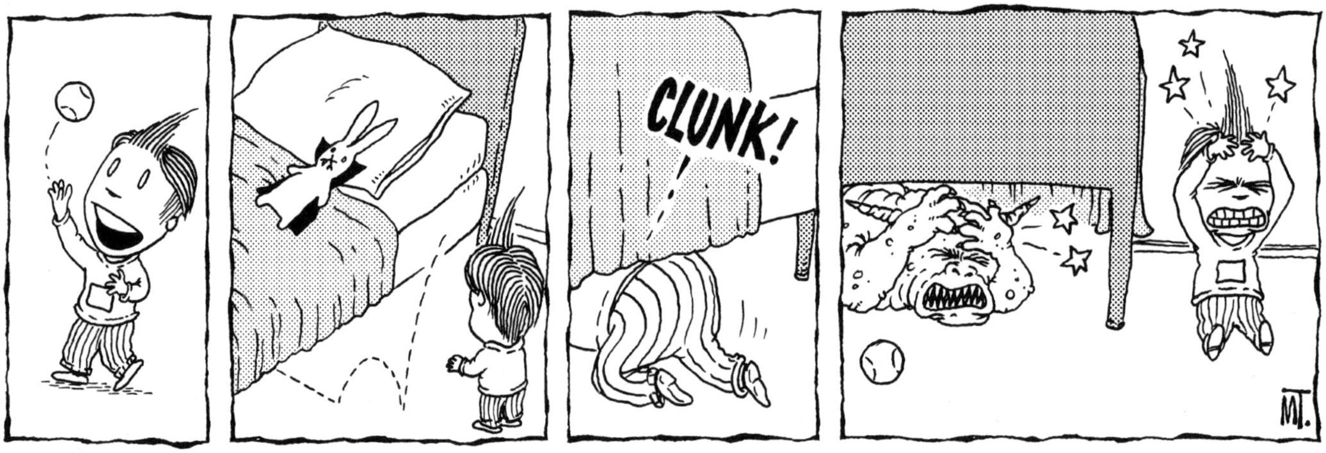
CLUNK!
MT.

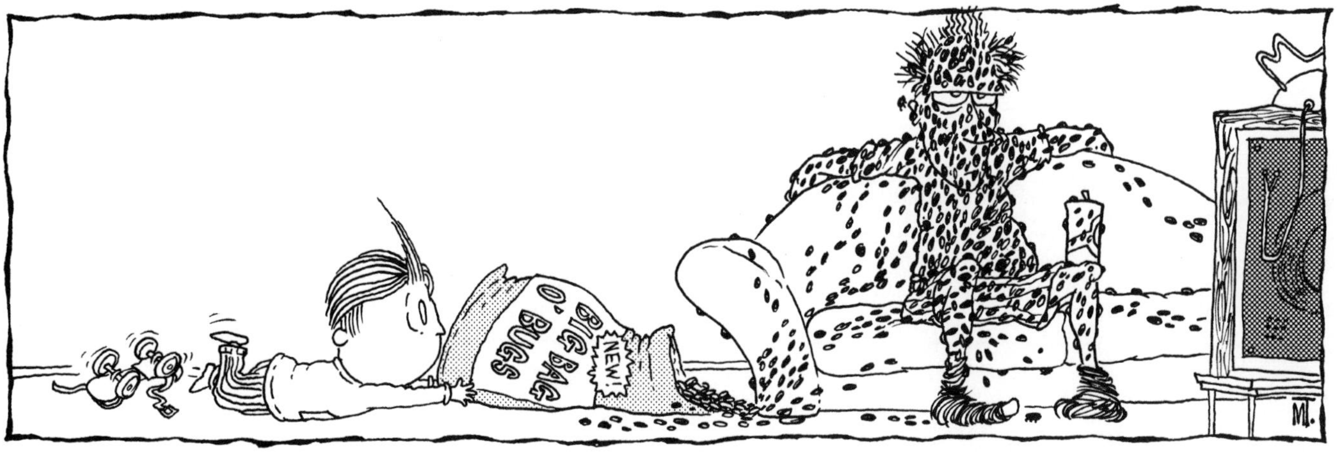
BIG BAG O' BUGS
NEW!

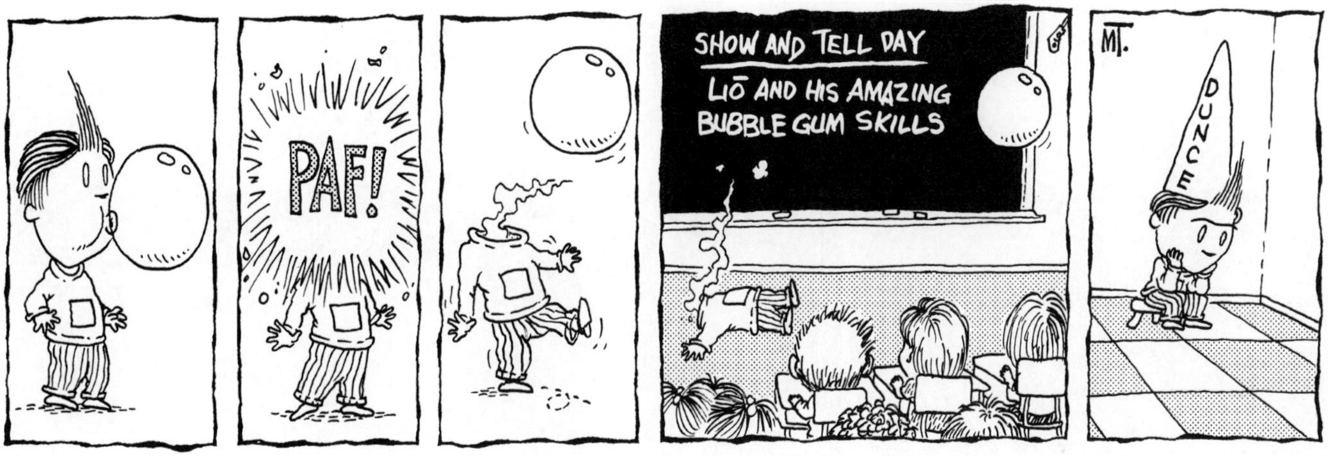
PAF!
SHOW AND TELL DAY
LIŌ AND HIS AMAZING BUBBLE GUM SKILLS
DUNCE

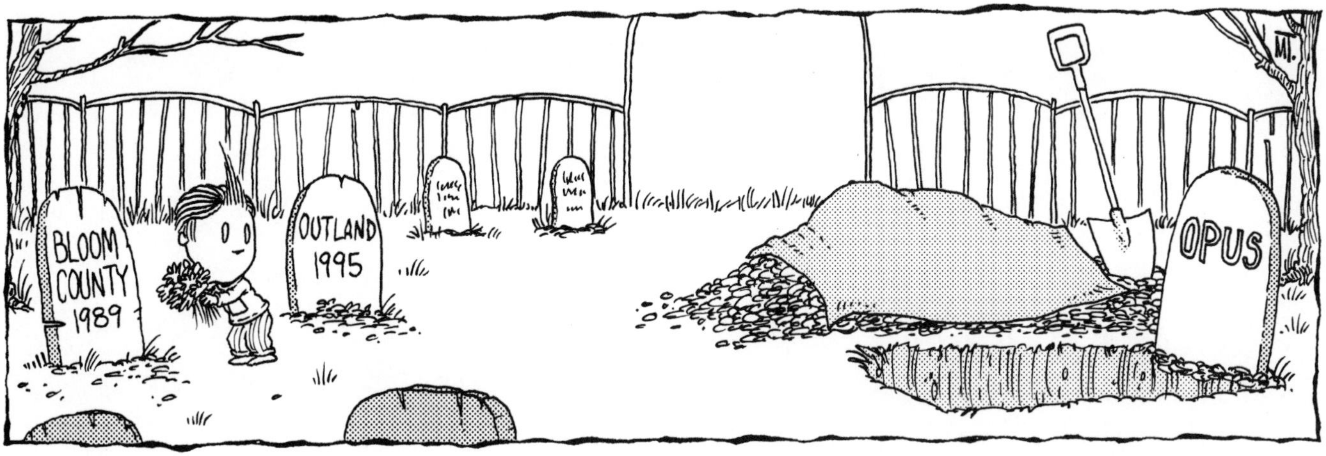
BLOOM COUNTY 1989
OUTLAND 1995
OPUS

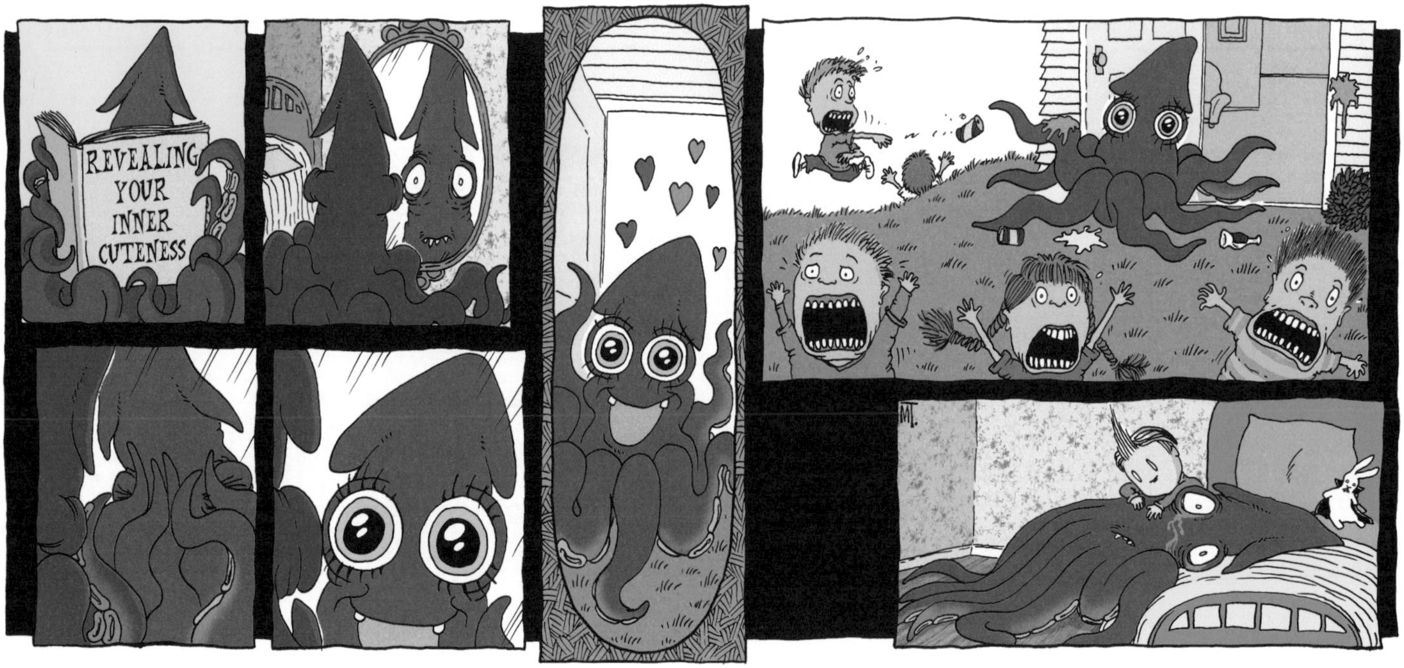
REVEALING YOUR INNER CUTENESS
MT.

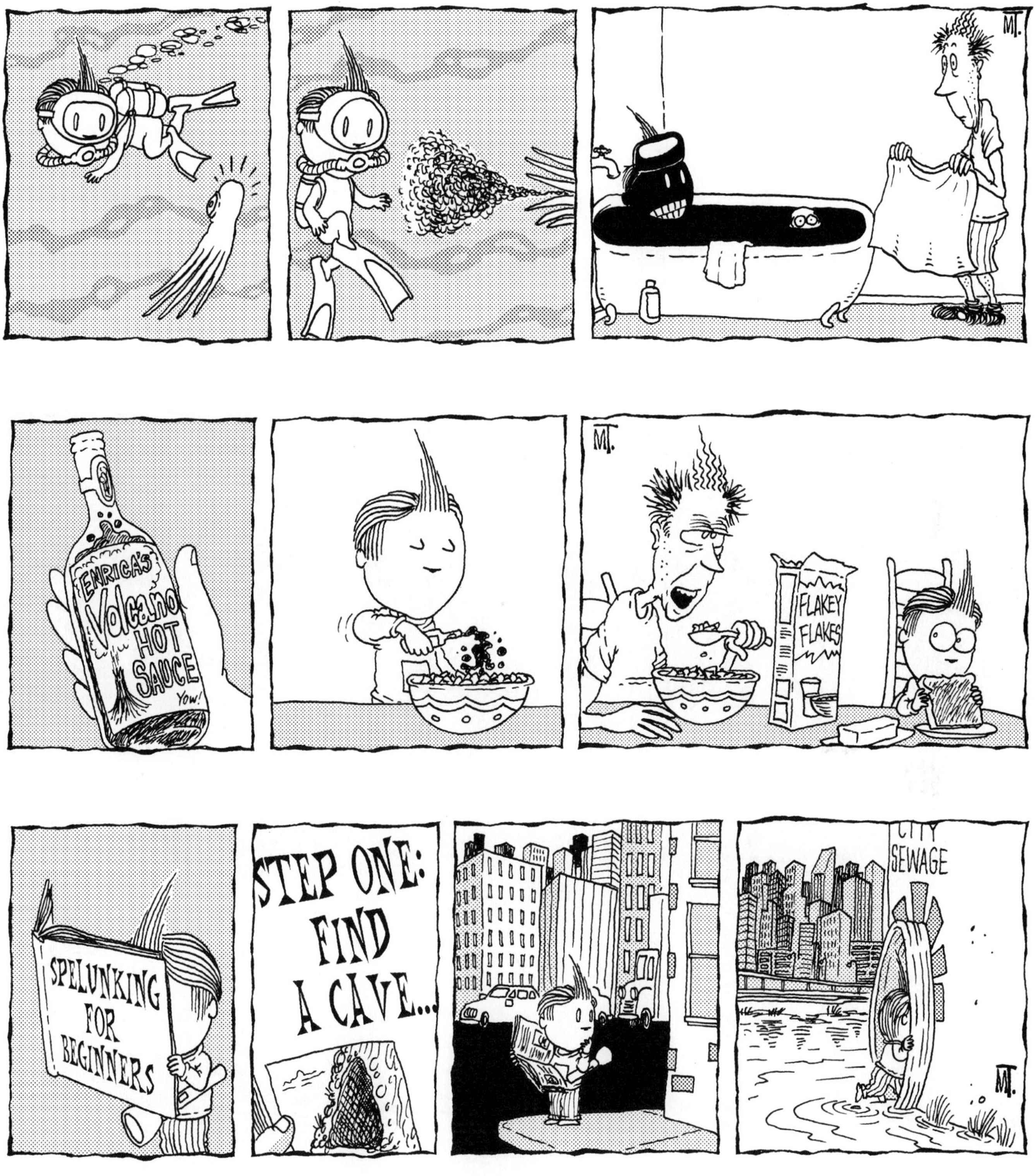
MT.
ENRICA'S
Volcano
HOT
SAUCE
YOW!
MT.
FLAKEY
FLAKES
SPELUNKING
FOR
BEGINNERS
STEP ONE:
FIND
A CAVE...
CITY
SEWAGE
MT.

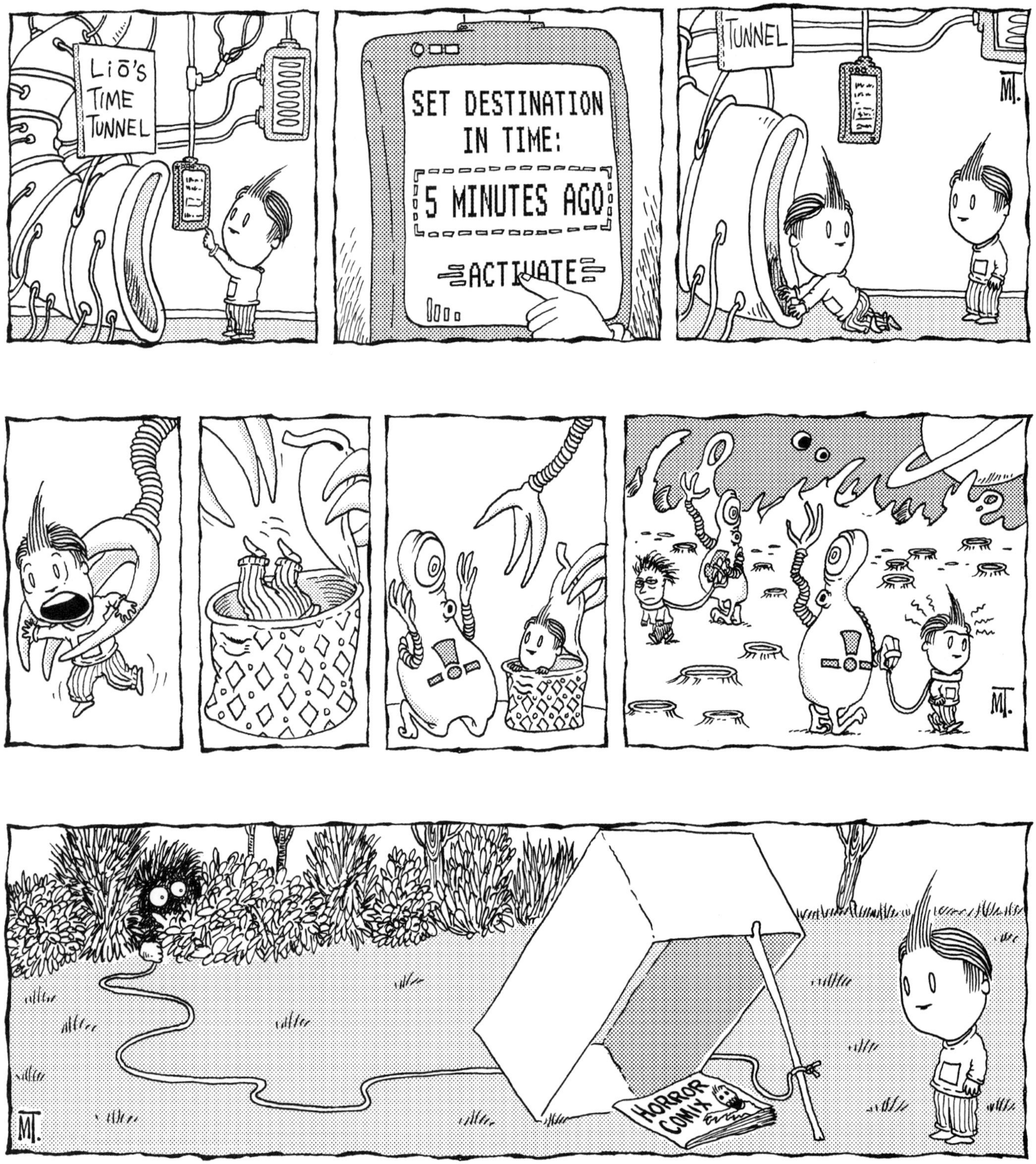
LIŌ'S TIME TUNNEL
SET DESTINATION IN TIME:
5 MINUTES AGO
ACTIVATE
TUNNEL
HORROR COMIX
MT.

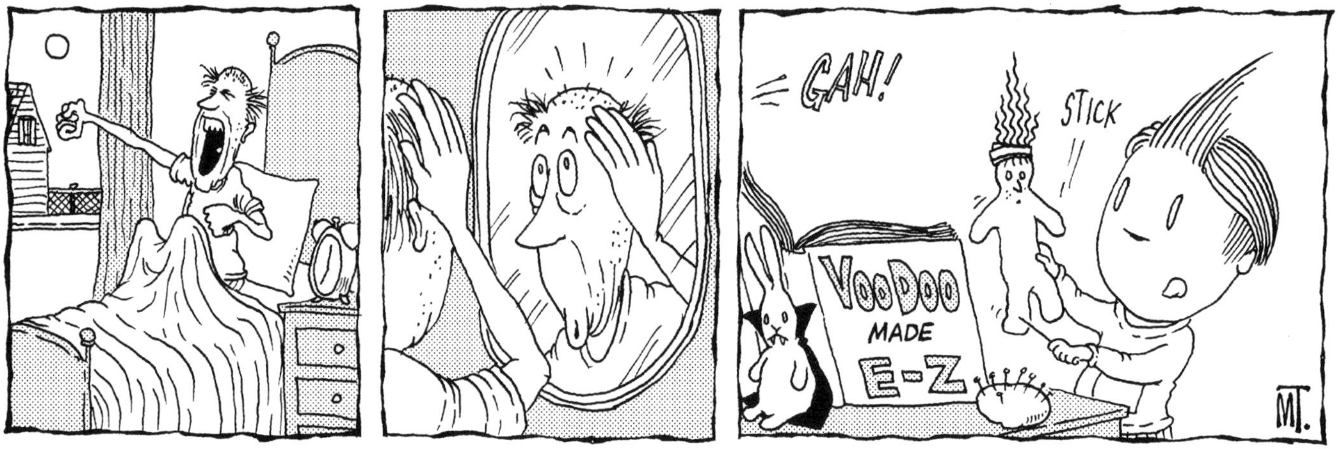
GAH!
STICK
VOODOO MADE E-Z
MT.

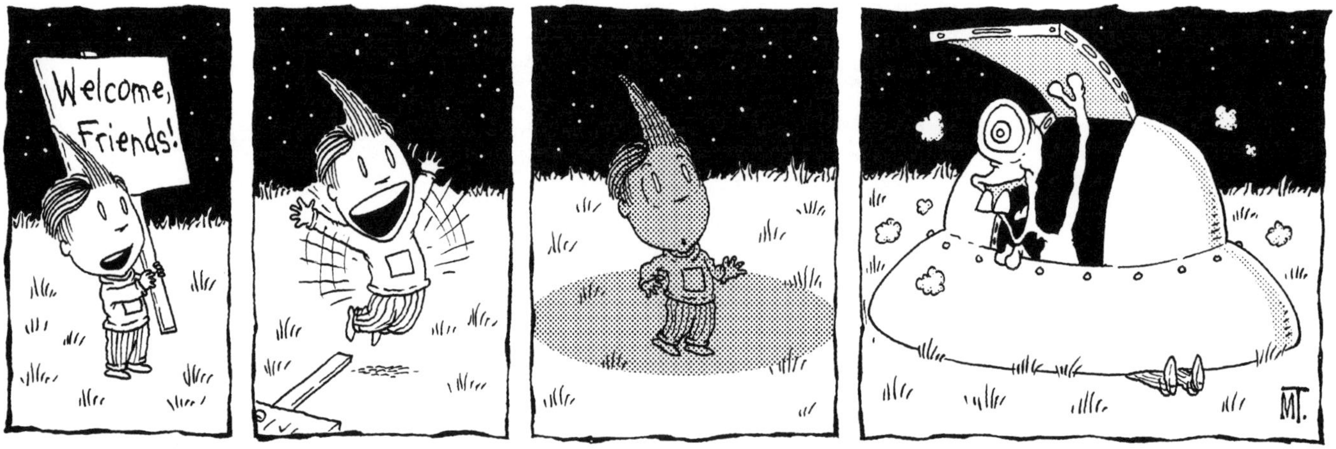
Welcome, Friends!
MT.

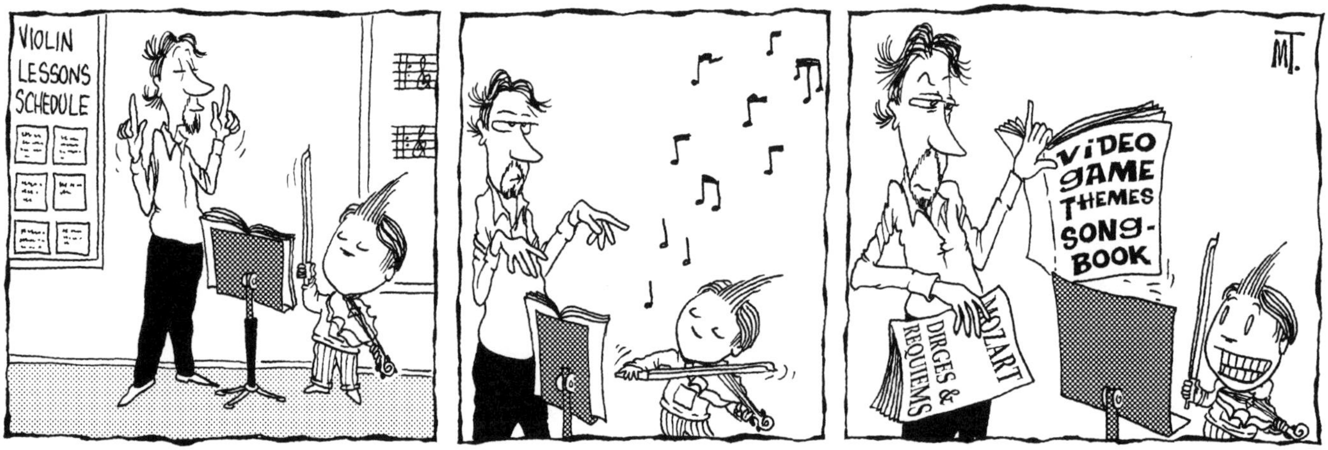
VIOLIN LESSONS SCHEDULE
MT.
VIDEO GAME THEMES SONG-BOOK
MOZART
DIRGES & REQUIEMS

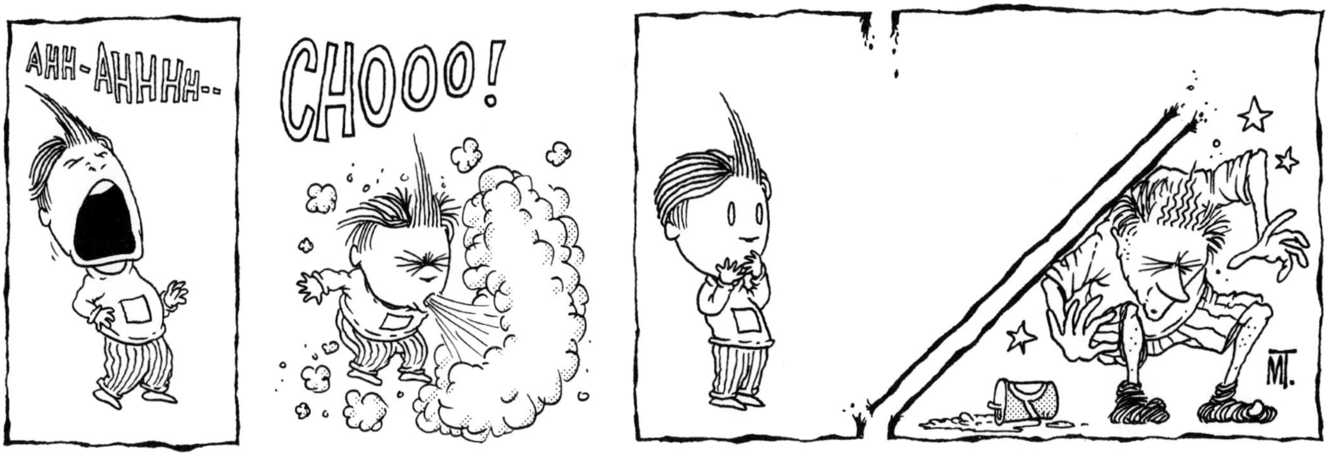
AHH-AHHHHH--
CHOOO!

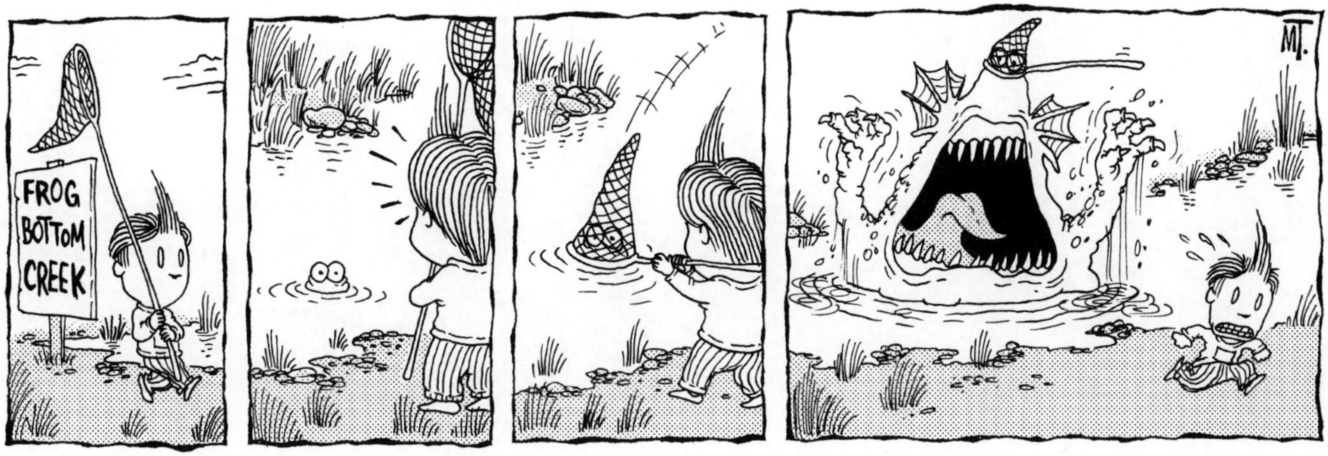
FROG BOTTOM CREEK

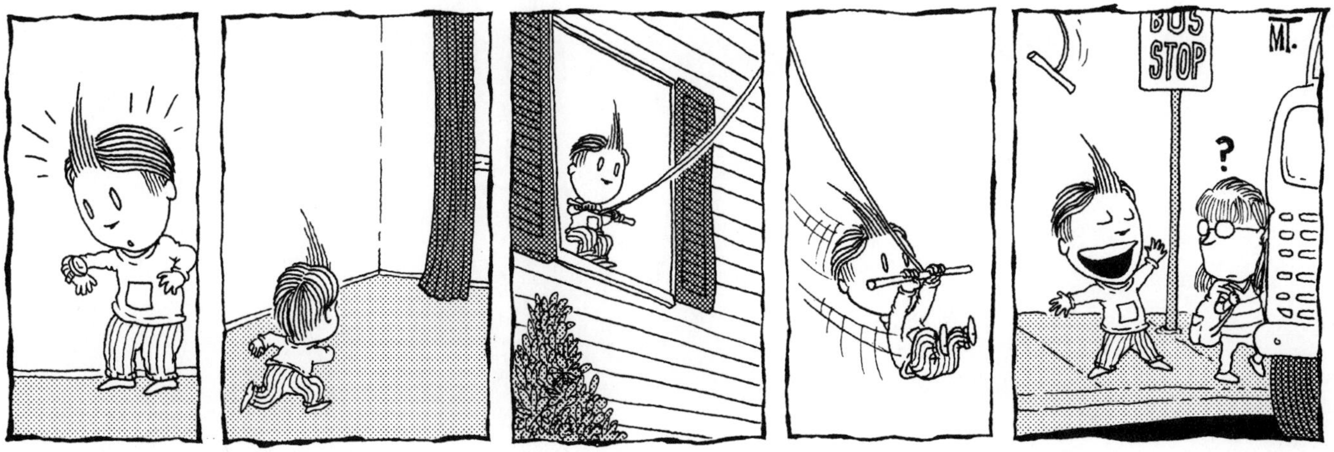
BUS STOP
?

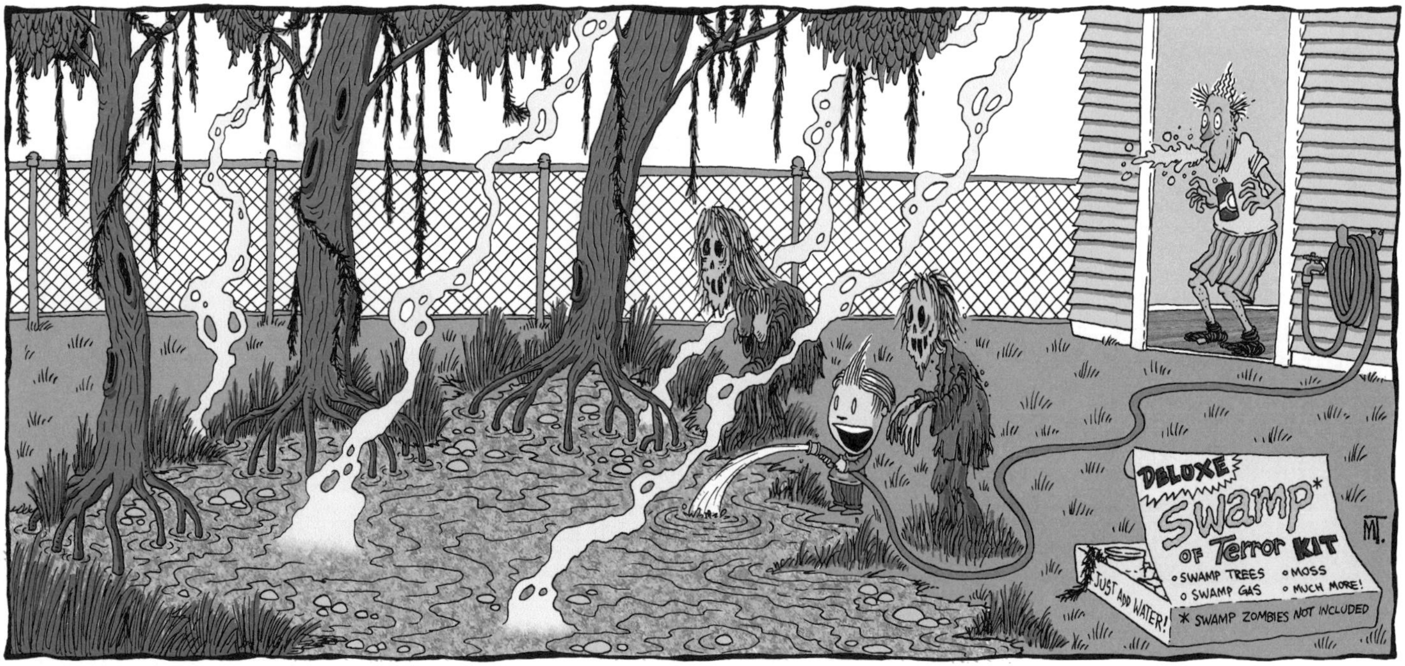
DELUXE
Swamp*
OF Terror KIT
SWAMP TREES
MOSS
SWAMP GAS
MUCH MORE!
JUST ADD WATER!
* SWAMP ZOMBIES NOT INCLUDED
MT.

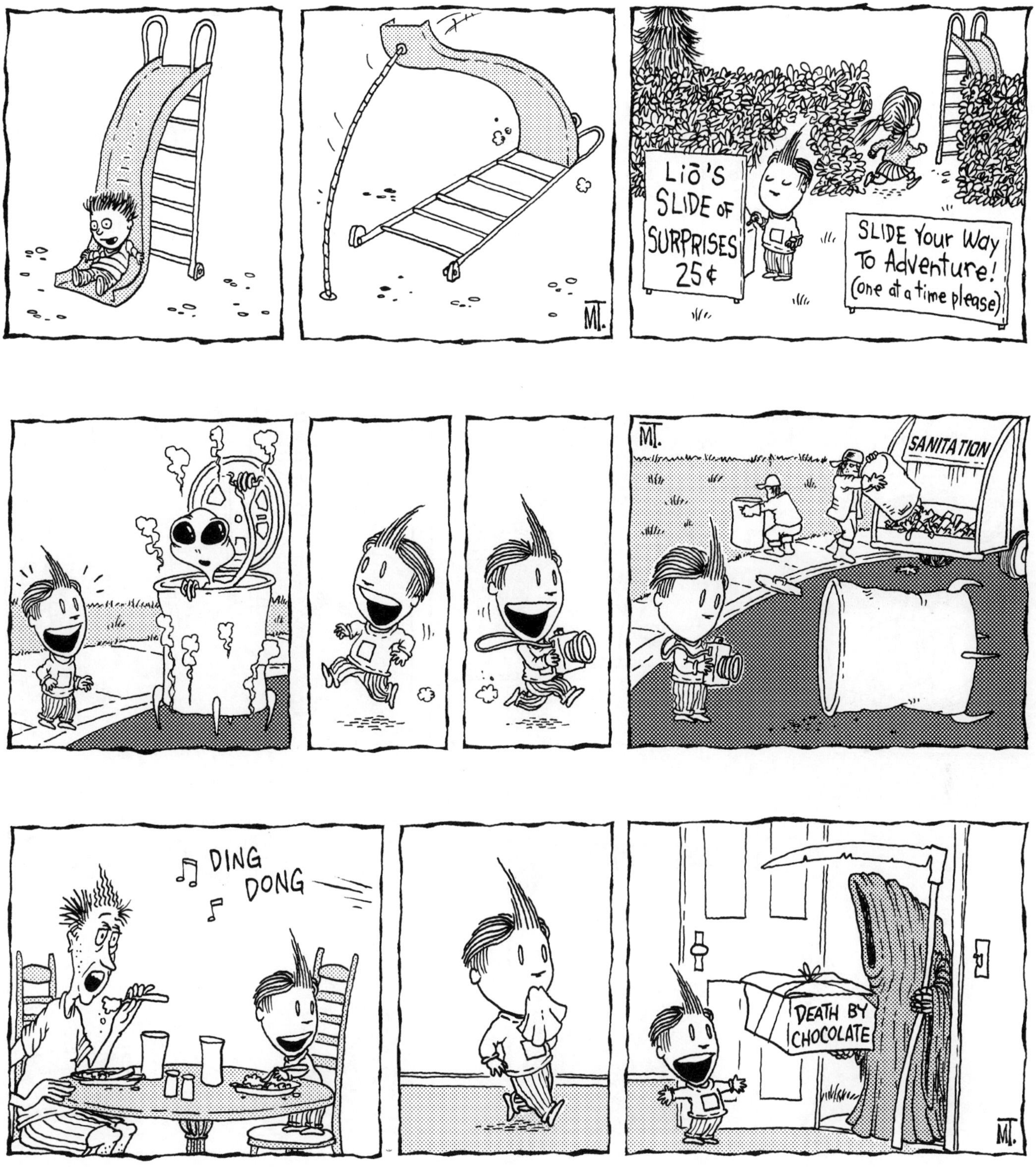
MT.
LIŌ'S
SLIDE OF
SURPRISES
25¢
SLIDE Your Way
To Adventure!
(one at a time please)
MT.
SANITATION
DING
DONG
DEATH BY
CHOCOLATE
MT.

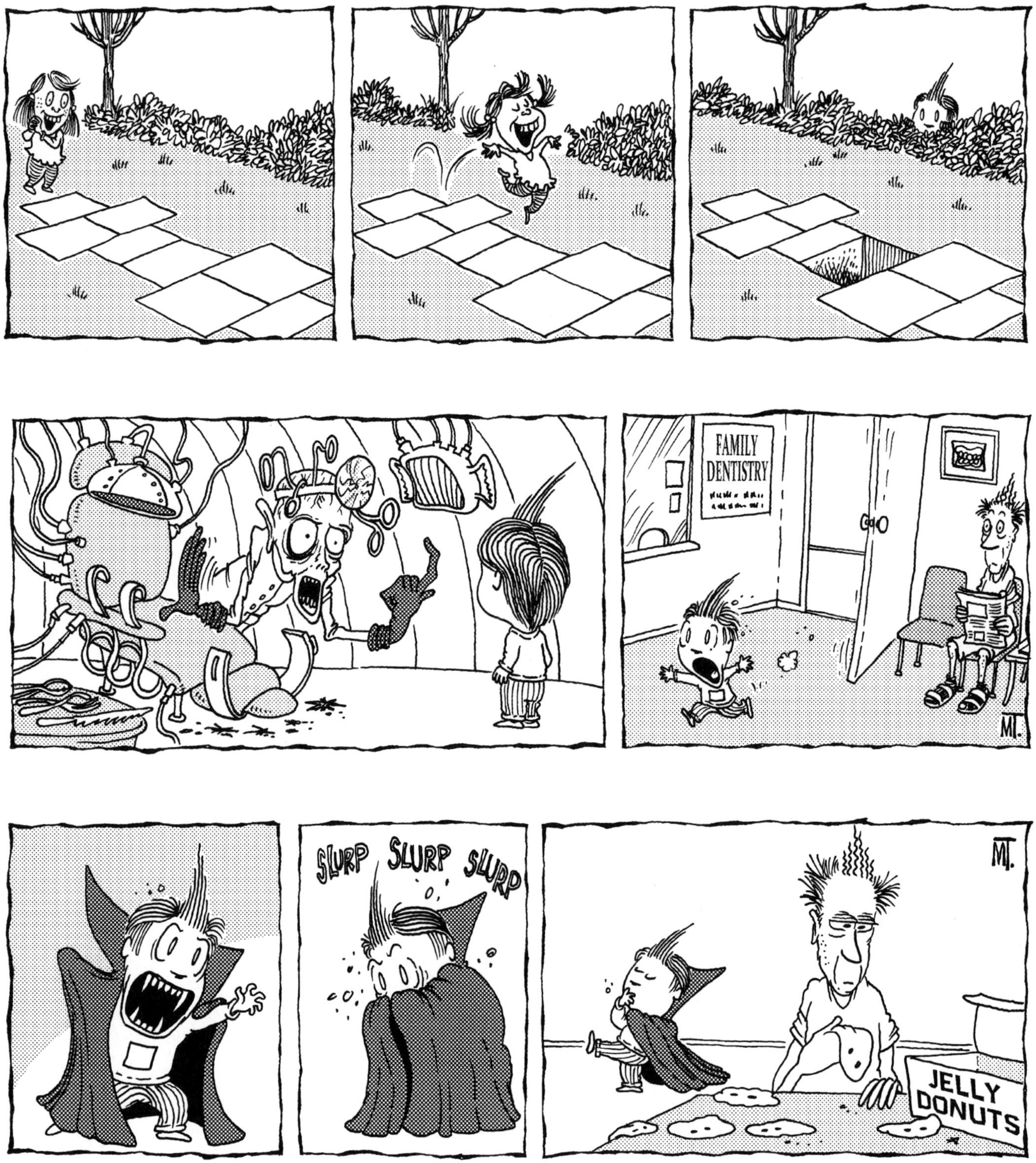
FAMILY DENTISTRY
SLURP SLURP SLURP
JELLY DONUTS
MT.

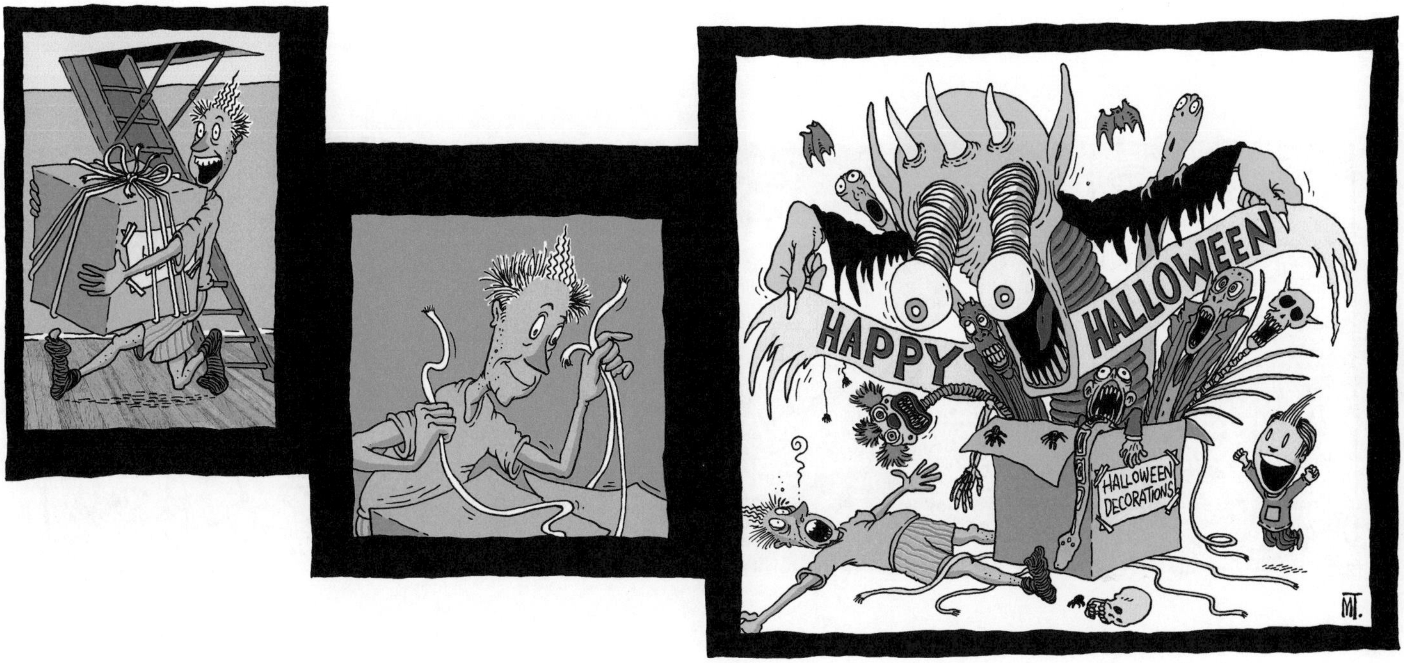
HAPPY HALLOWEEN
HALLOWEEN DECORATIONS
MT.

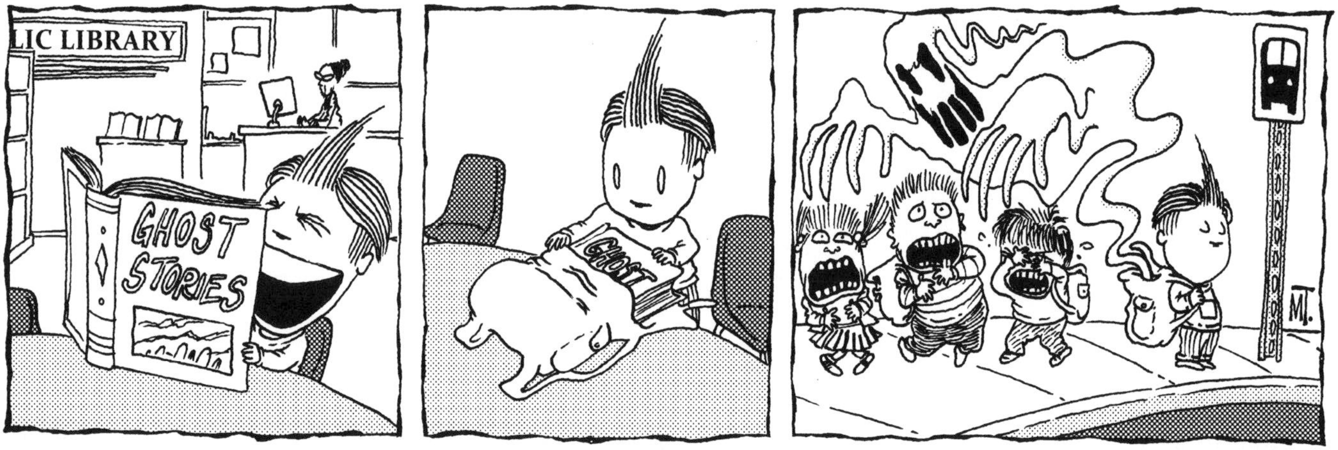
LIC LIBRARY
GHOST STORIES
GHOST
MT.

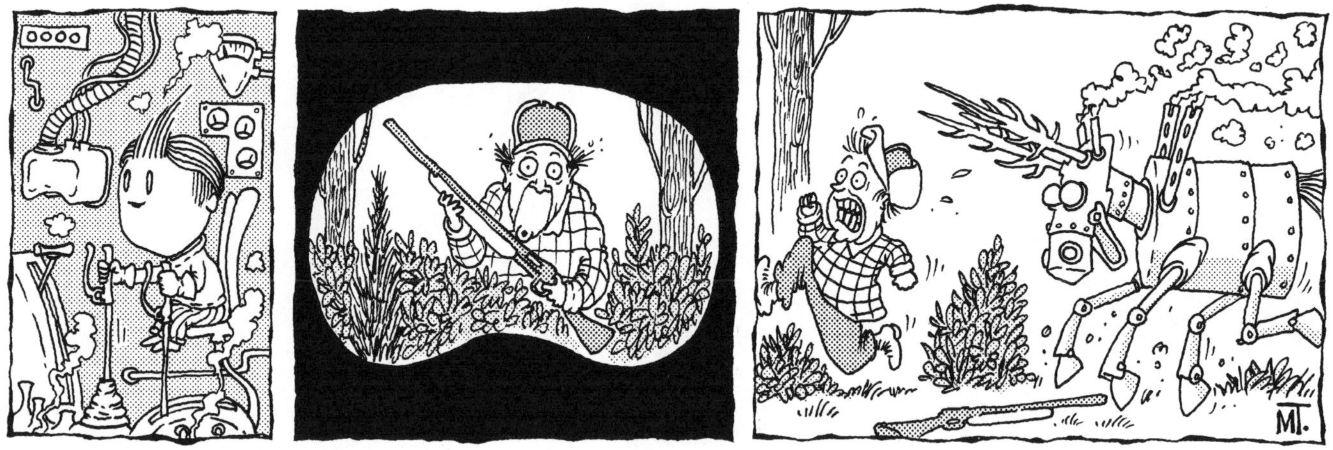
MT.

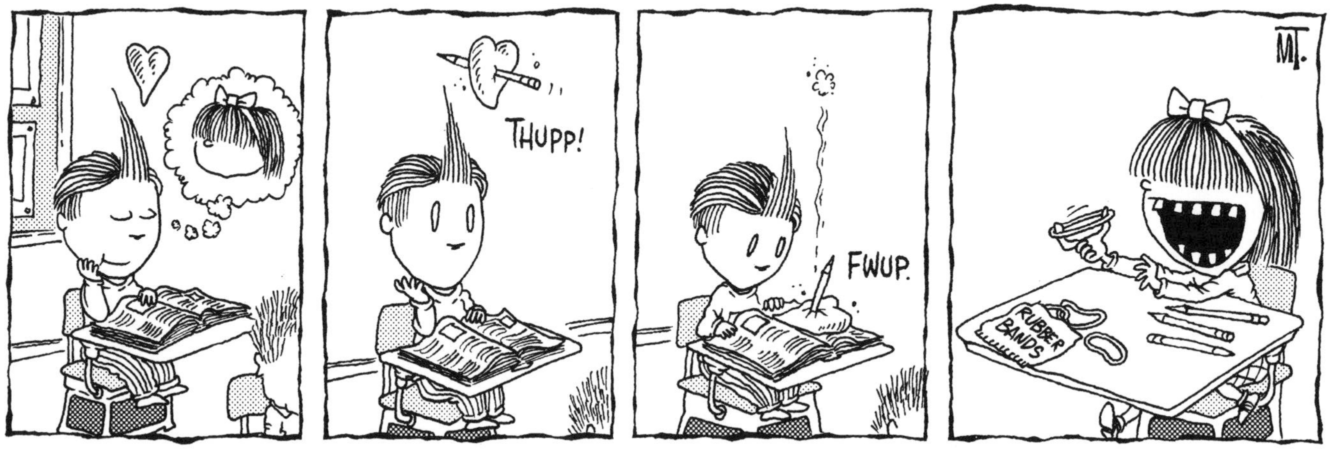
MT.
THUPP!
FWUP.
RUBBER BANDS

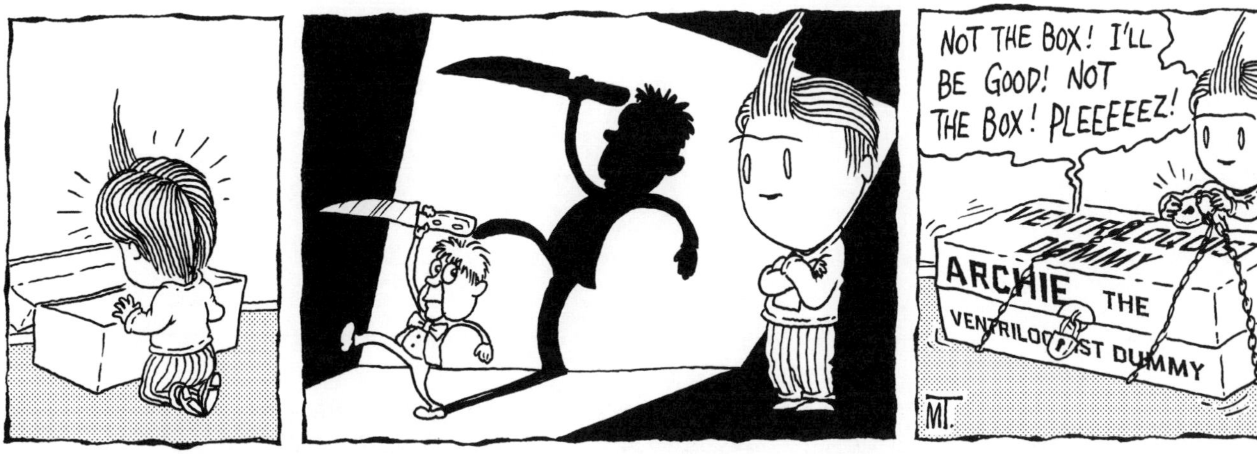
NOT THE BOX! I'LL BE GOOD! NOT THE BOX! PLEEEEEZ!
VENTRILOQUIST DUMMY
ARCHIE THE VENTRILOQUIST DUMMY
MT.

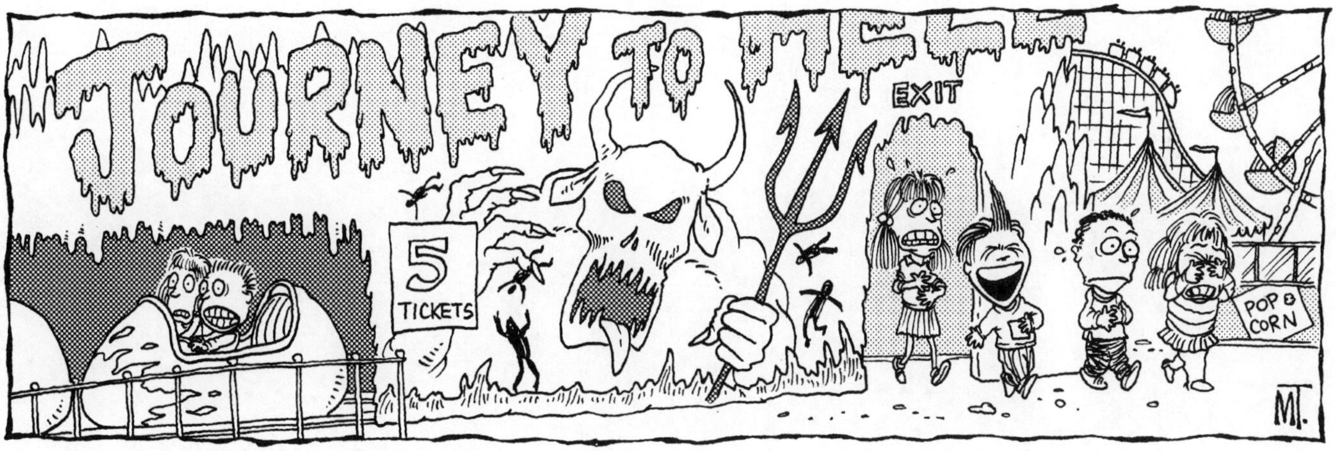
JOURNEY TO
EXIT
5 TICKETS
POP CORN
MT.

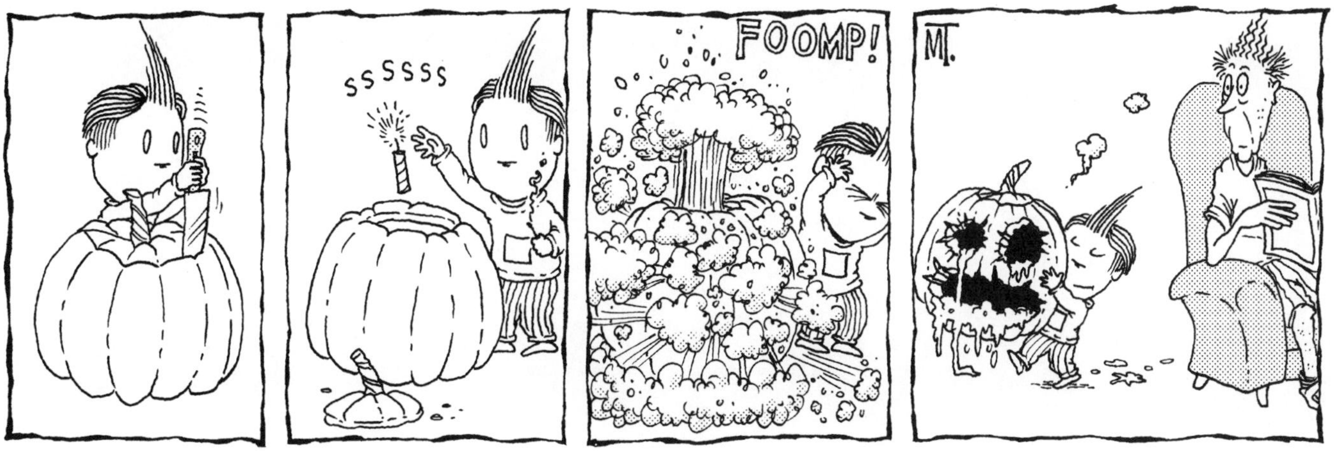
SSSSSS
FOOMP!
MT.

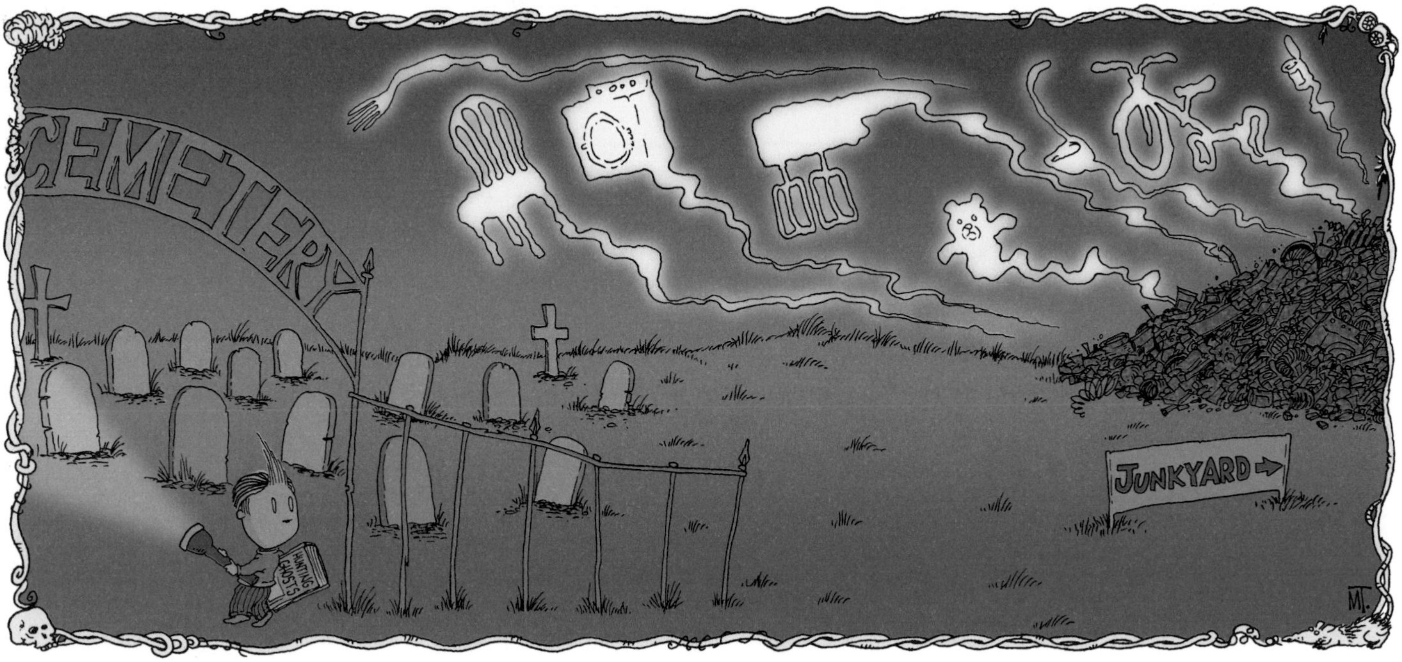
CEMETERY
HUNTING GHOSTS
JUNKYARD
MT.

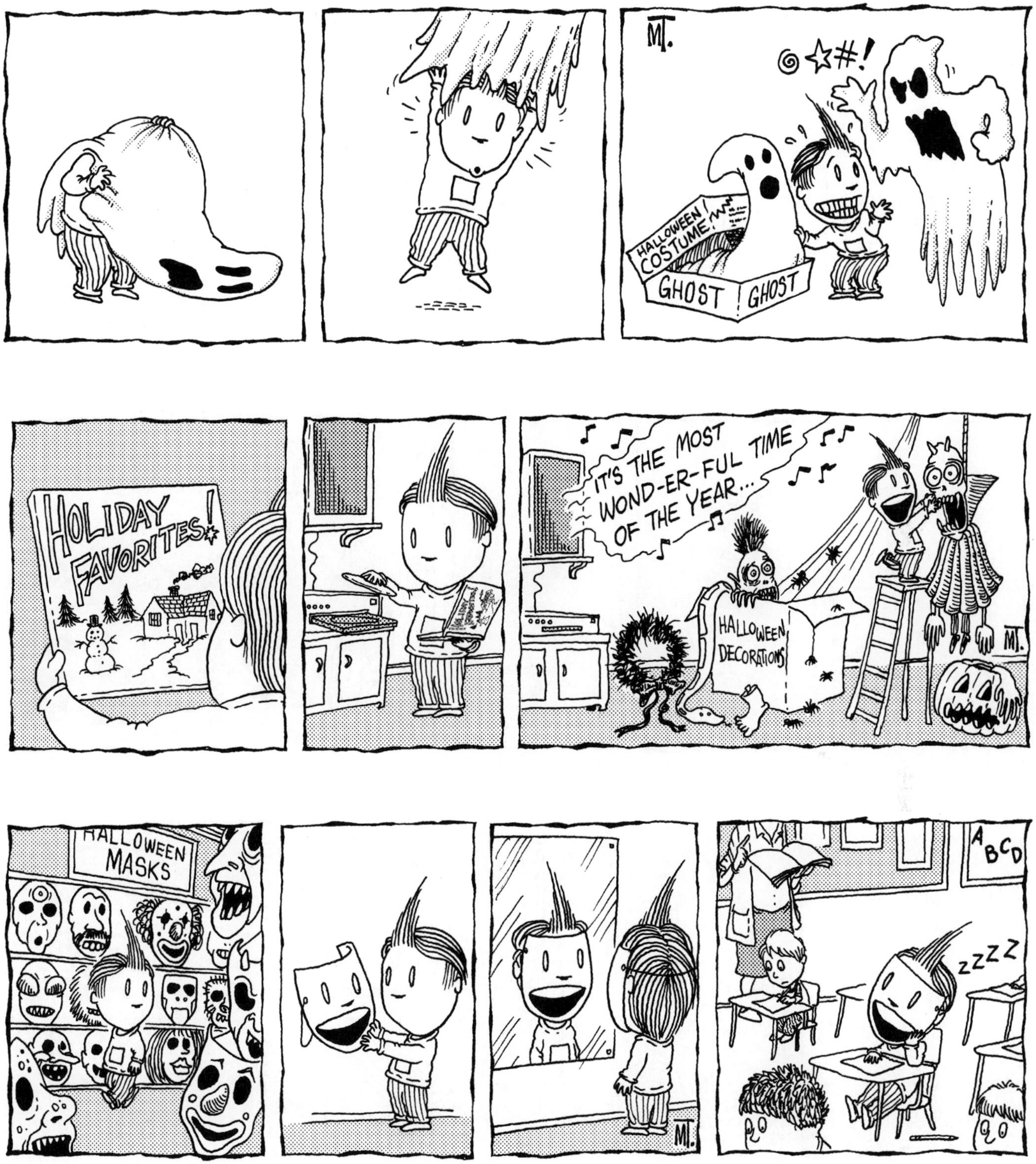
HALLOWEEN COSTUME
GHOST
GHOST
HOLIDAY FAVORITES!
IT'S THE MOST WOND-ER-FUL TIME OF THE YEAR...
HALLOWEEN DECORATIONS
HALLOWEEN MASKS
ABCD
ZZZZ

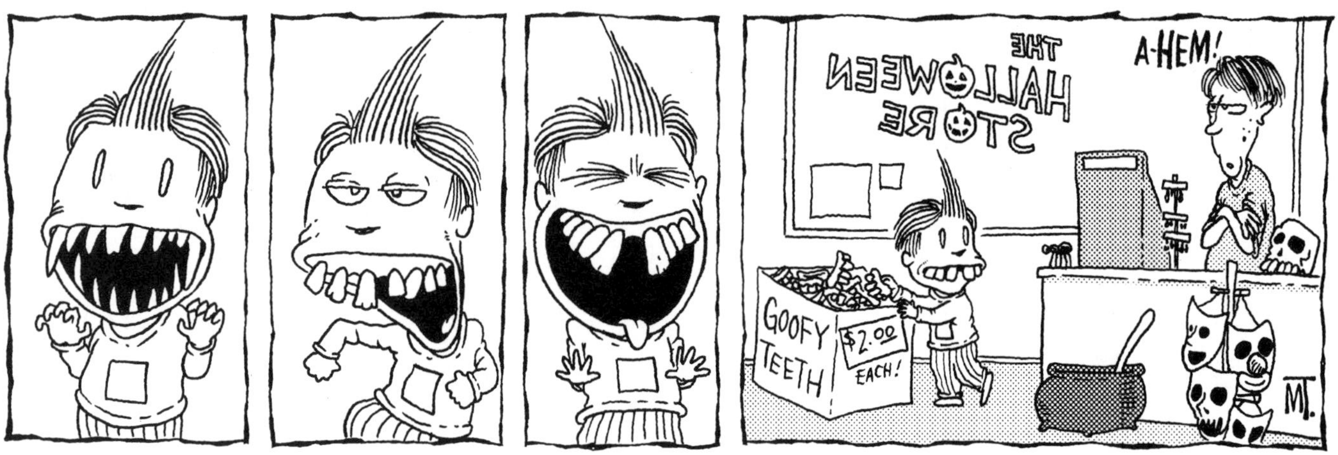
THE HALLOWEEN STORE
A-HEM!
GOOFY TEETH
$2.00 EACH!
MT.

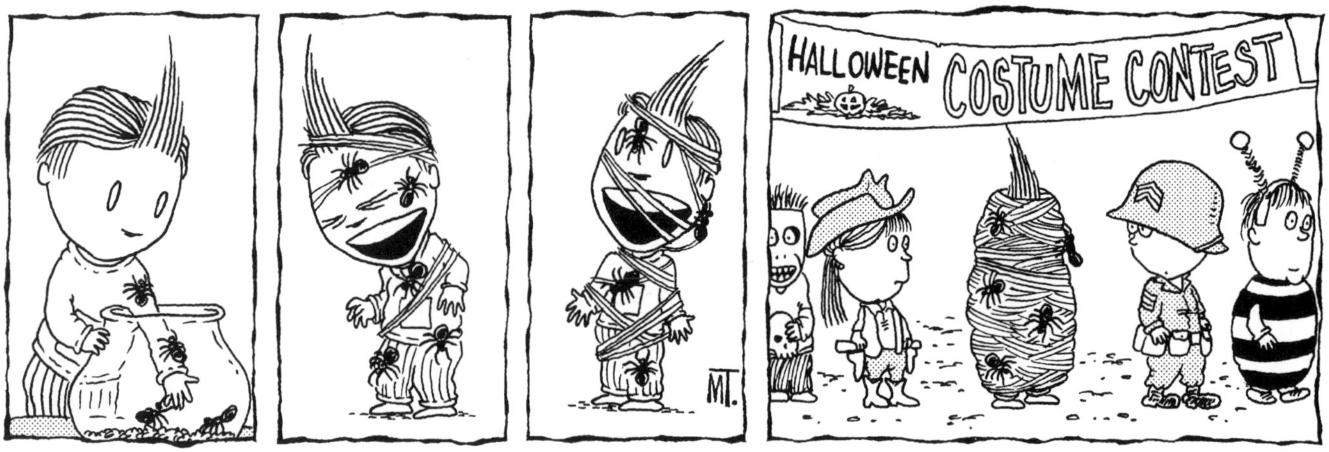
HALLOWEEN COSTUME CONTEST
MT.

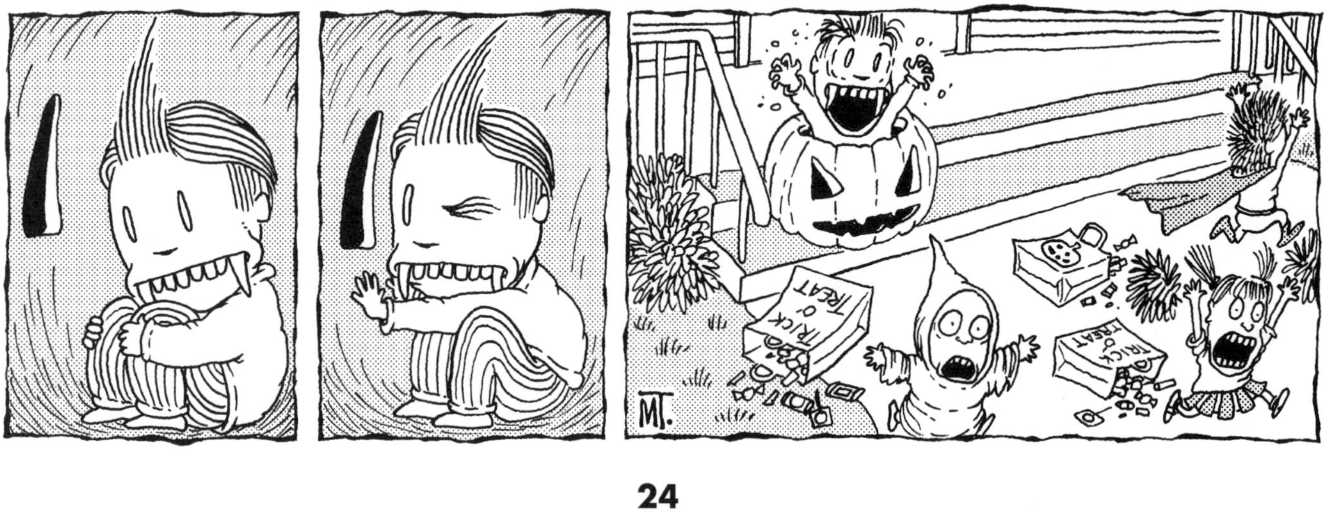
TRICK O' TREAT
TRICK O' TREAT
MT.

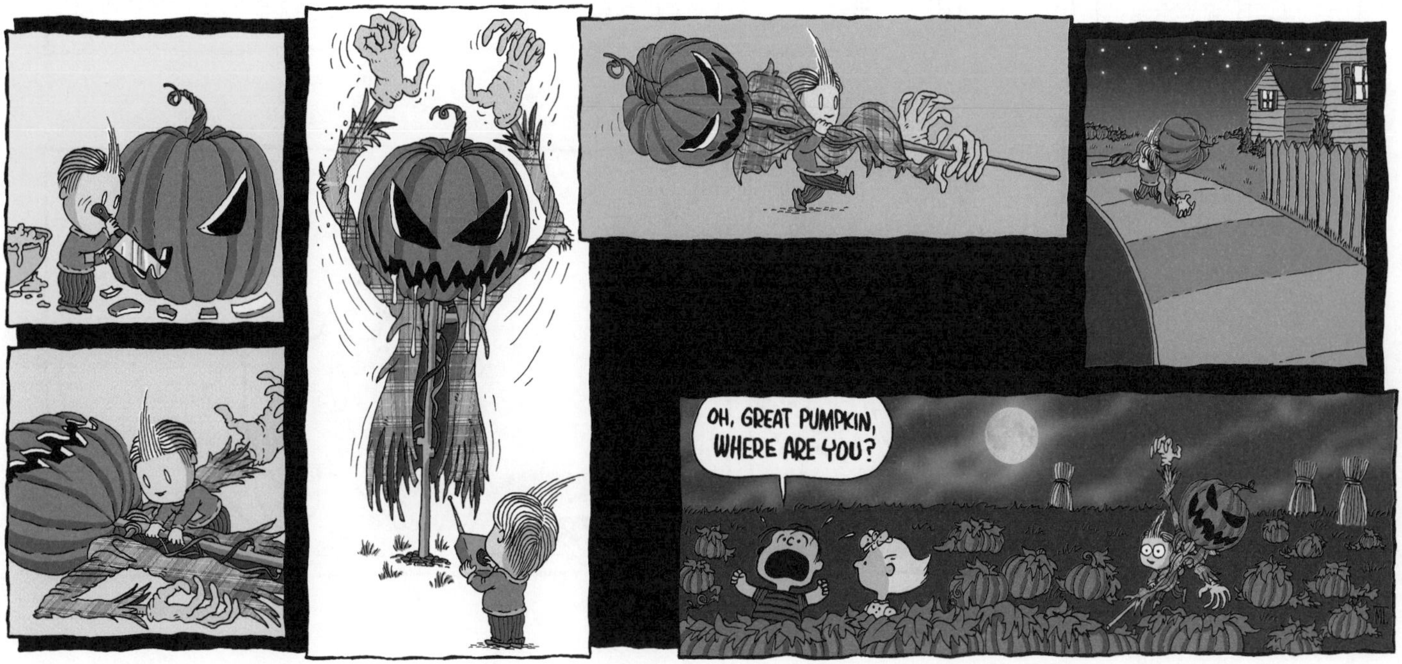
OH, GREAT PUMPKIN,
WHERE ARE YOU?

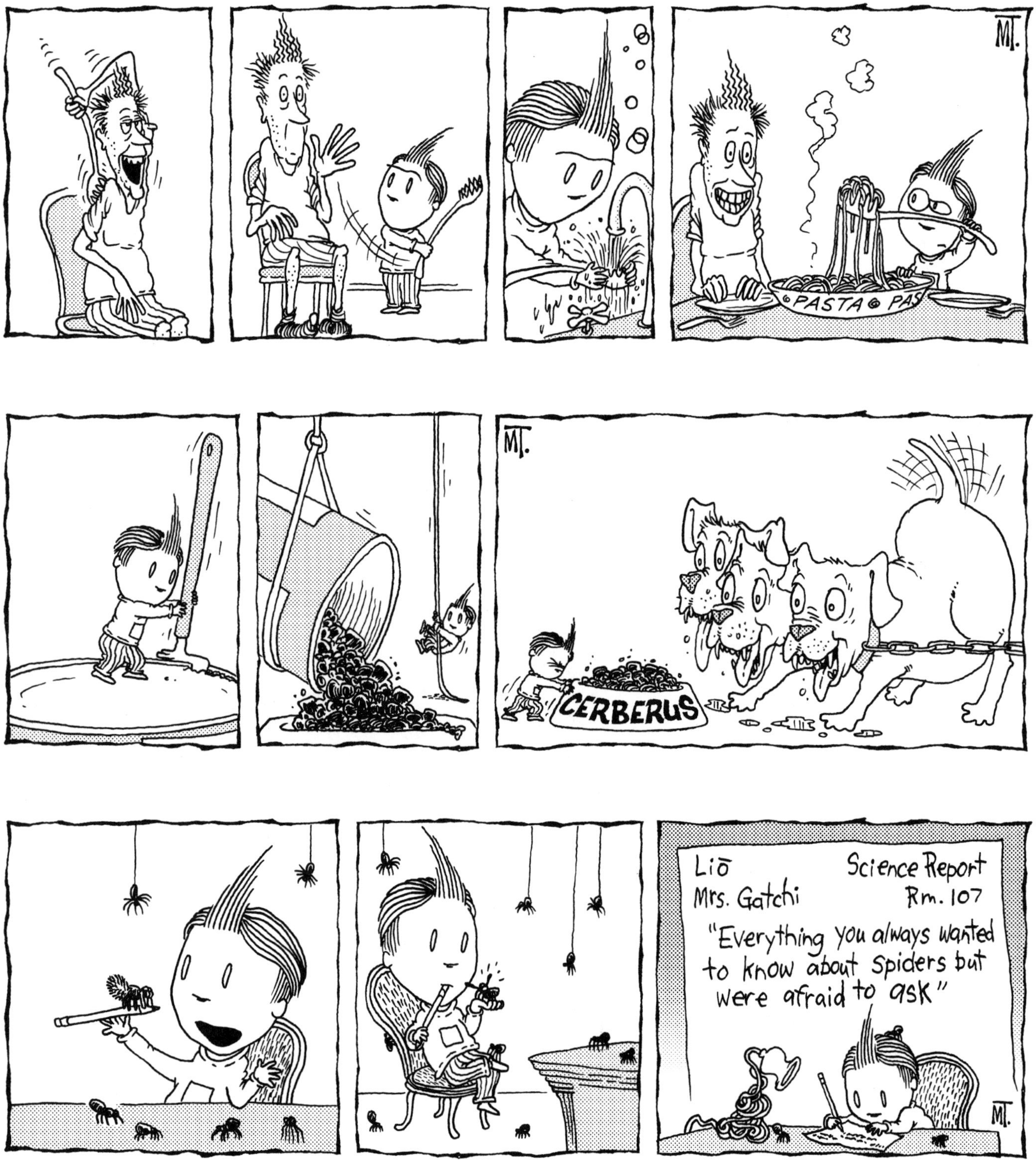
PASTA PAS
CERBERUS
Liō
Science Report
Mrs. Gatchi
Rm. 107
"Everything you always wanted to know about Spiders but were afraid to ask"

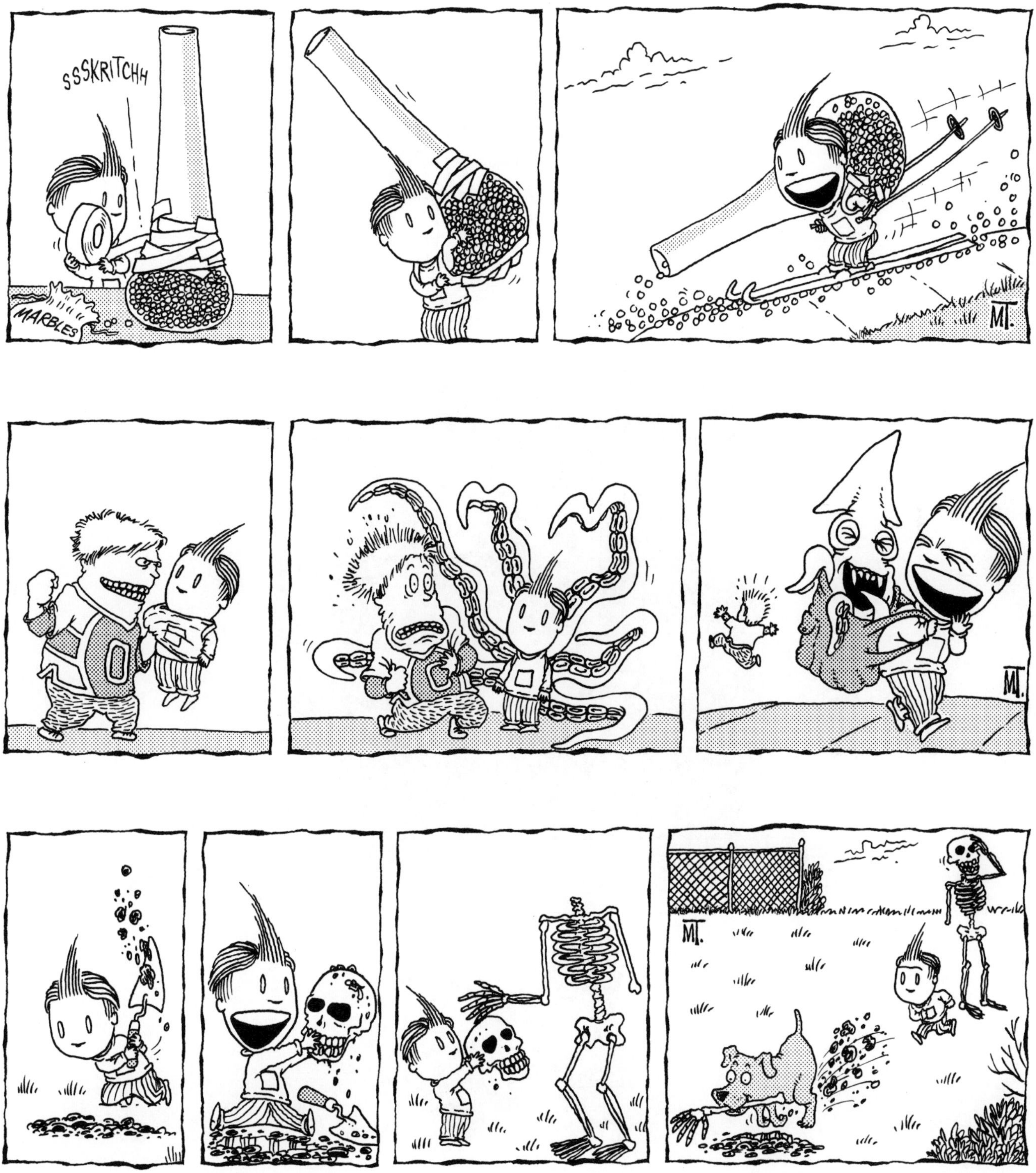
SSSKRITCHH
MARBLES
MT.
MT.
MT.

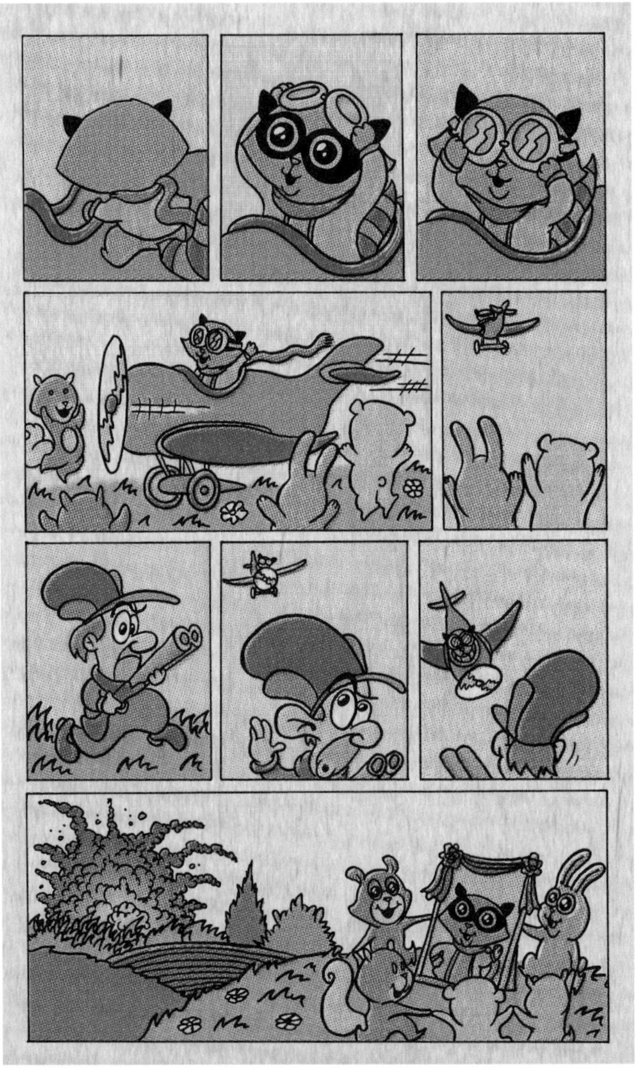

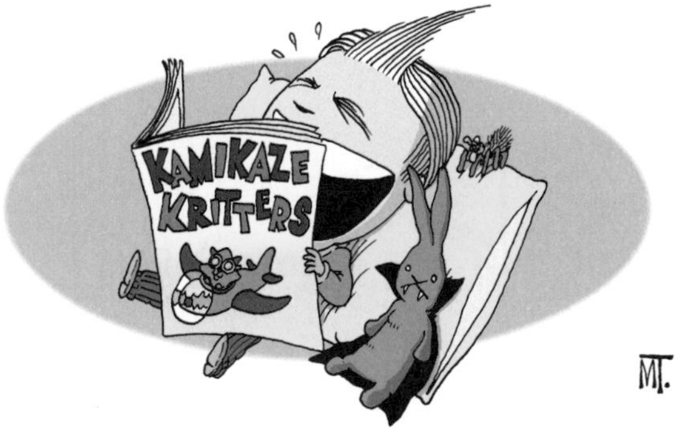
KAMIKAZE
KRITTERS
MT.

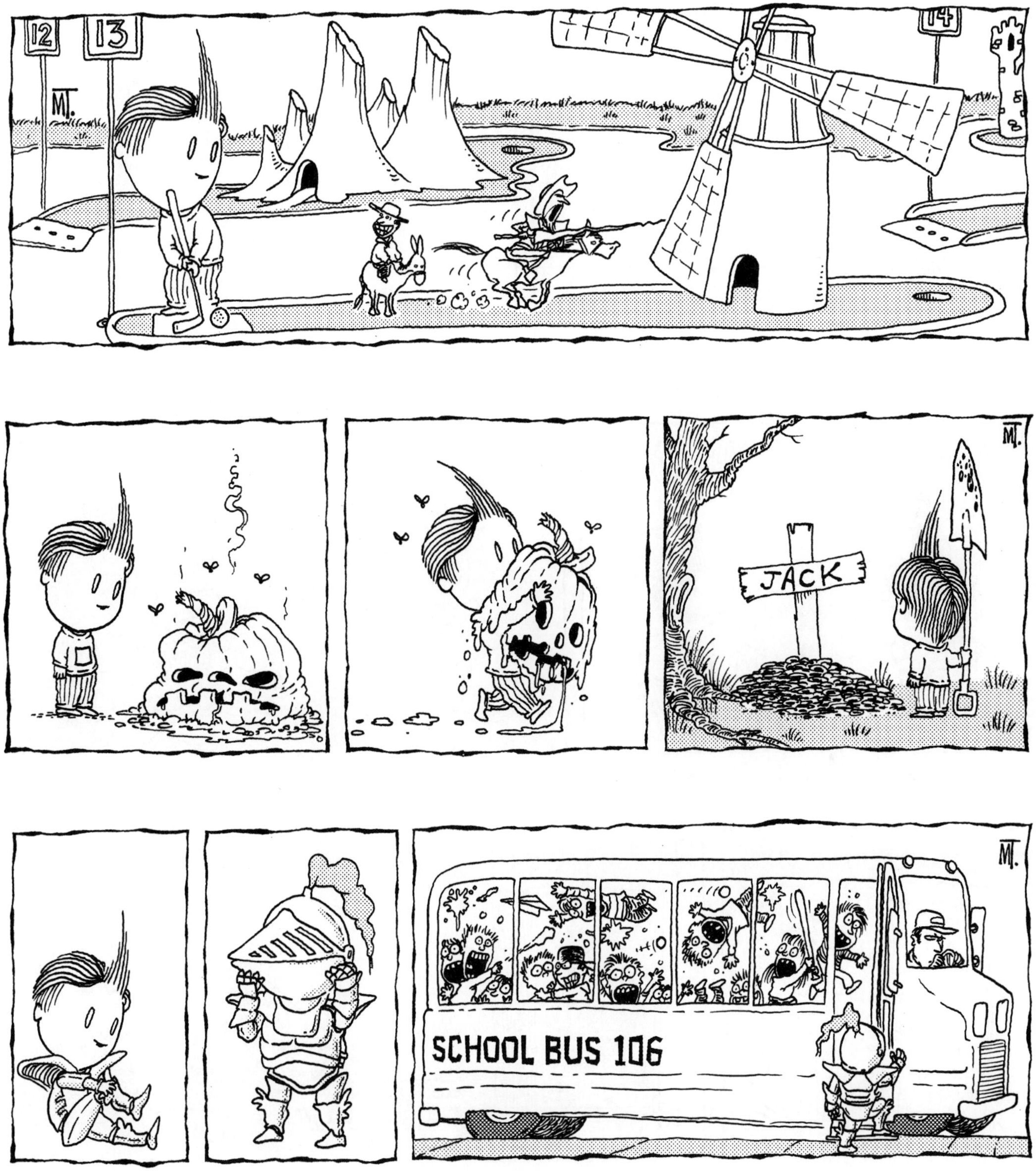
12
13
14
MT.
JACK
MT.
SCHOOL BUS 106
MT.

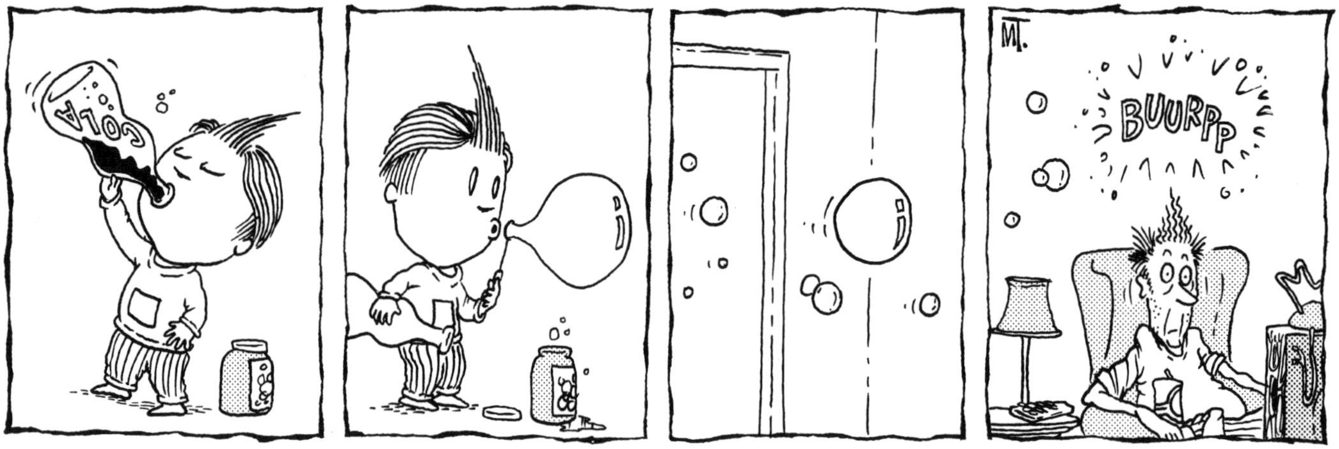
COLA
MT.
BUURPPP

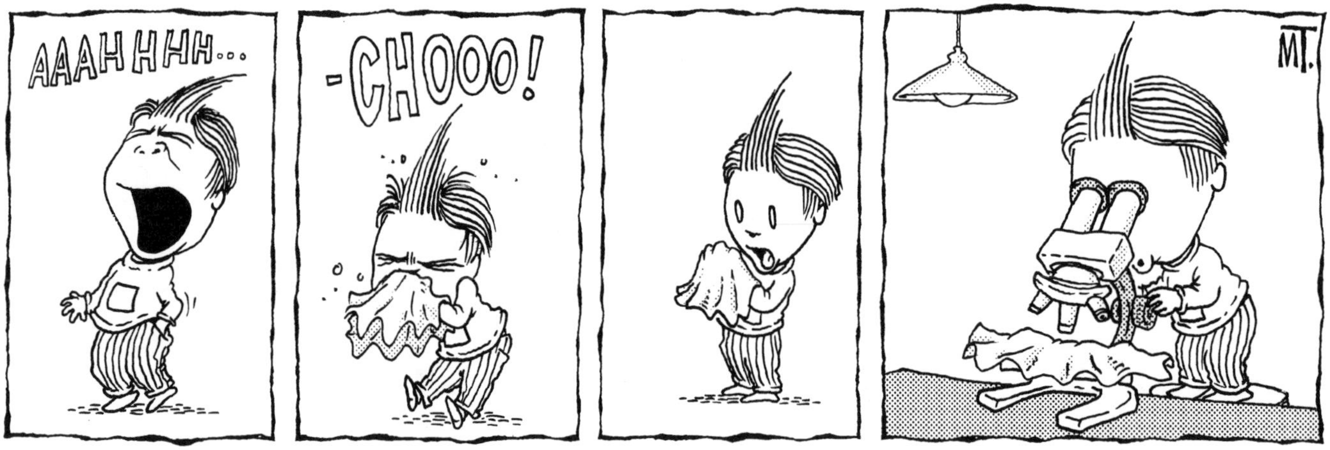
AAAHHHH...
-CHOOO!
MT.

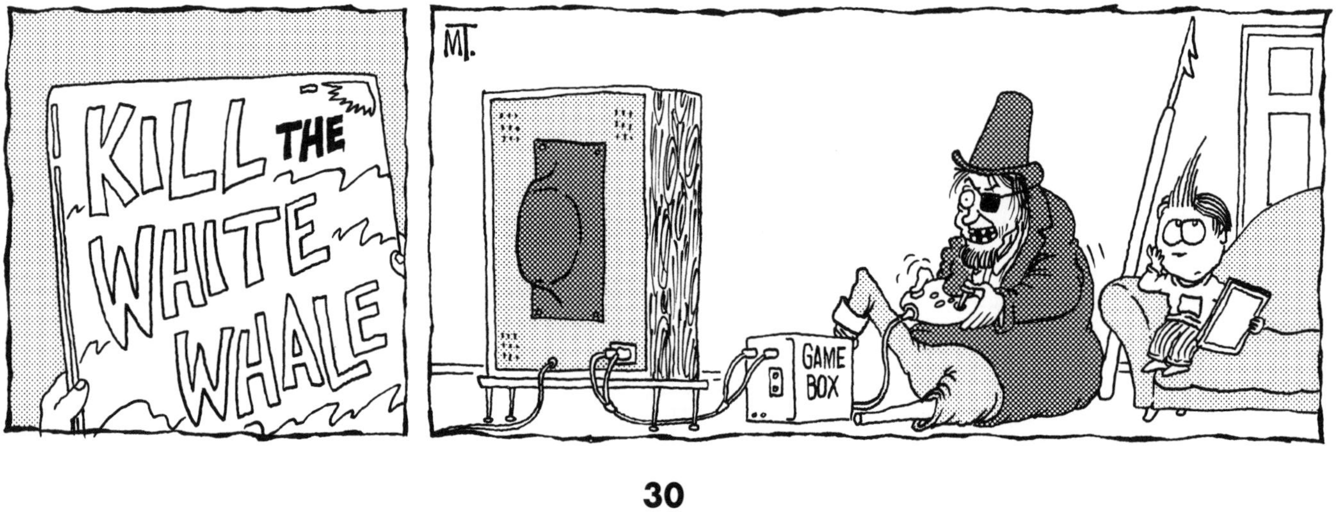
KILL THE WHITE WHALE
MT.
GAME BOX

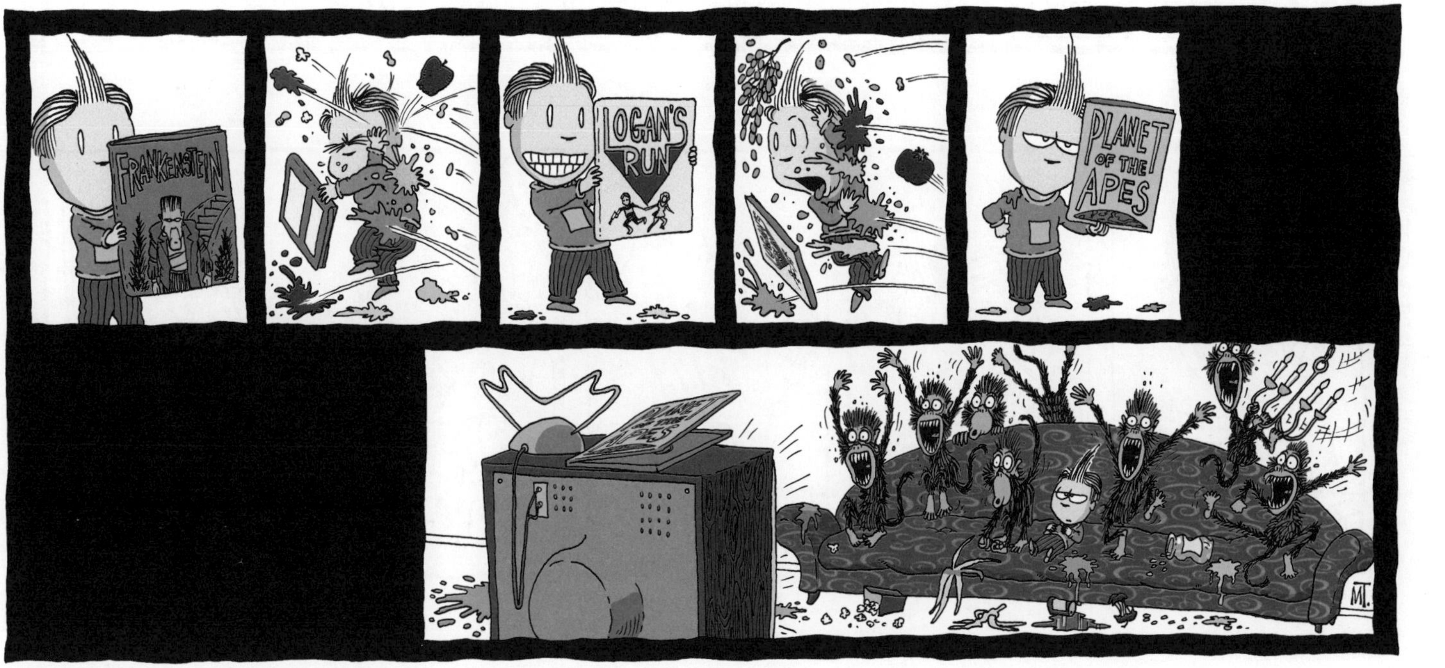
FRANKENSTEIN
LOGAN'S RUN
PLANET OF THE APES
MT.

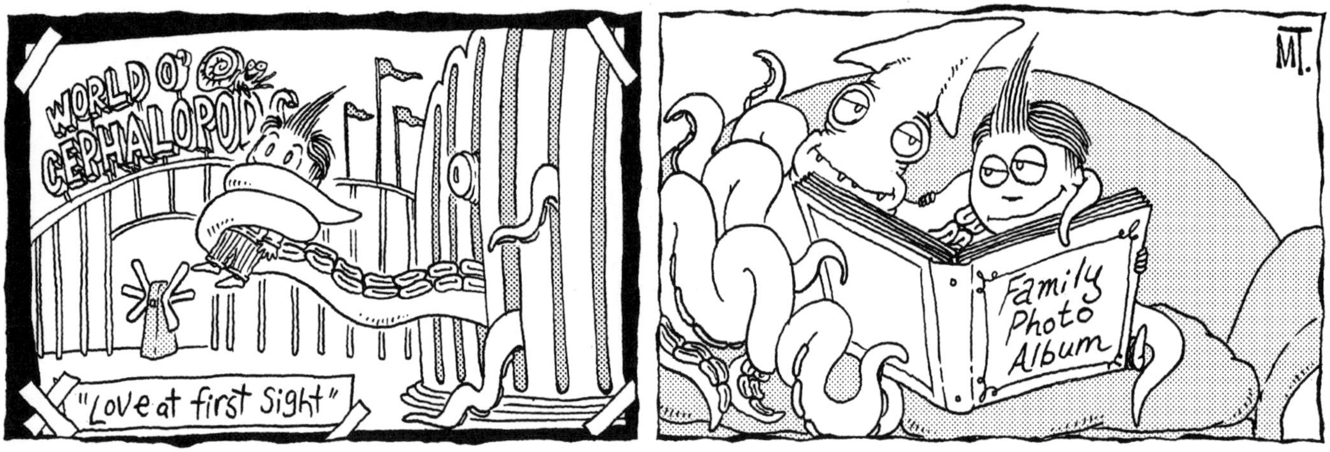
WORLD O' CEPHALOPODS
"Love at first Sight"
Family Photo Album
MT.

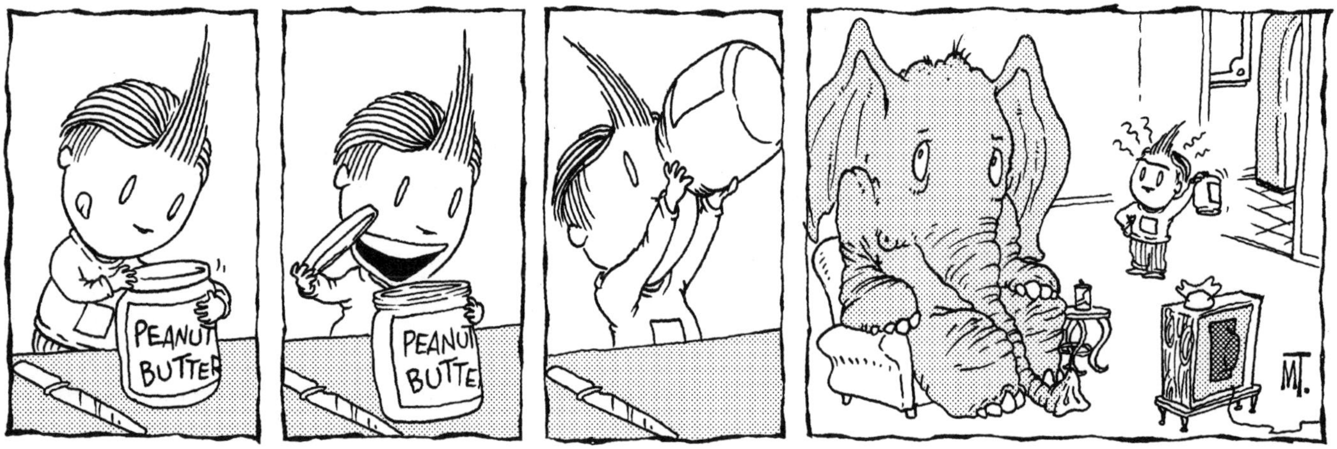
PEANUT BUTTER
MT.

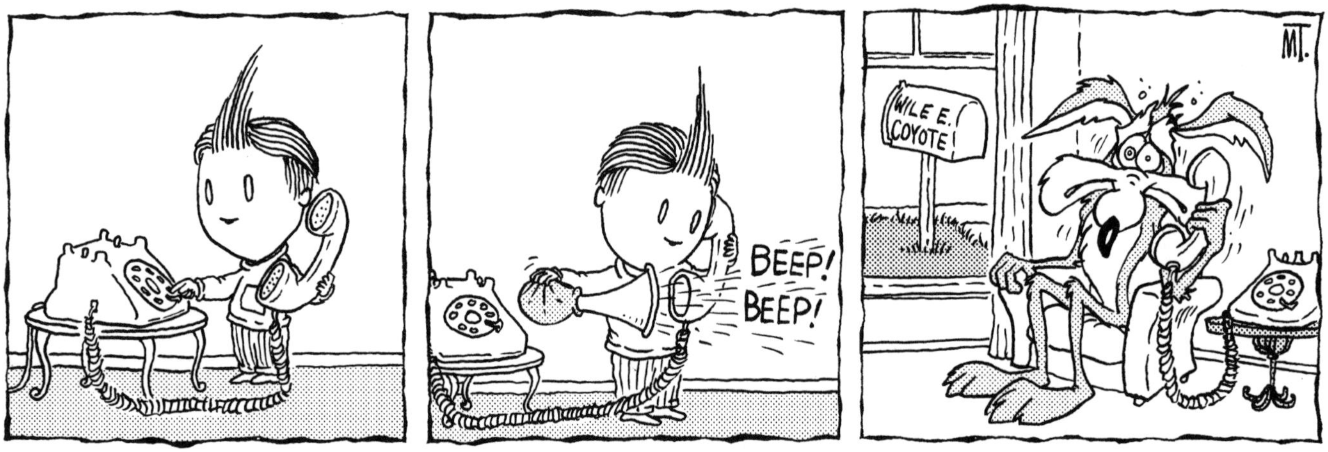
BEEP! BEEP!
WILE E. COYOTE
MT.

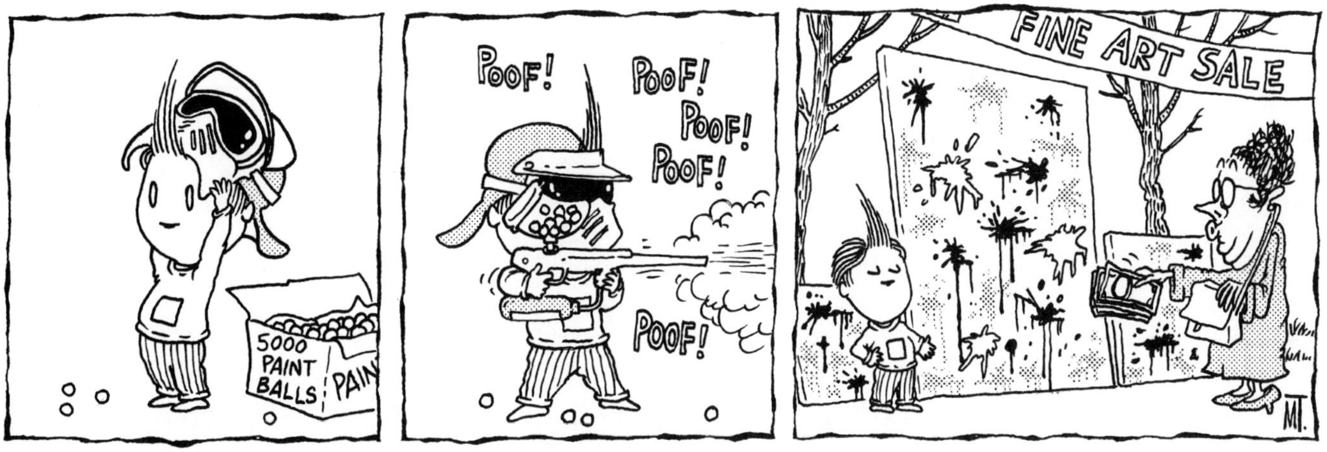
5000
PAINT
BALLS
PAIN
POOF!
POOF!
POOF!
POOF!
POOF!
FINE ART SALE
MT.

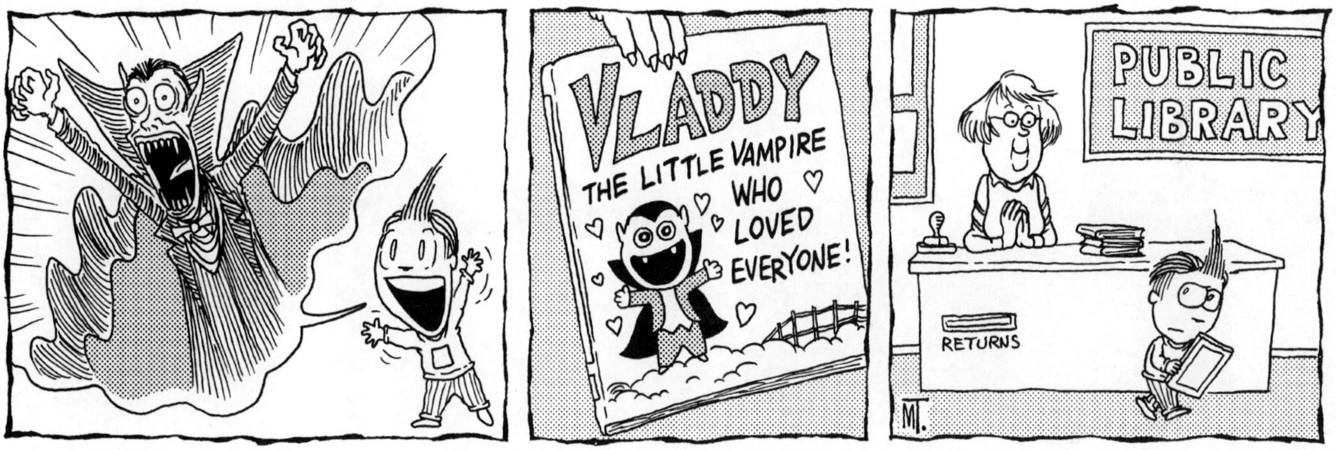
VLADDY
THE LITTLE VAMPIRE
WHO
LOVED
EVERYONE!
PUBLIC
LIBRARY
RETURNS
MT.

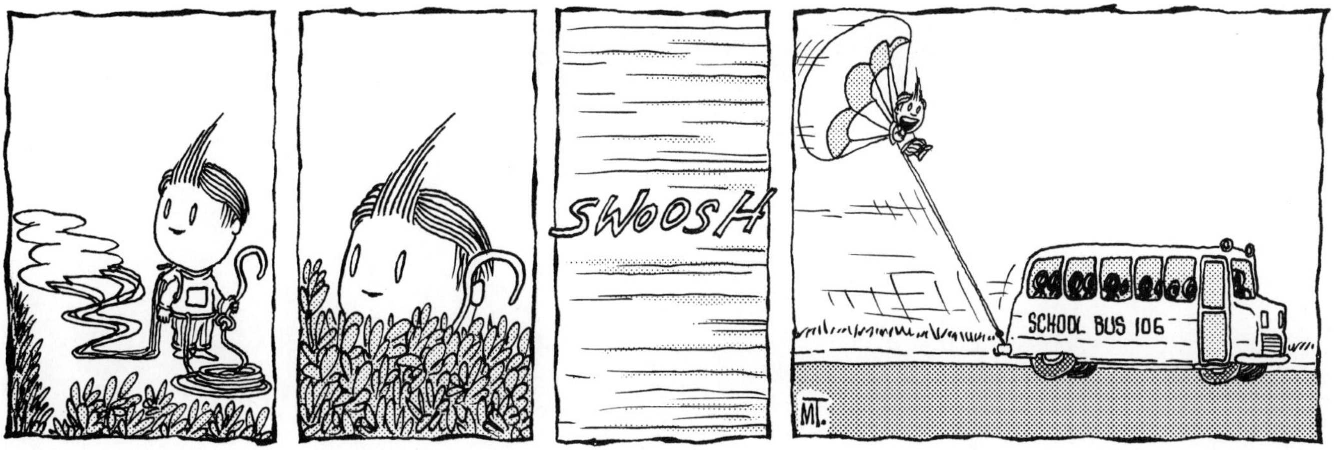
SWOOSH
SCHOOL BUS 106
MT.

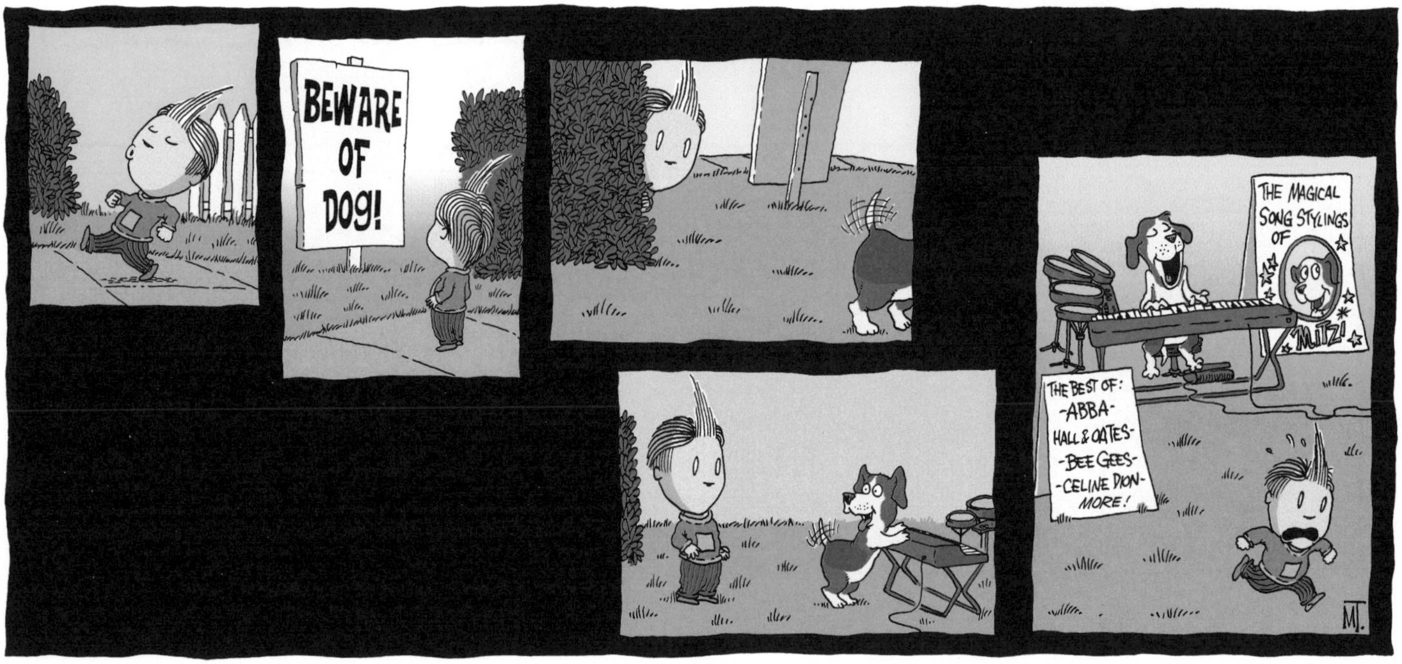
BEWARE OF DOG!
THE MAGICAL SONG STYLINGS OF "MITZI"
THE BEST OF:
-ABBA-
HALL & OATES-
-BEE GEES-
-CELINE DION-
MORE!
MT.

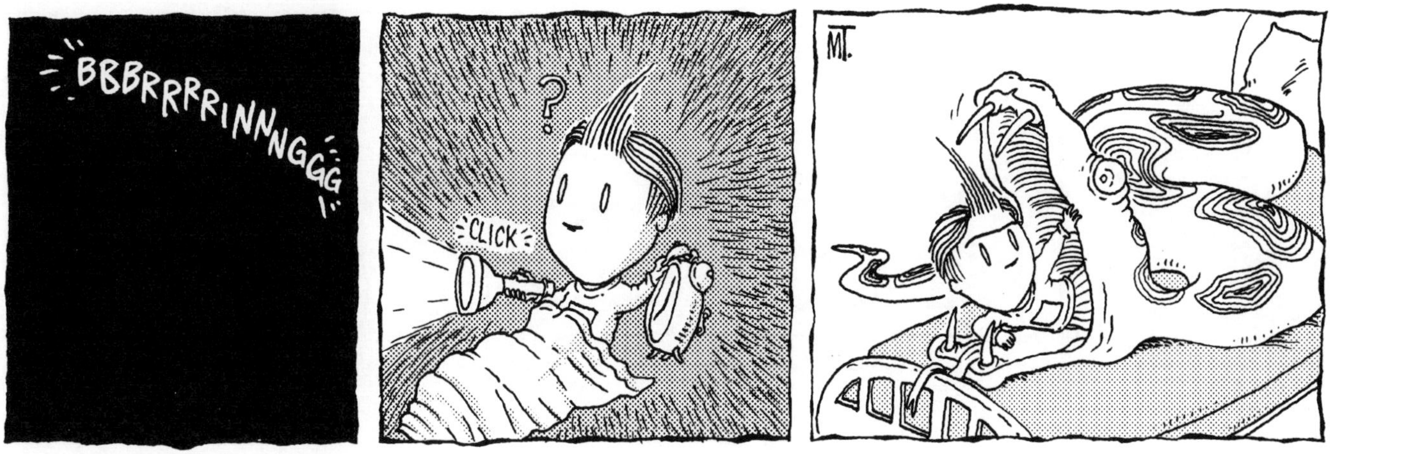
BBBRRRRINNNGGG
?
CLICK

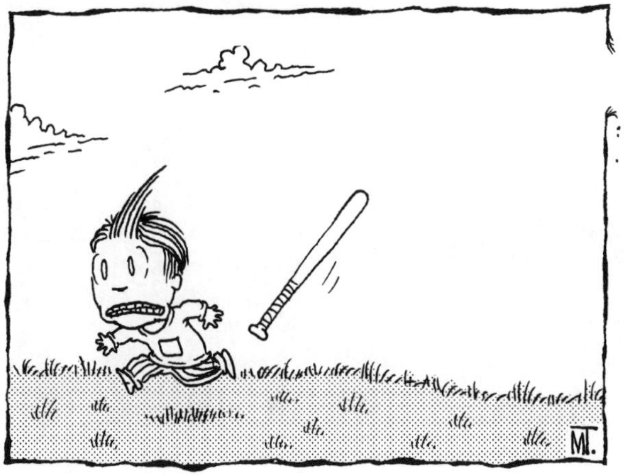

Family Circus

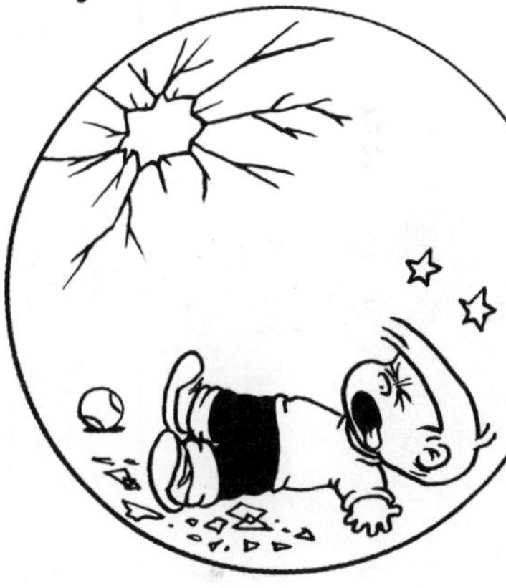

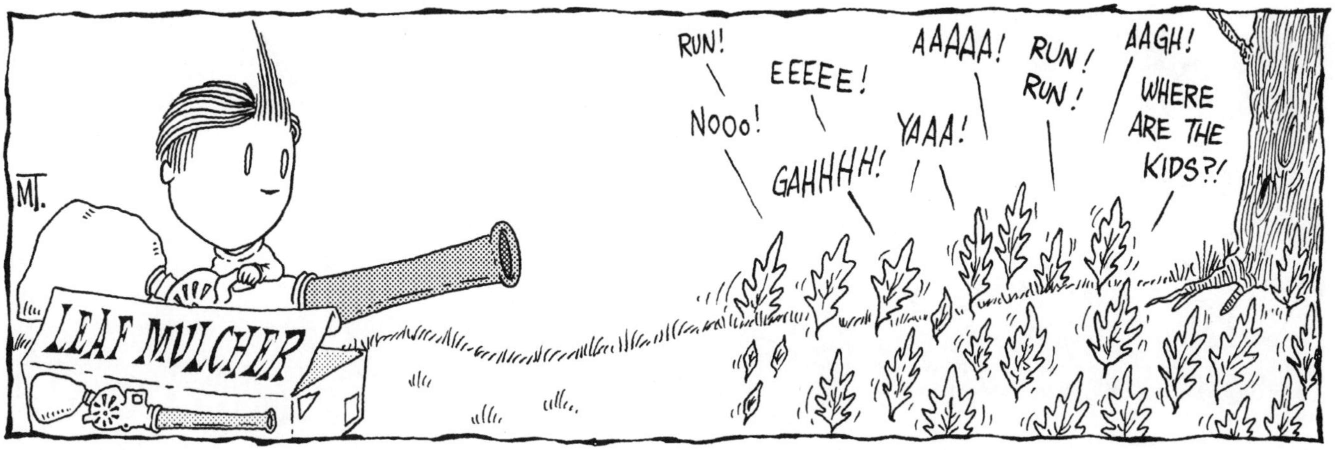
LEAF MULCHER
RUN!
NOoo!
EEEEE!
GAHHHH!
YAAA!
AAAAA!
RUN! RUN!
AAGH!
WHERE ARE THE KIDS?!

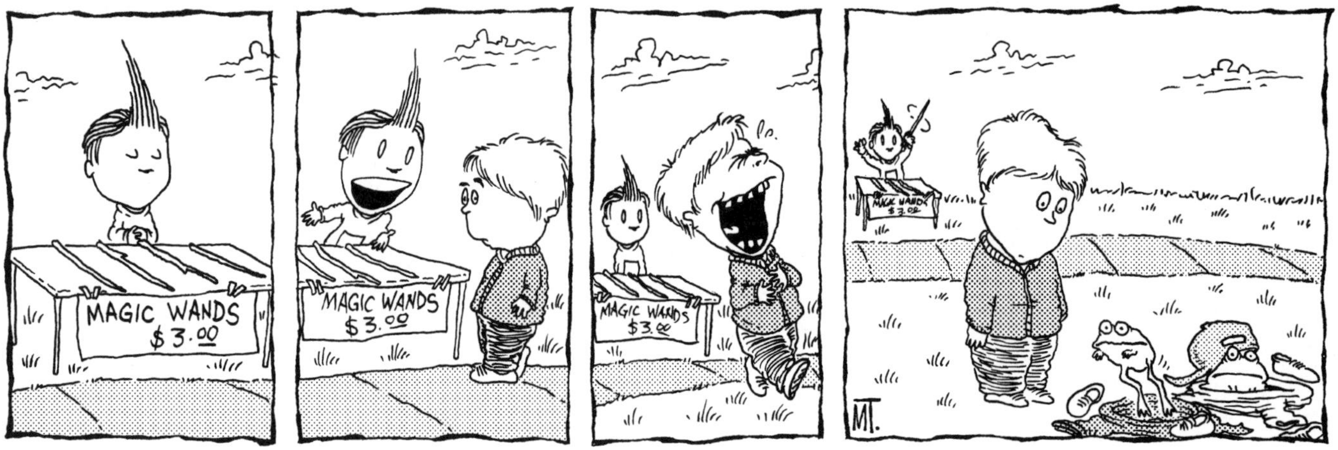
MAGIC WANDS $3.00
MAGIC WANDS $3.00
MAGIC WANDS $3.00
MT.

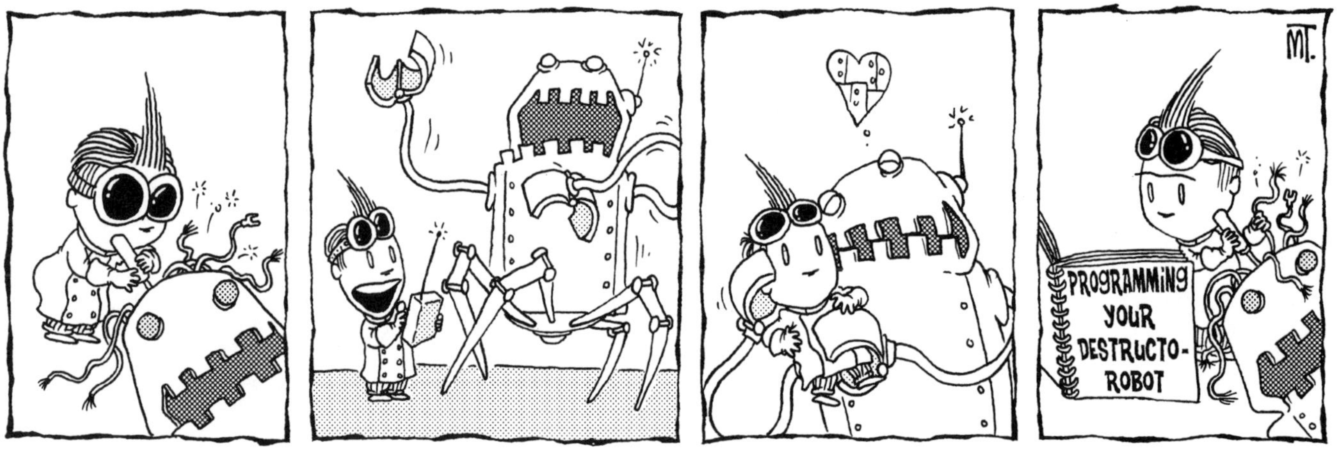
MT.
PROGRAMMING YOUR DESTRUCTO-ROBOT

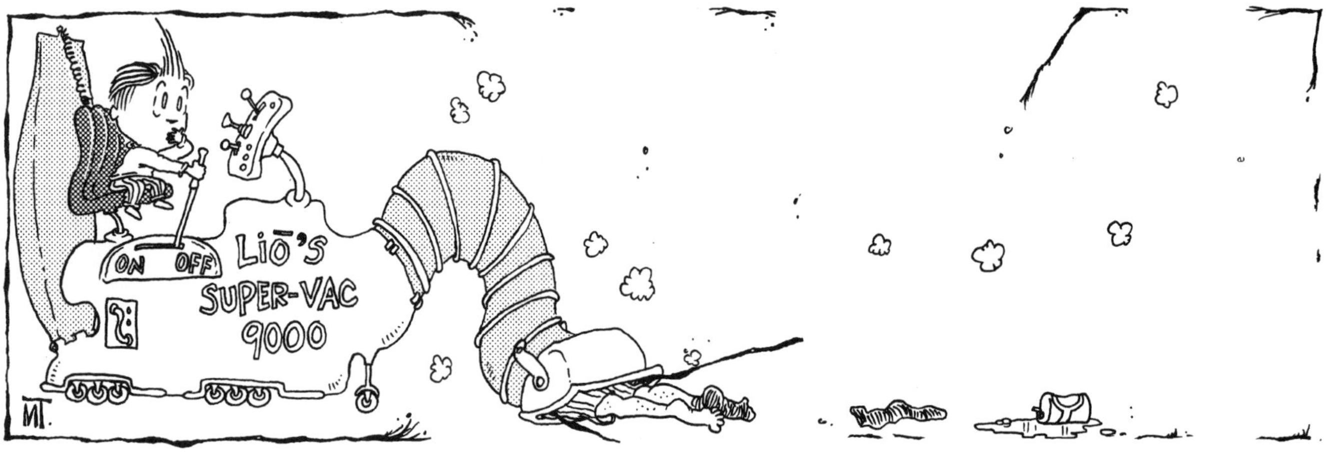
ON OFF
LIŌ'S SUPER-VAC 9000
MT.

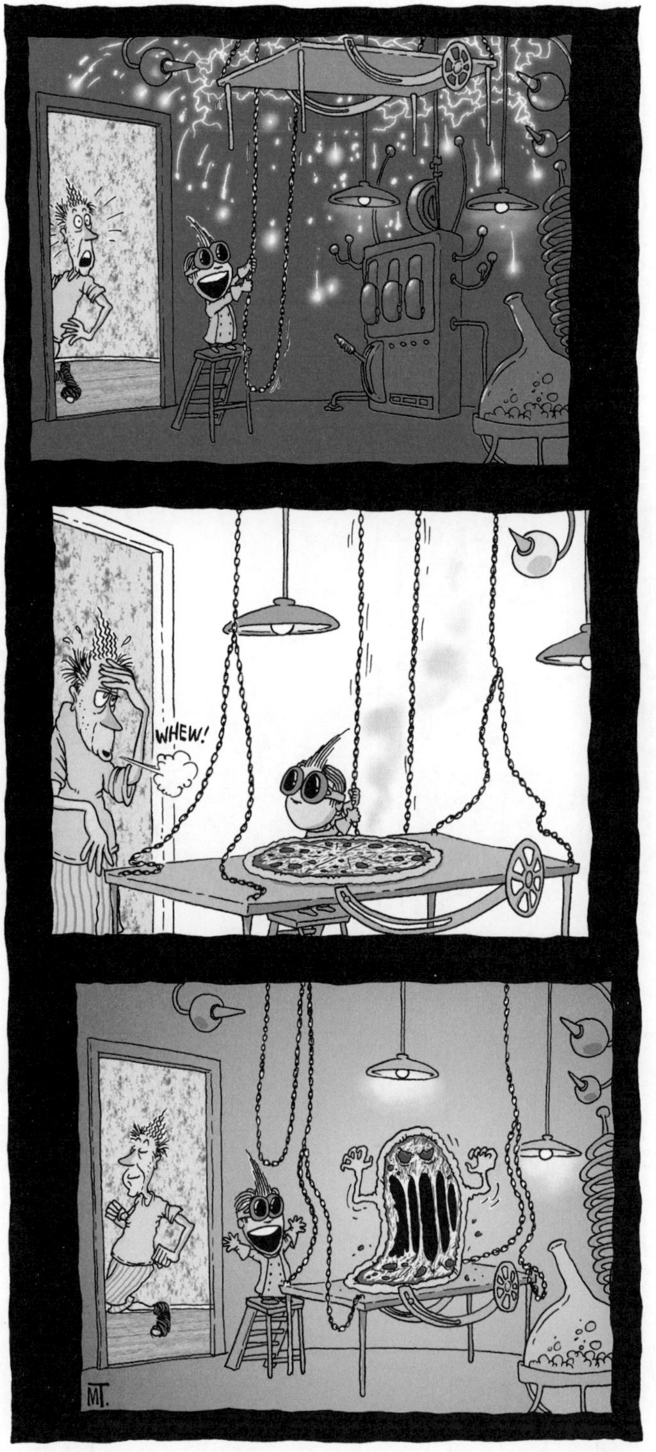
WHEW!
MT.

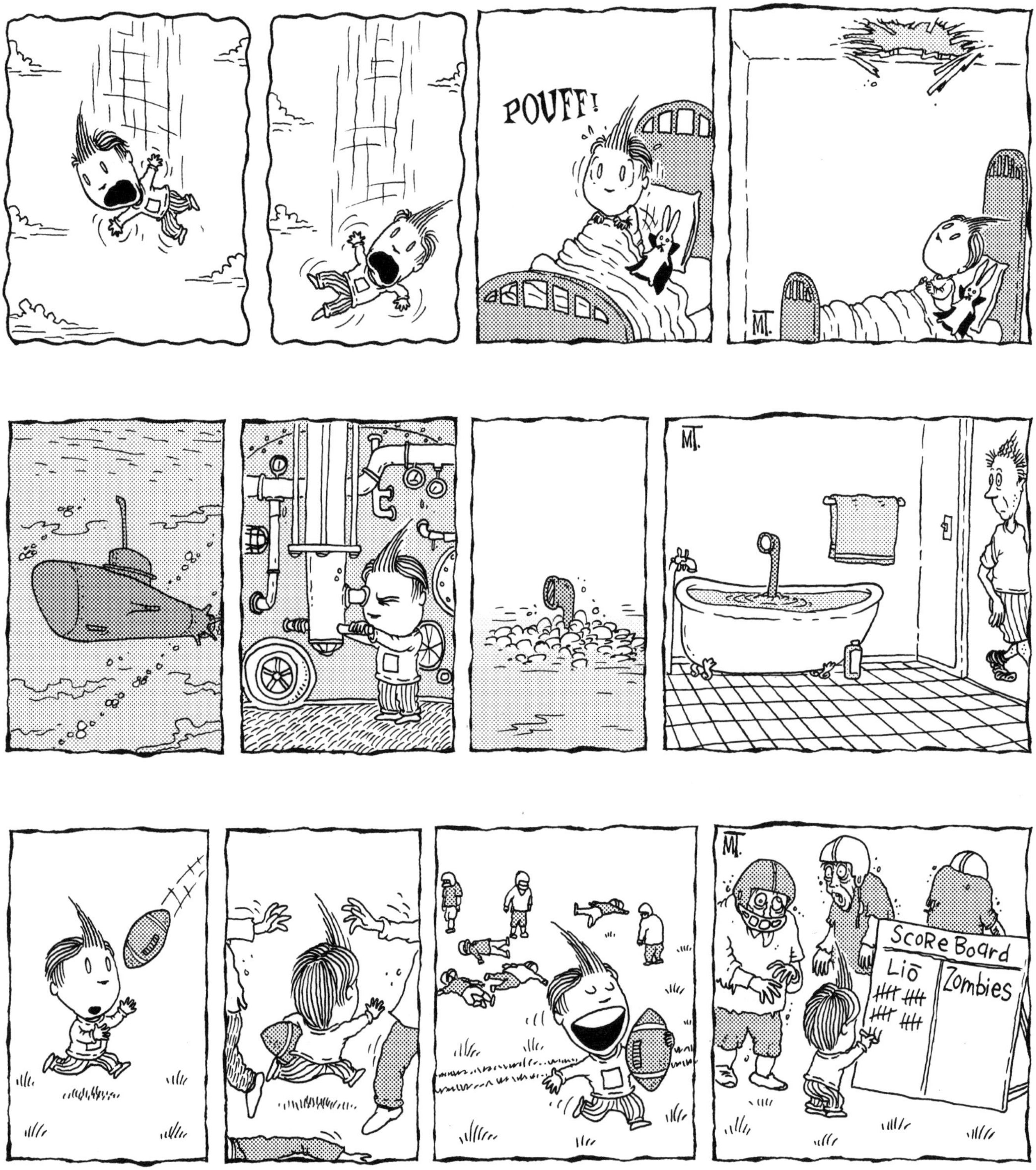
POUFF!
MT.
MT.
MT.
ScoReBoard
Lio
Zombies

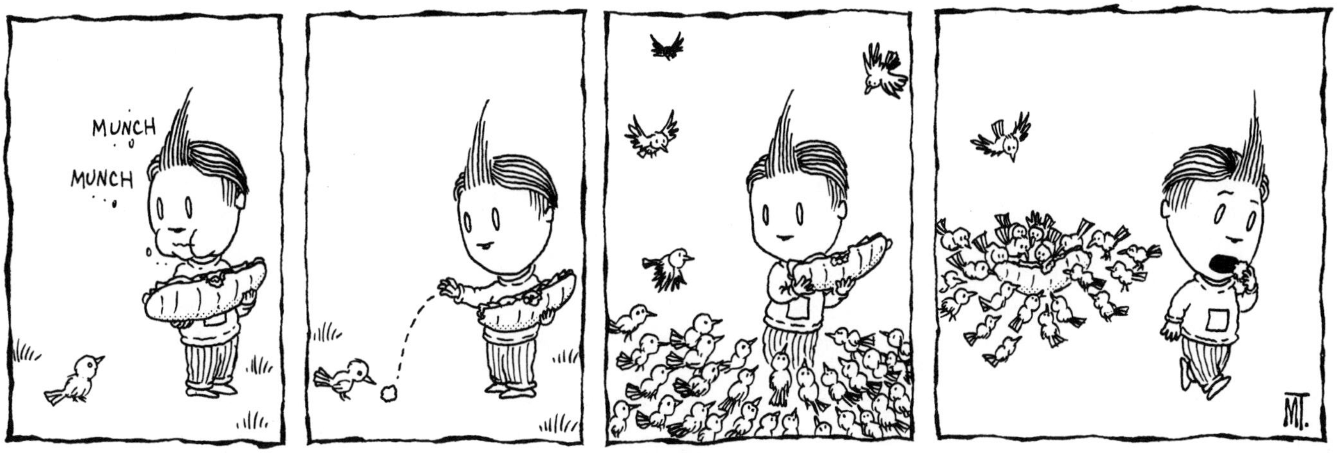
MUNCH
MUNCH

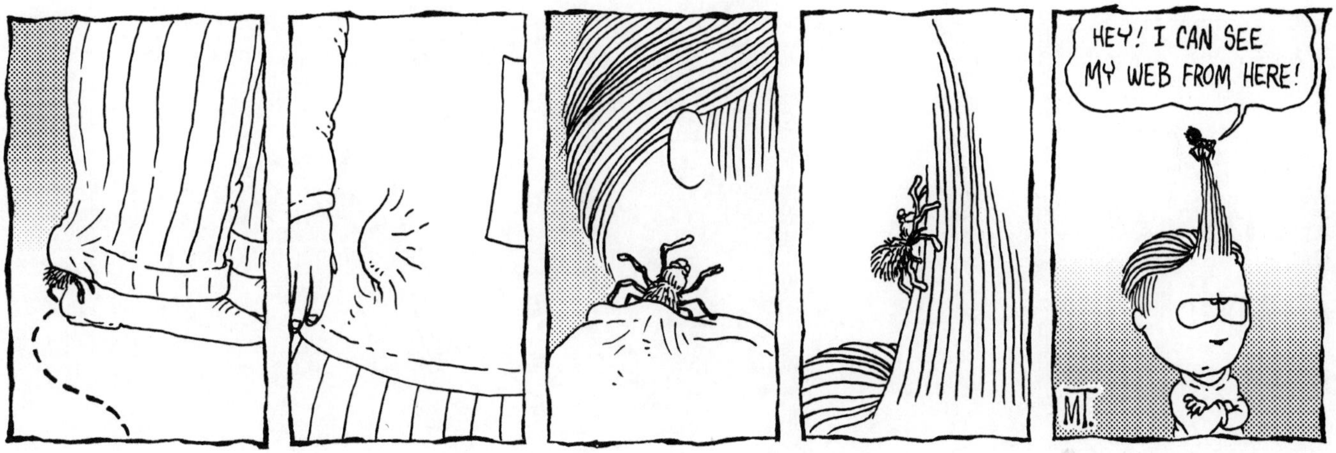
HEY! I CAN SEE MY WEB FROM HERE!

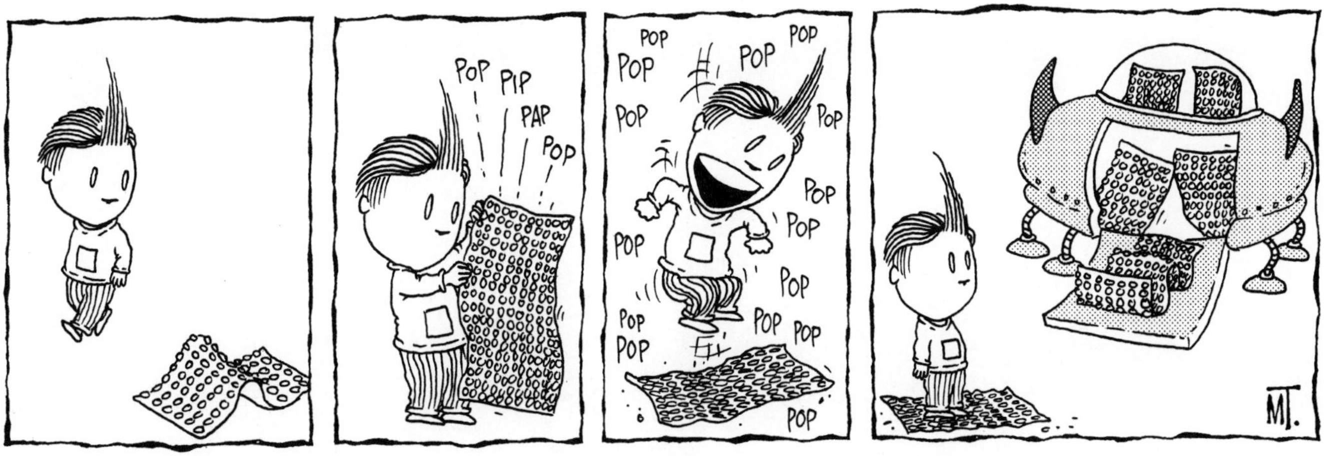
POP PIP PAP POP
POP POP POP POP POP POP POP POP POP POP POP POP POP POP POP

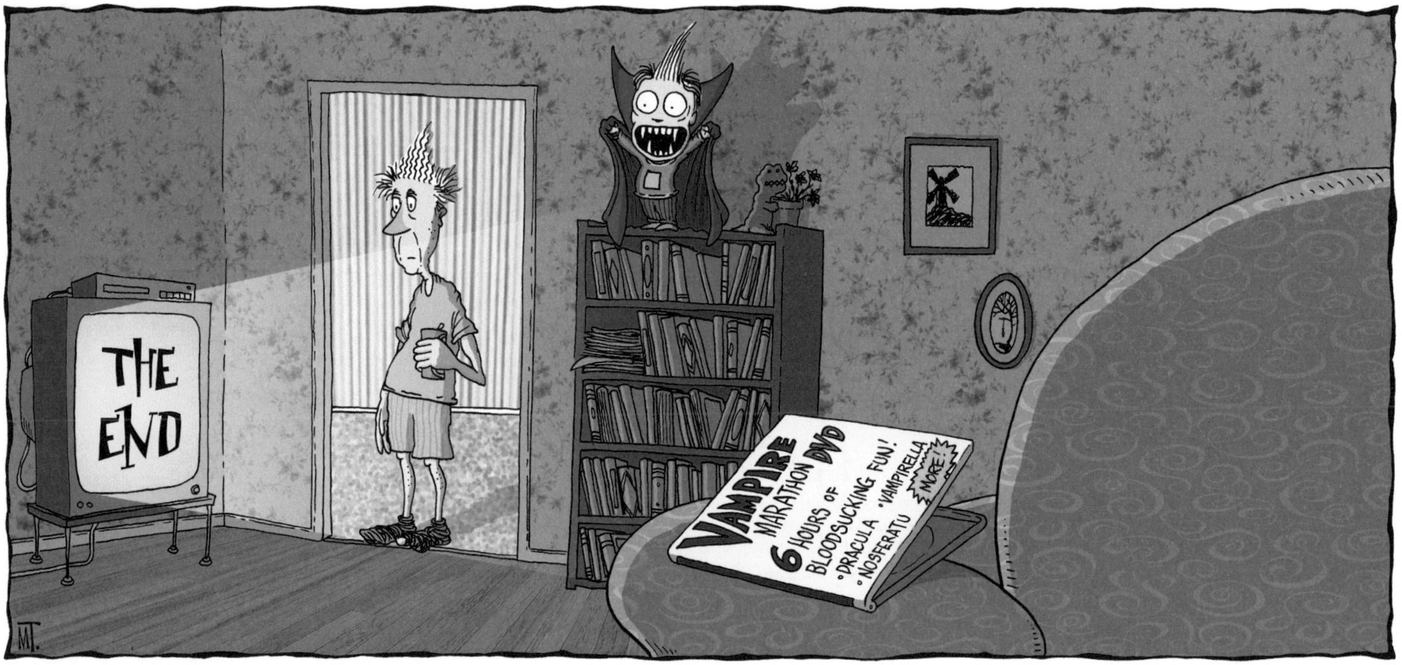
THE END
VAMPIRE MARATHON DVD
6 HOURS OF BLOODSUCKING FUN!
•DRACULA •VAMPIRELLA
•NOSFERATU
MORE!
MT.

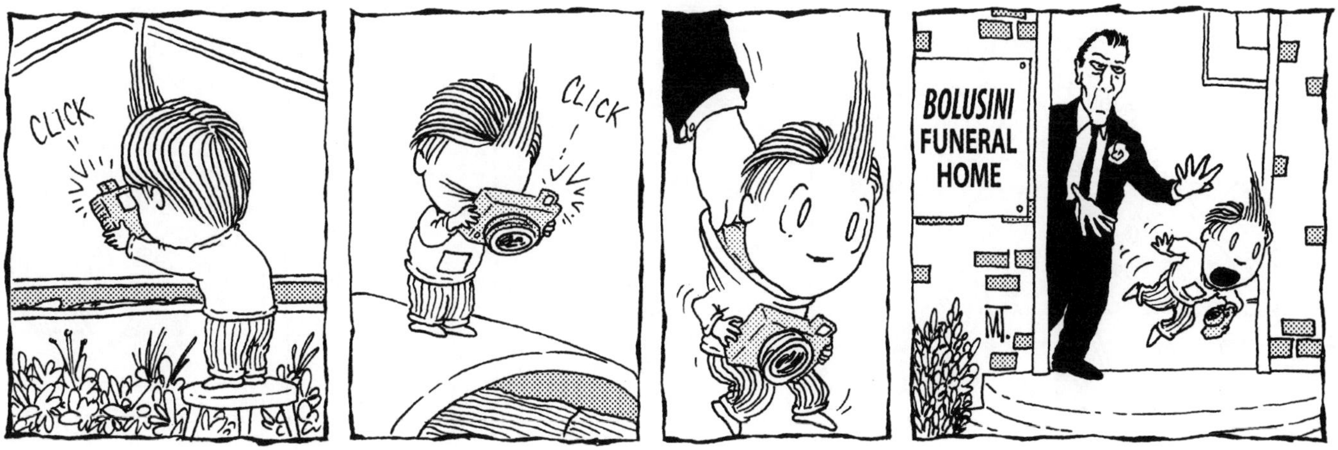
CLICK
CLICK
BOLUSINI
FUNERAL
HOME
MT.

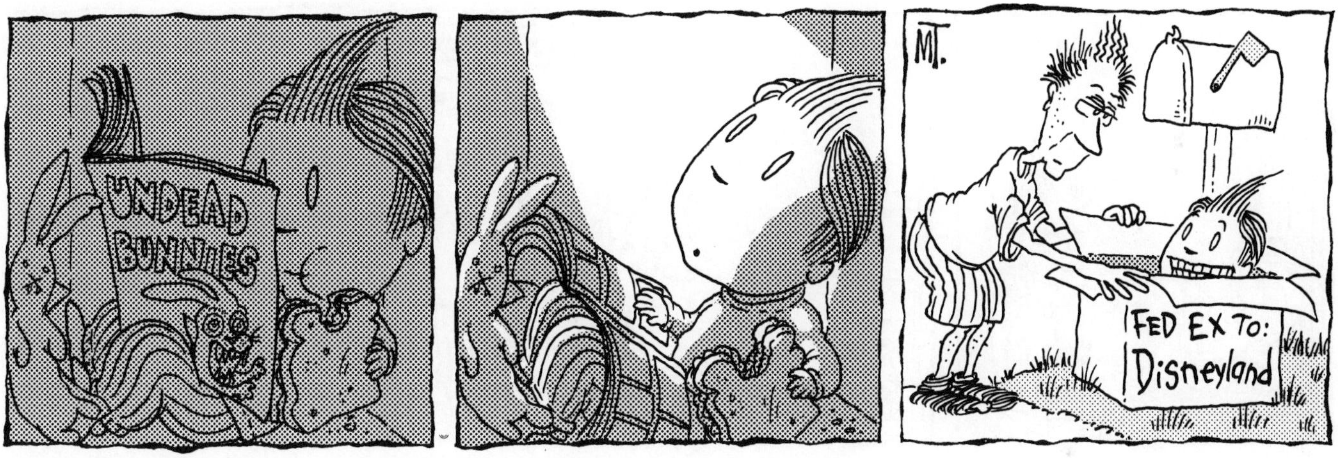
UNDEAD
BUNNIES
MT.
FED EX To:
Disneyland

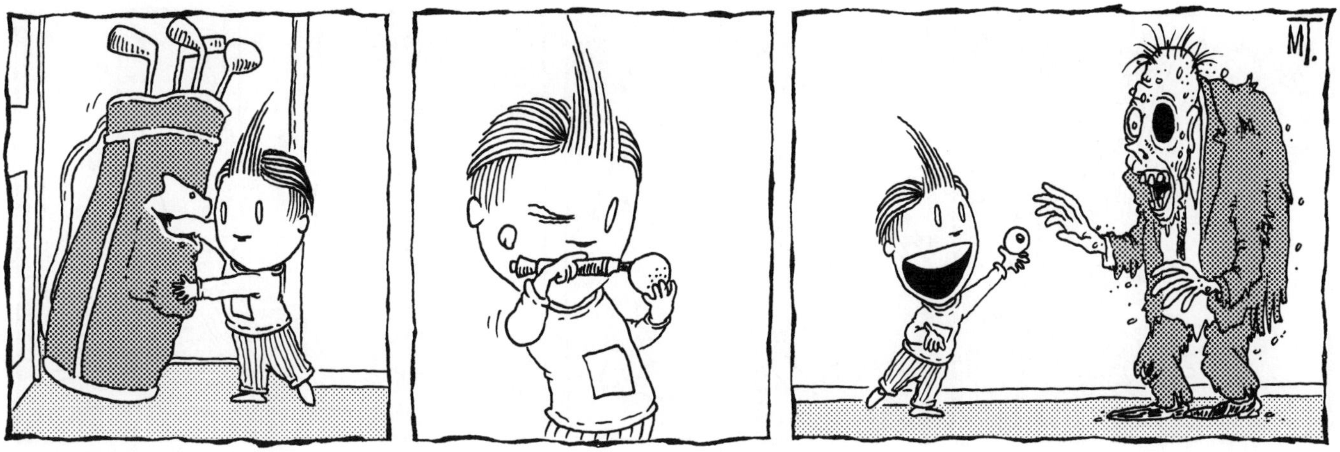
MT.

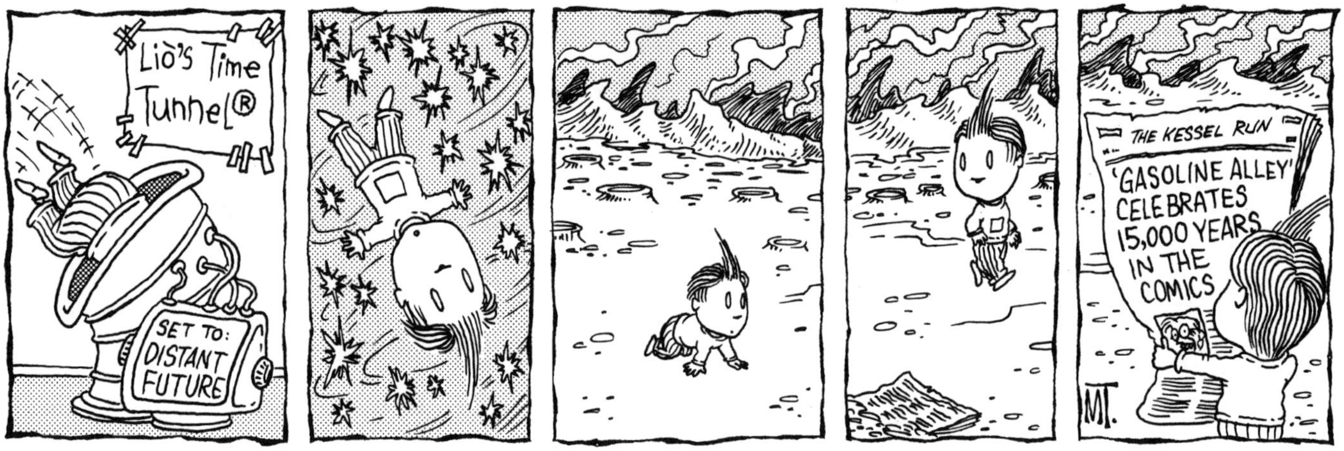
Lio's Time Tunnel®
SET TO: DISTANT FUTURE
THE KESSEL RUN
'GASOLINE ALLEY' CELEBRATES 15,000 YEARS IN THE COMICS
MT.

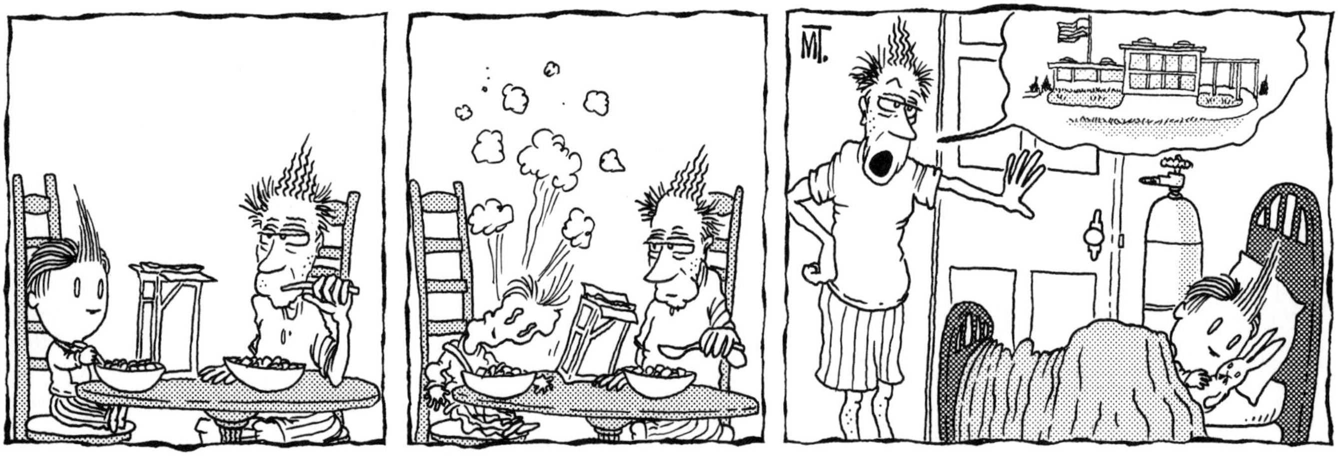
MT.

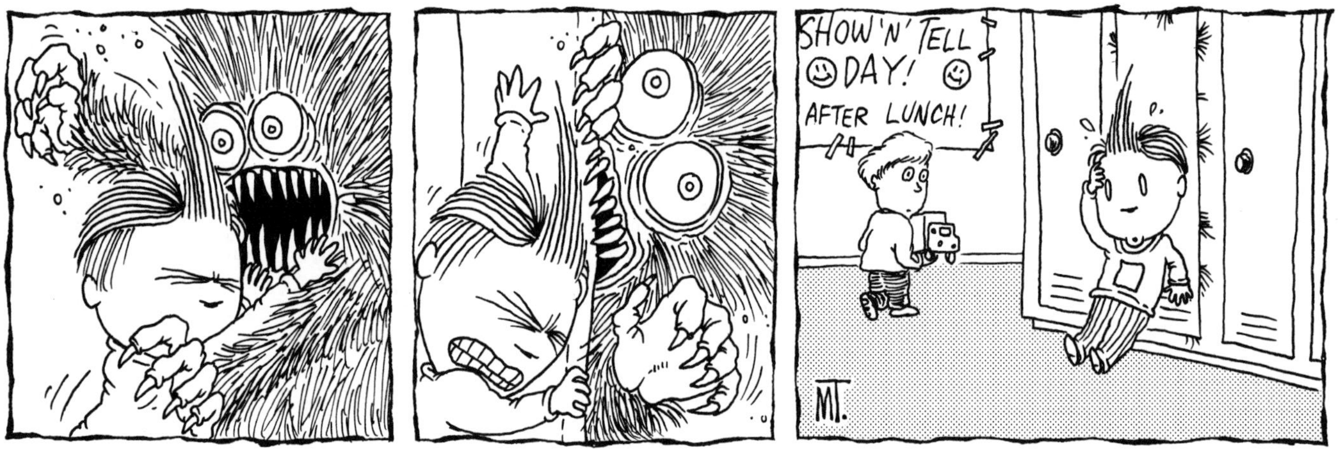
SHOW 'N' TELL DAY!
AFTER LUNCH!
MT.

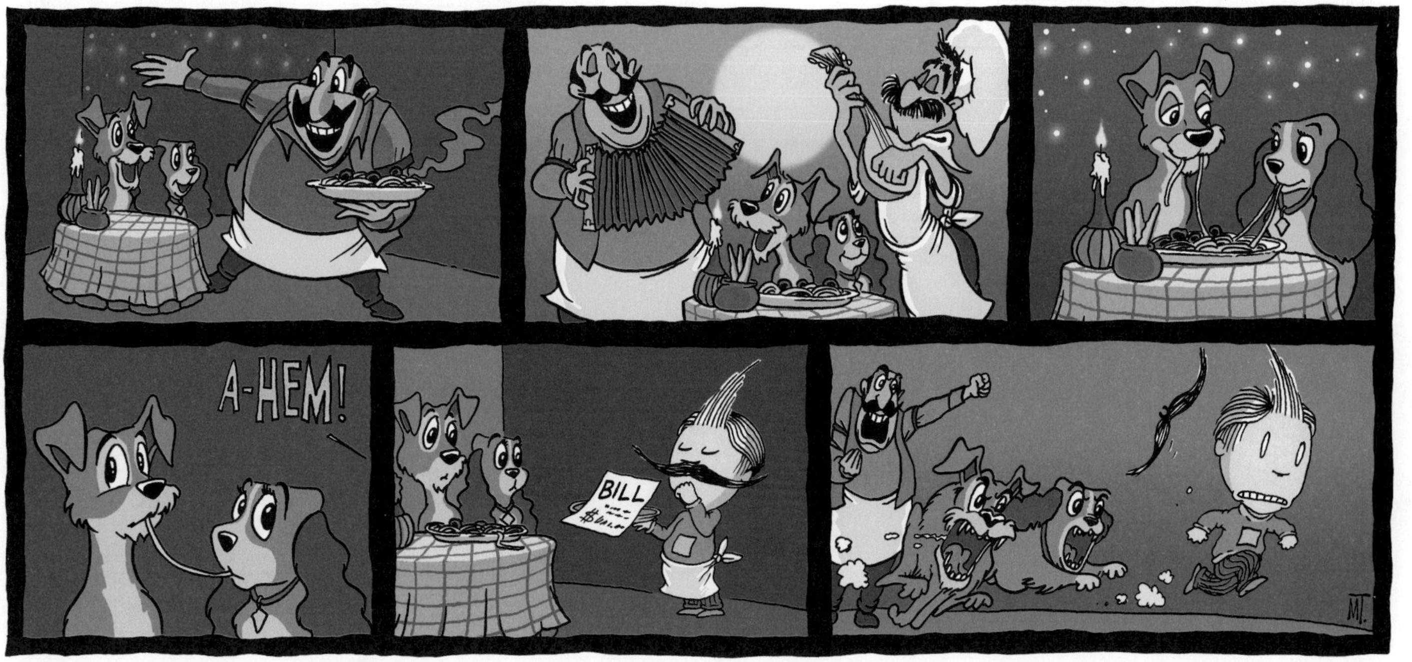
A-HEM!
BILL

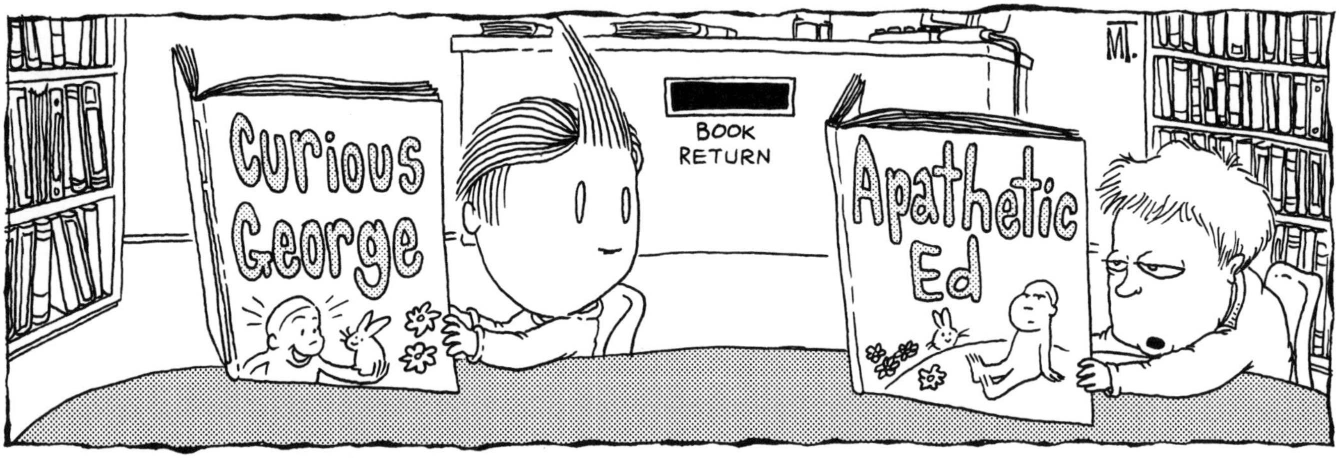
Curious George
BOOK RETURN
Apathetic Ed

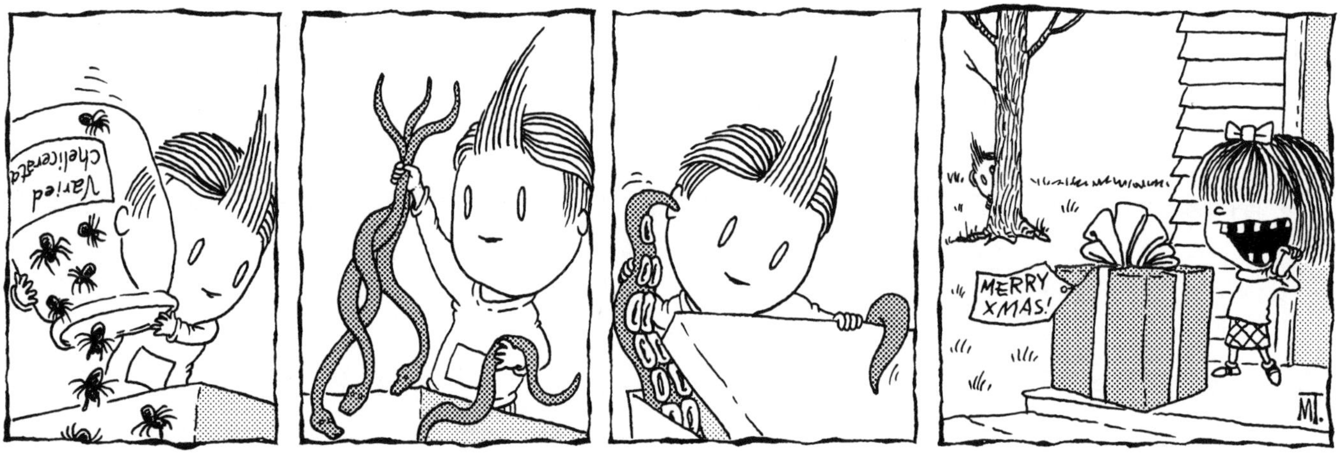
Varied chelicerata
MERRY XMAS!

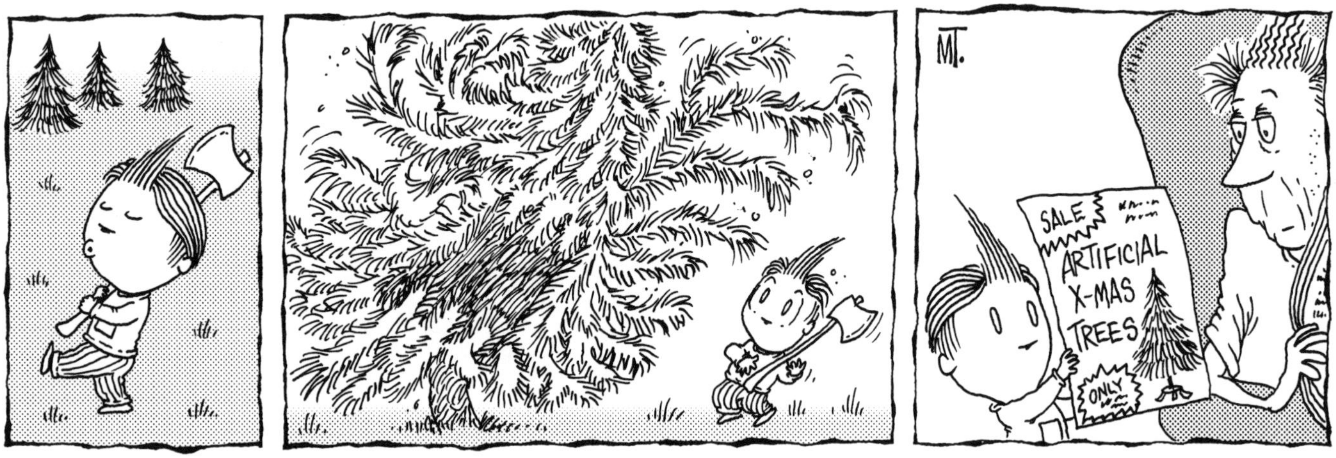
SALE
ARTIFICIAL X-MAS TREES
ONLY

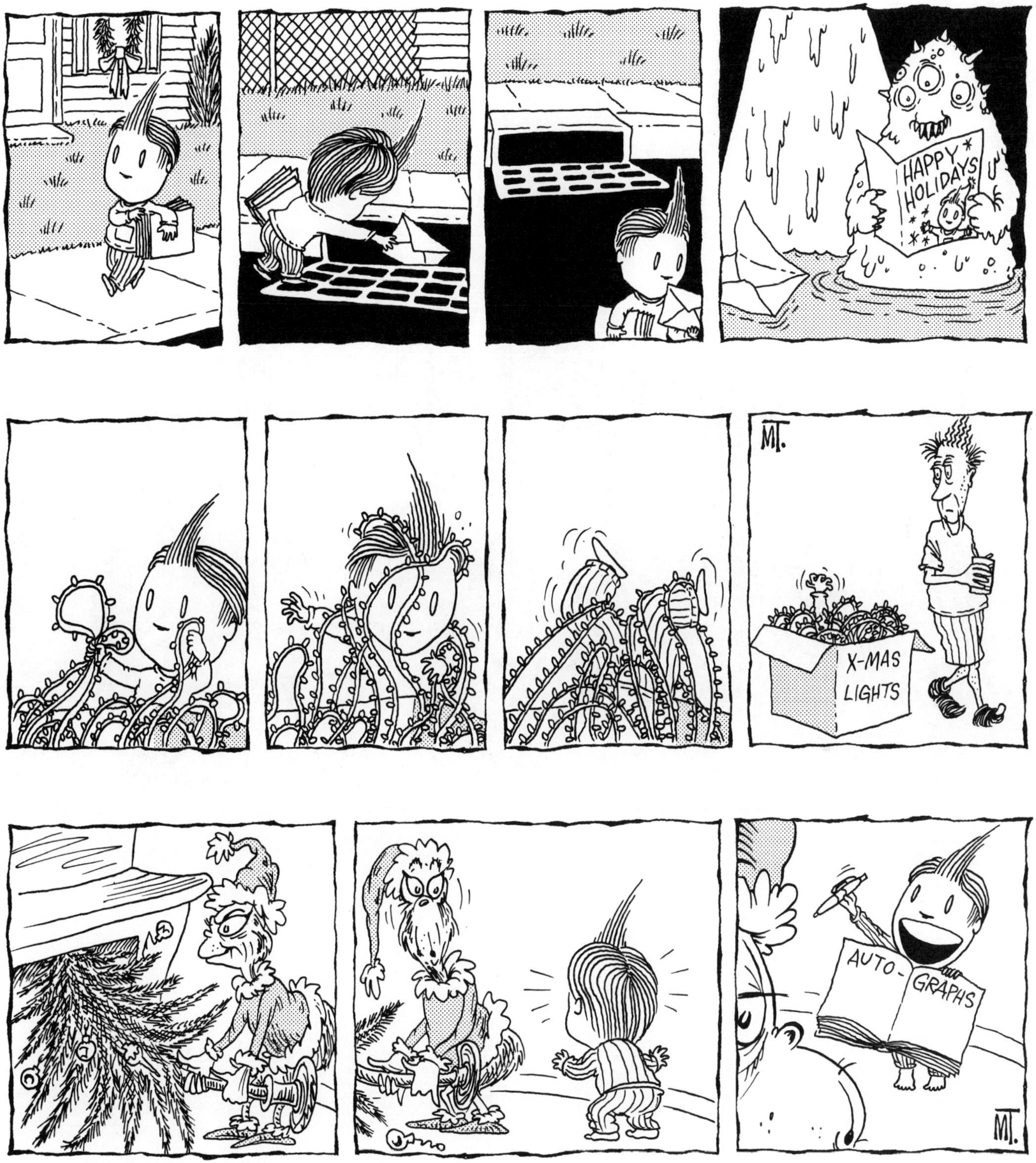
HAPPY HOLIDAYS
MT.
X-MAS LIGHTS
AUTO-GRAPHS
MT.

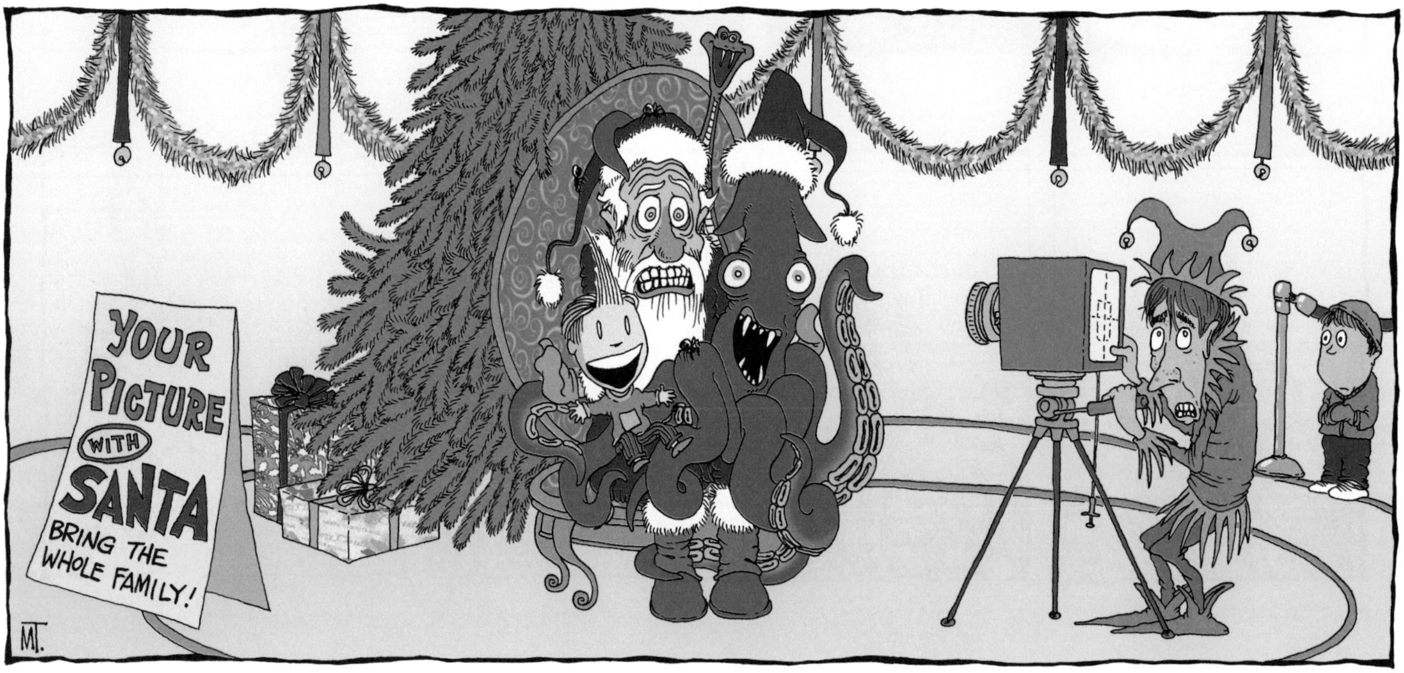
YOUR PICTURE WITH SANTA
BRING THE WHOLE FAMILY!
MT.

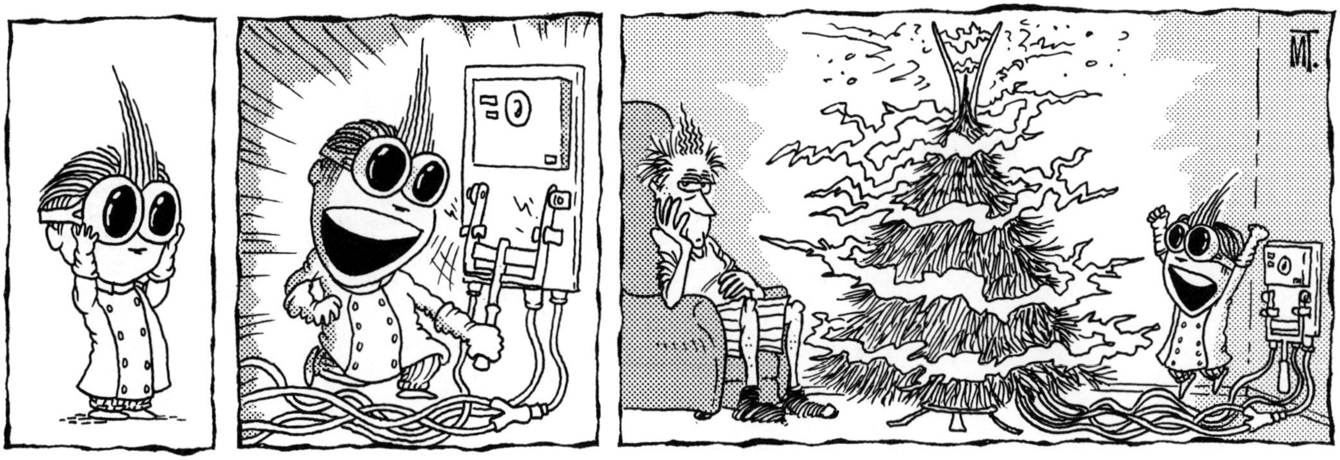
MT.

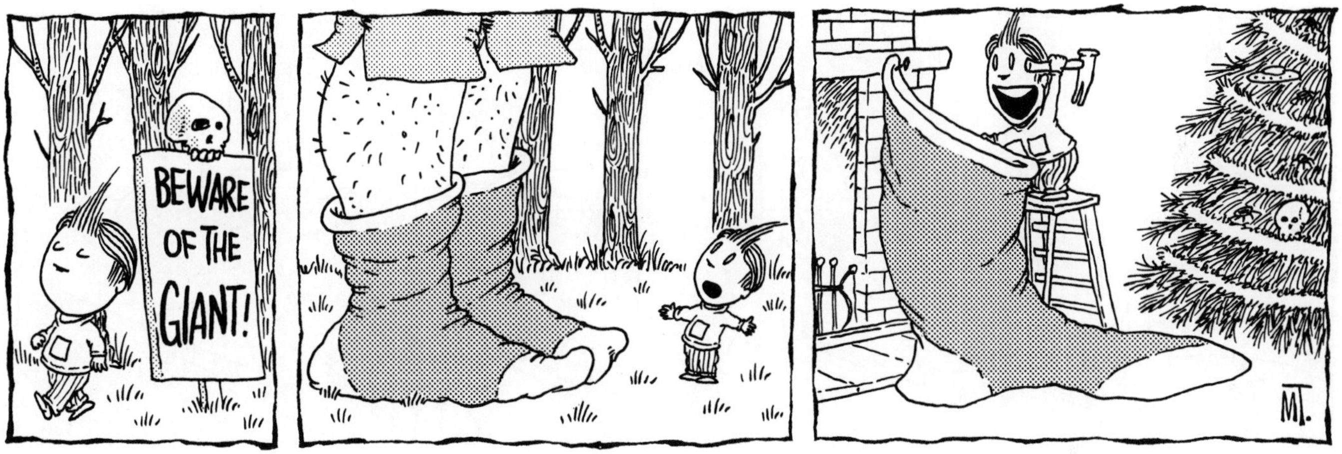
BEWARE OF THE GIANT!
MT.

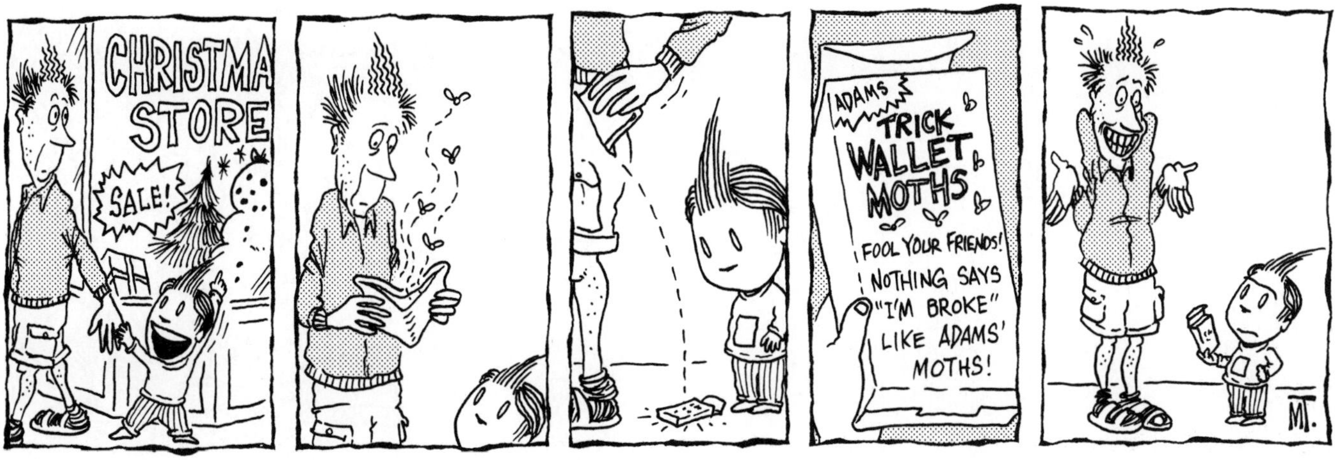
CHRISTMA STORE
SALE!
ADAMS TRICK WALLET MOTHS
FOOL YOUR FRIENDS!
NOTHING SAYS "I'M BROKE" LIKE ADAMS' MOTHS!
MT.

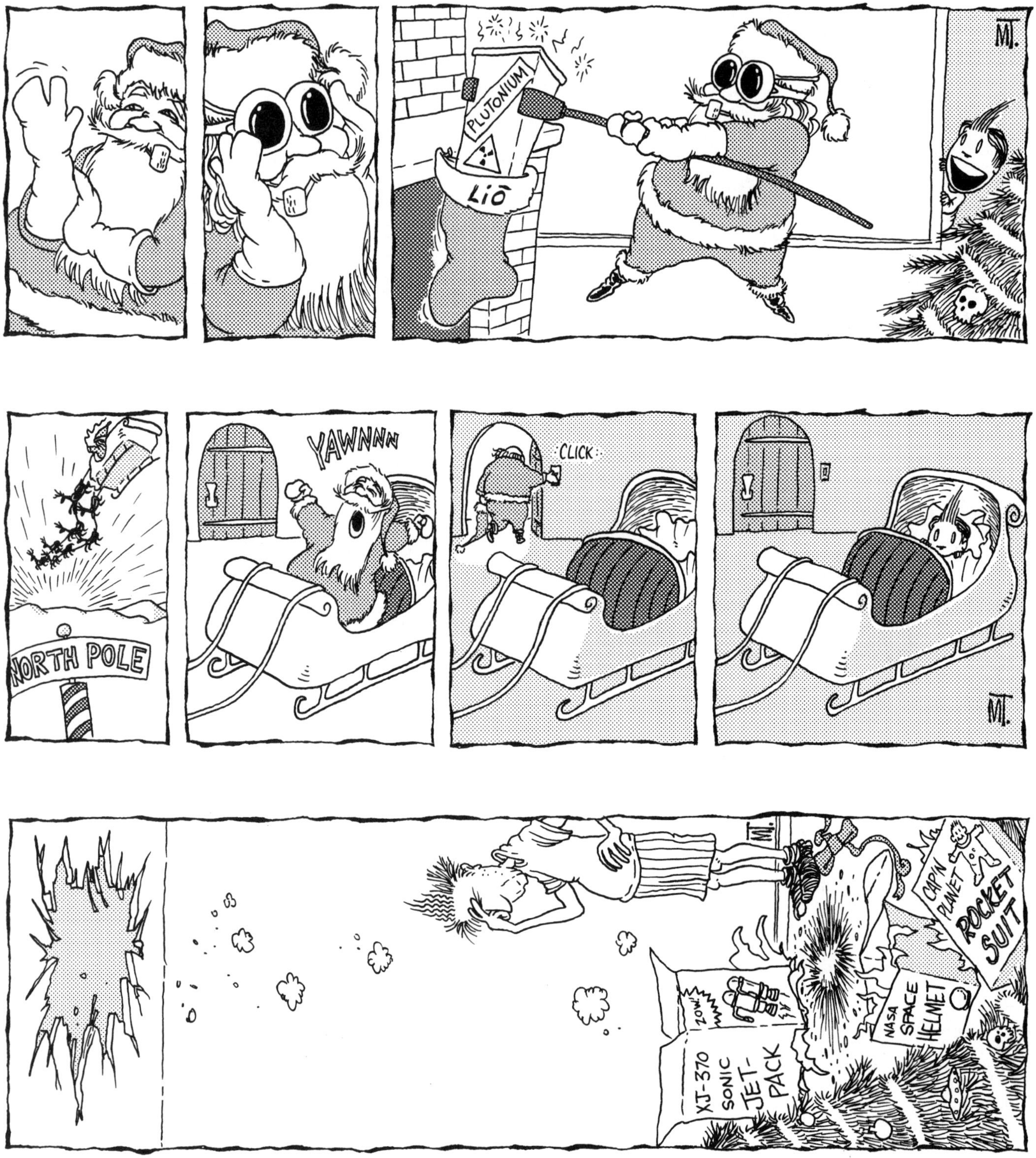
MT.
PLUTONIUM
LIO
NORTH POLE
YAWNNN
CLICK
MT.
MT.
ZOW!
XJ-370 SONIC JET-PACK
NASA SPACE HELMET
CAP'N PLANET ROCKET SUIT

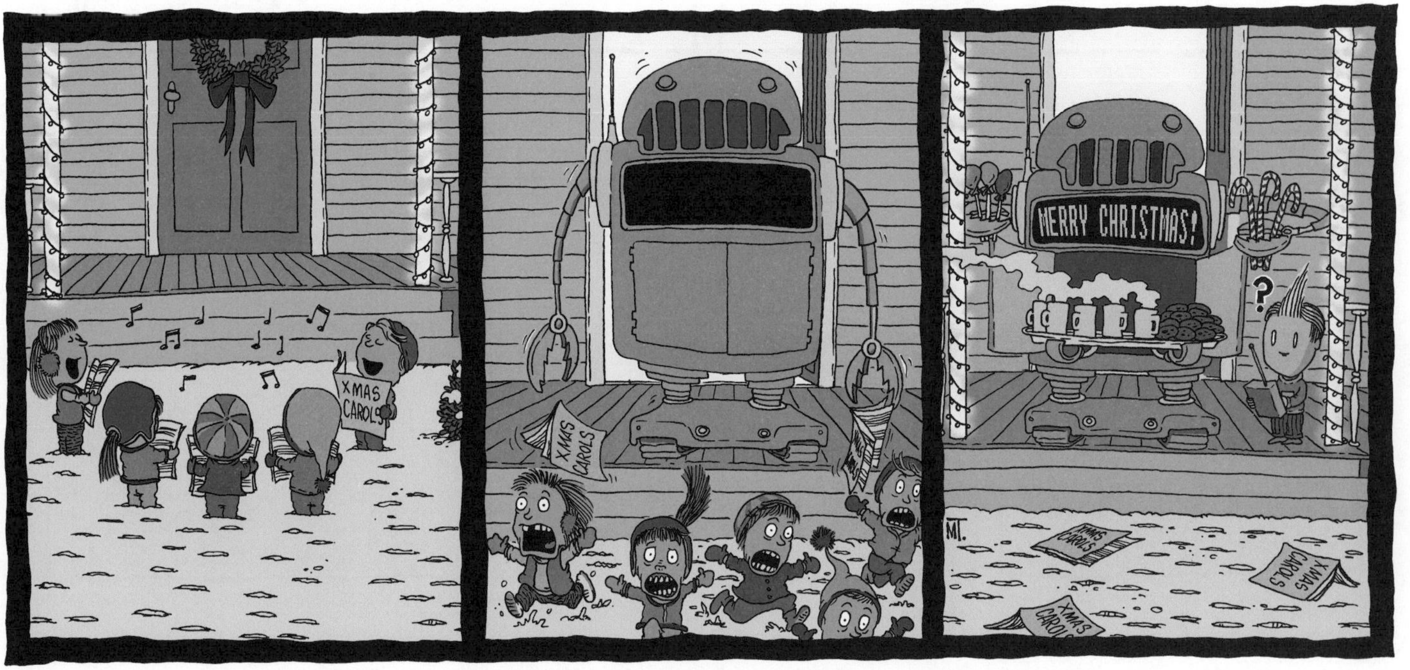
XMAS CAROLS
XMAS CAROLS
MERRY CHRISTMAS!
?
MT.
XMAS CAROLS
XMAS CAROLS
XMAS CAROLS

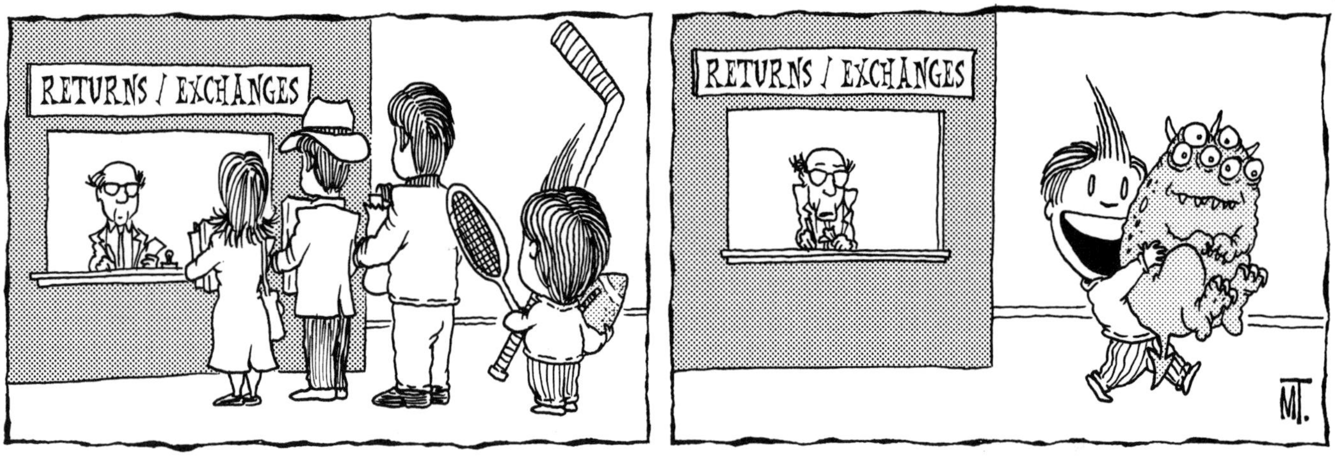
RETURNS / EXCHANGES
RETURNS / EXCHANGES

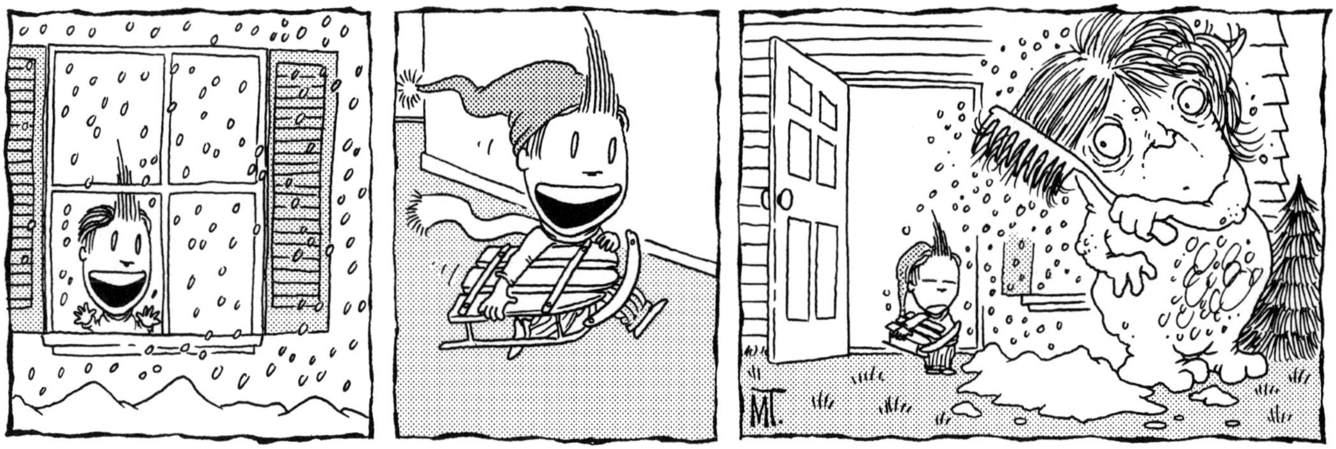

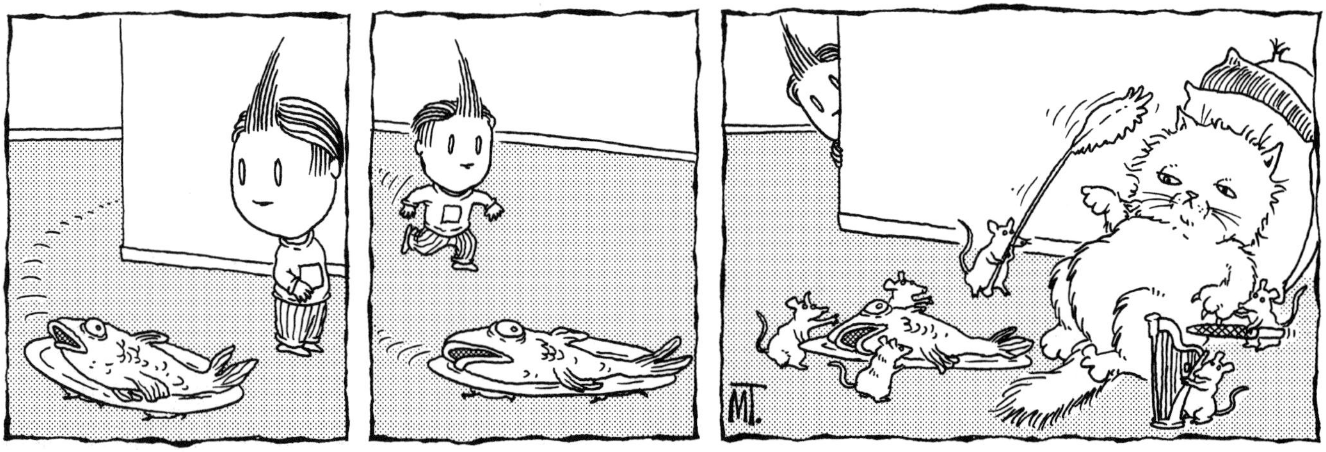

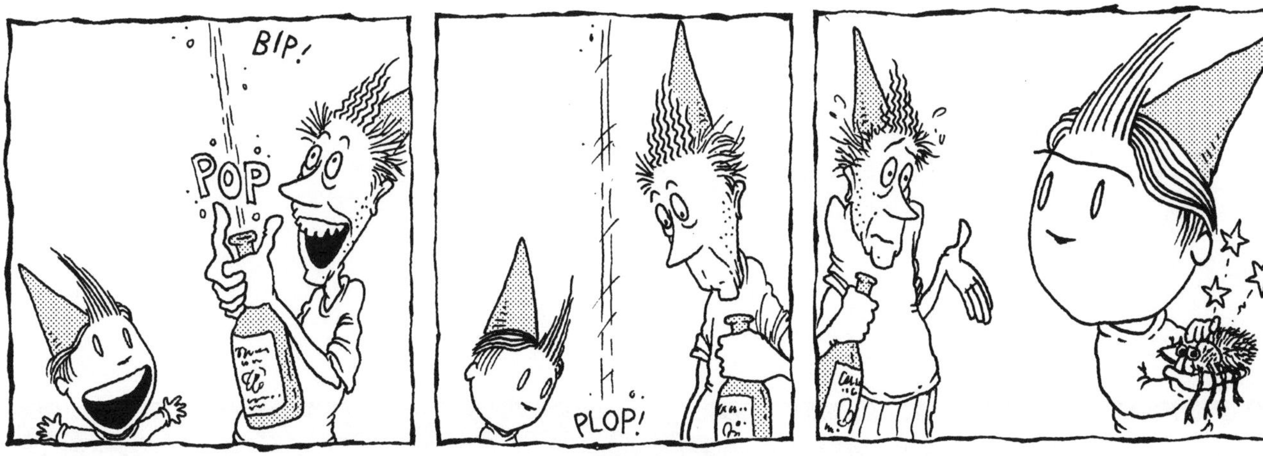
BIP!
POP
PLOP!
MT.

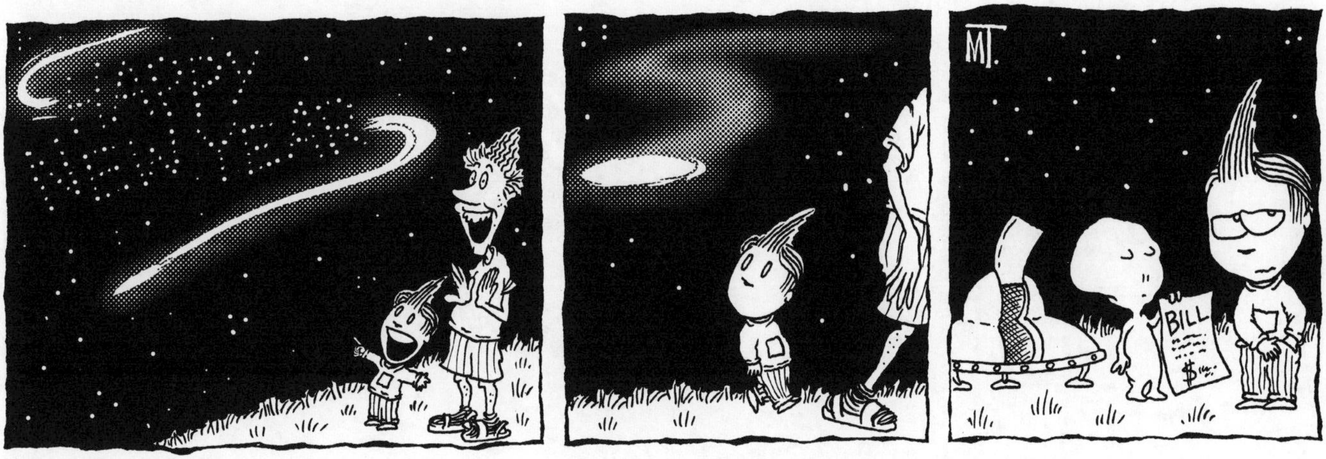
MT.
BILL
$

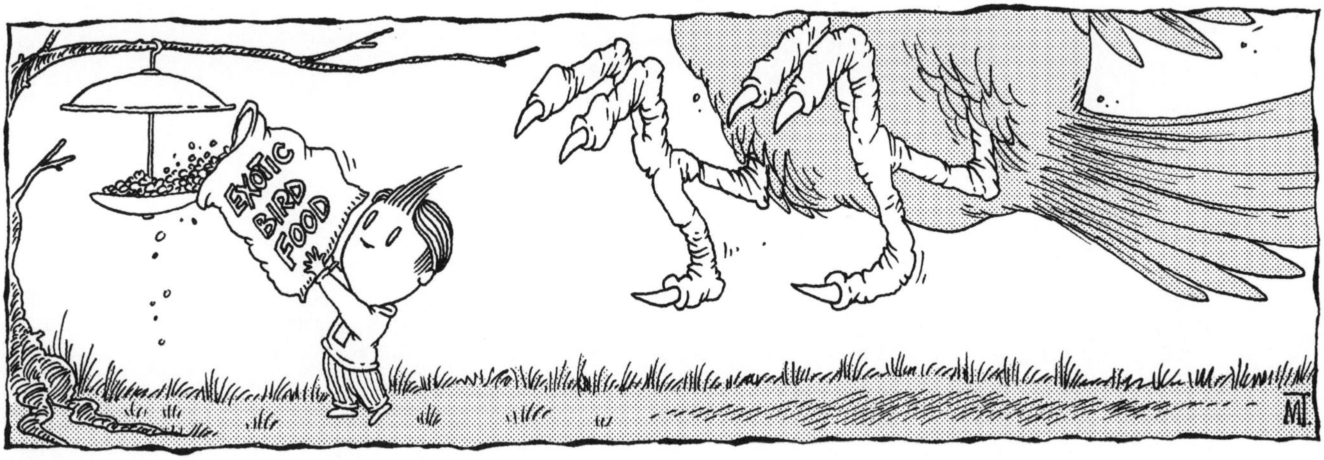
EXOTIC BIRD FOOD
MT.

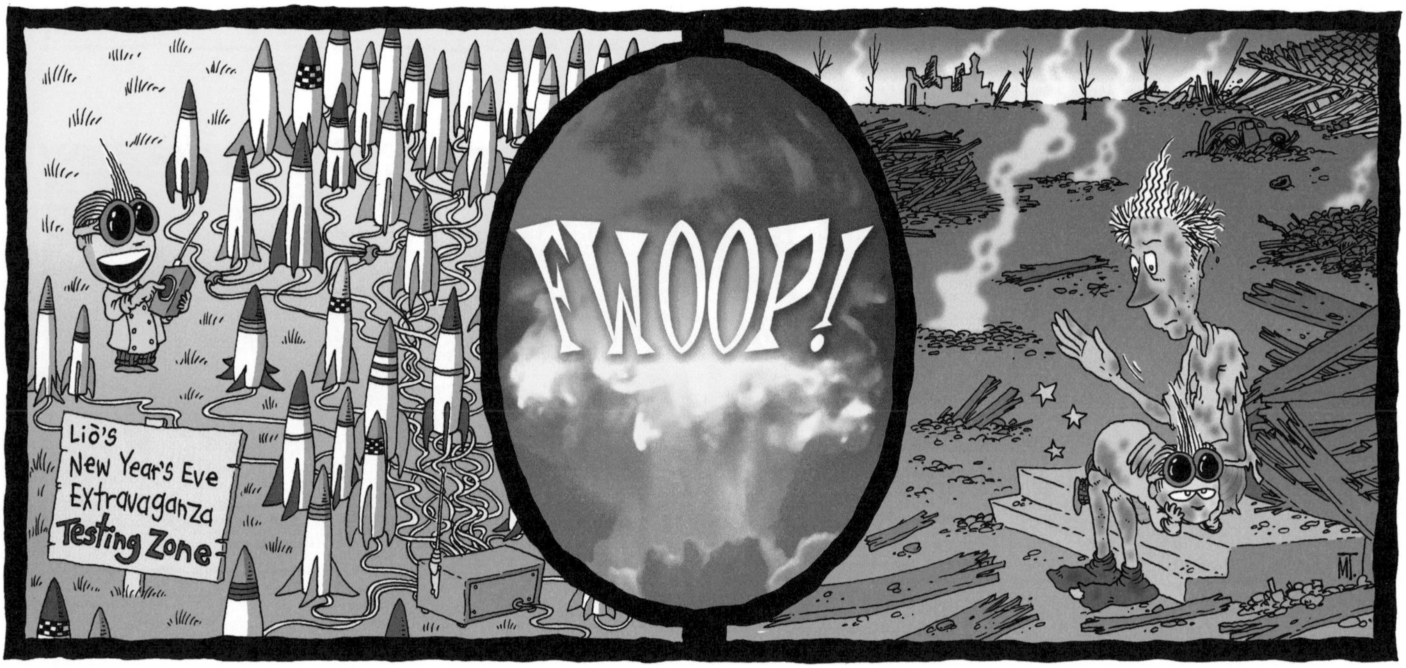
Lio's
New Year's Eve
Extravaganza
Testing Zone
FWOOP!
MT.

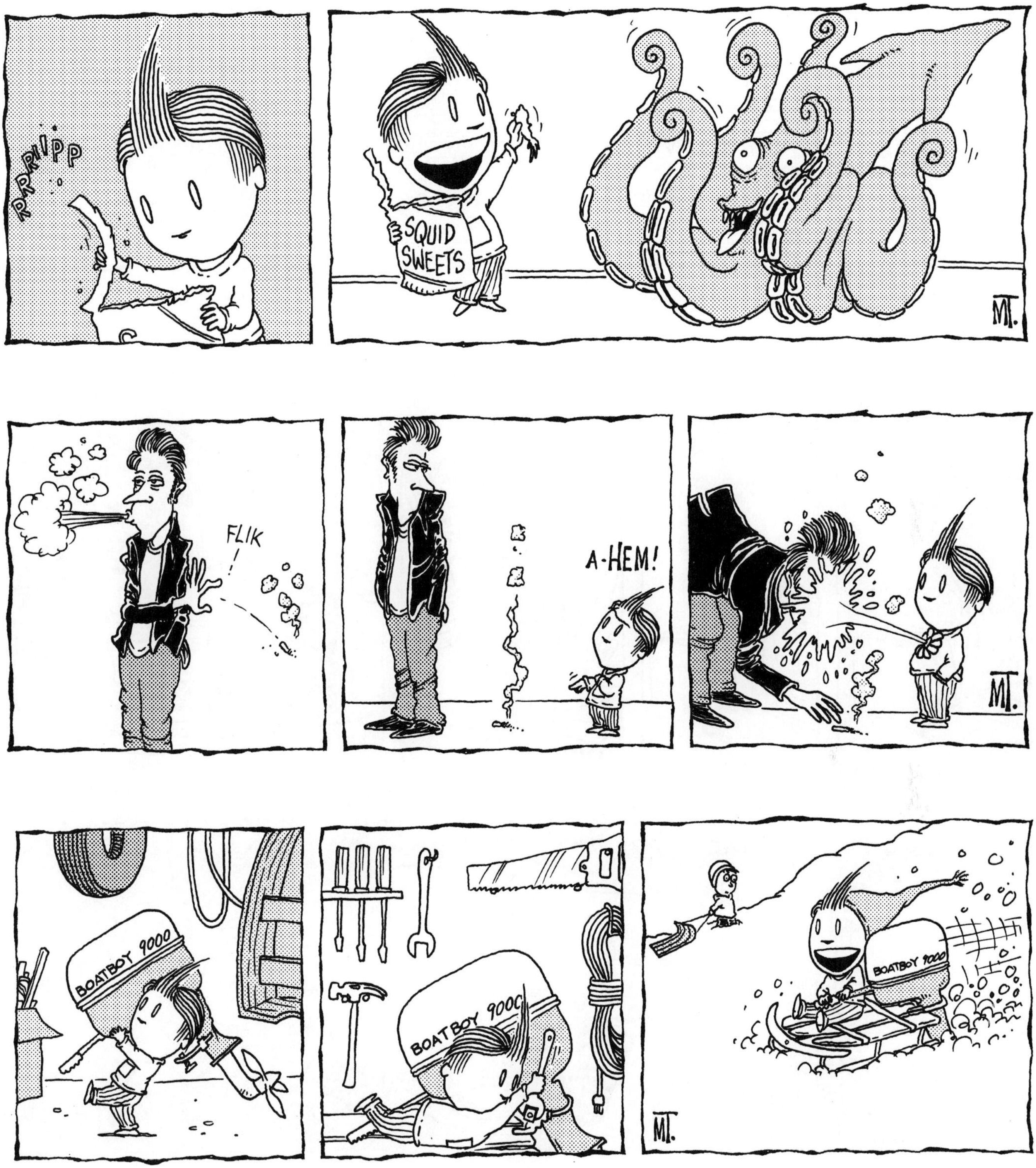
RRRIPP
SQUID SWEETS
MT.
FLIK
A-HEM!
MT.
BOATBOY 9000
BOATBOY 9000
BOATBOY 9000
MT.

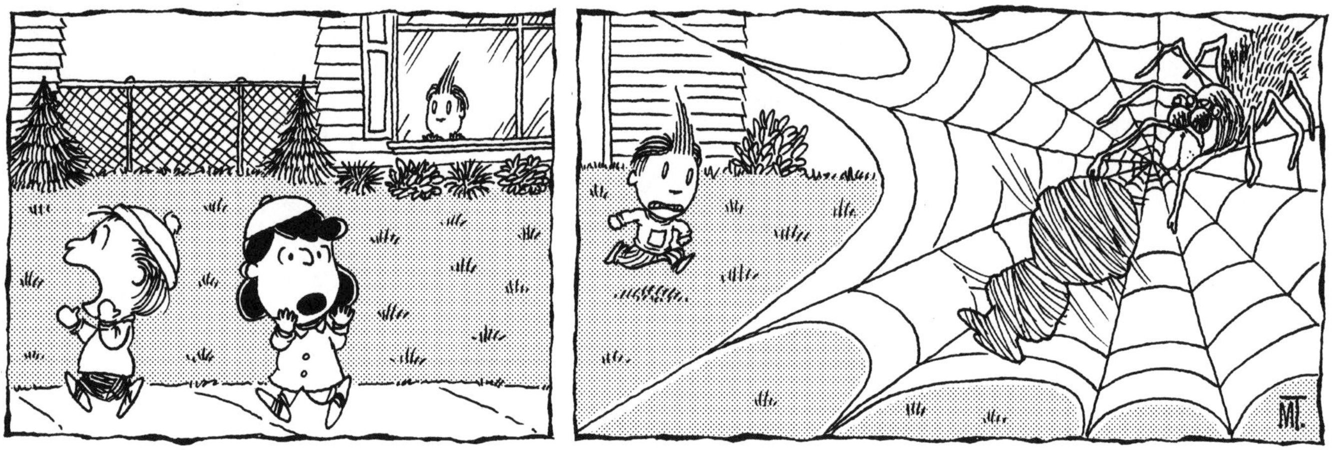

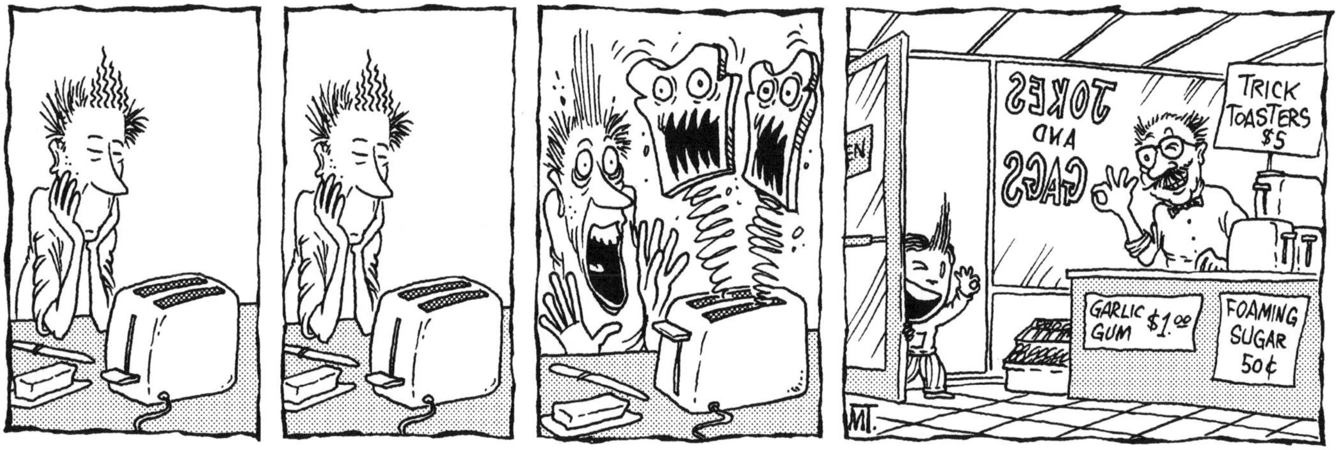
JOKES AND GAGS
TRICK TOASTERS $5
GARLIC GUM $1.00
FOAMING SUGAR 50¢

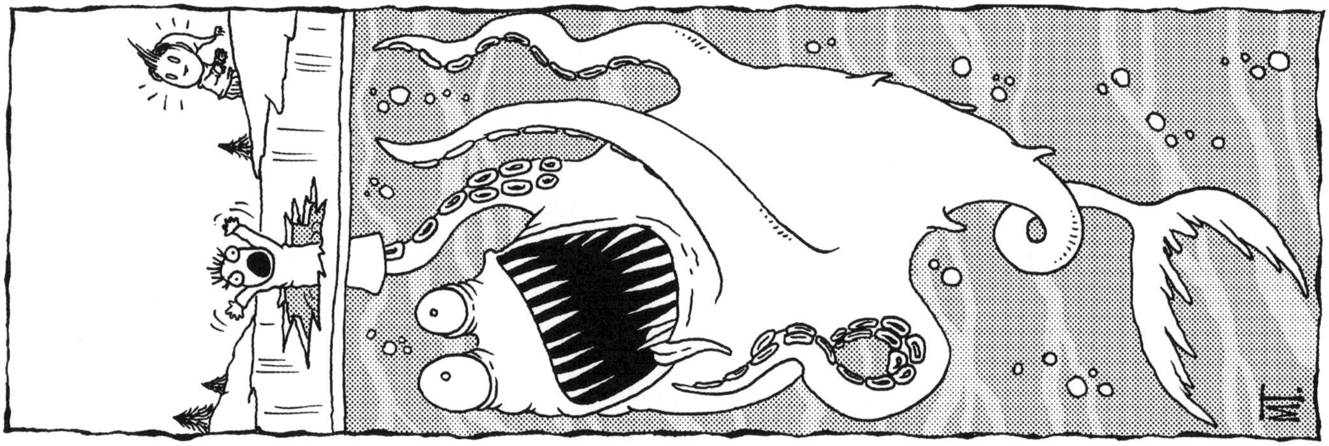

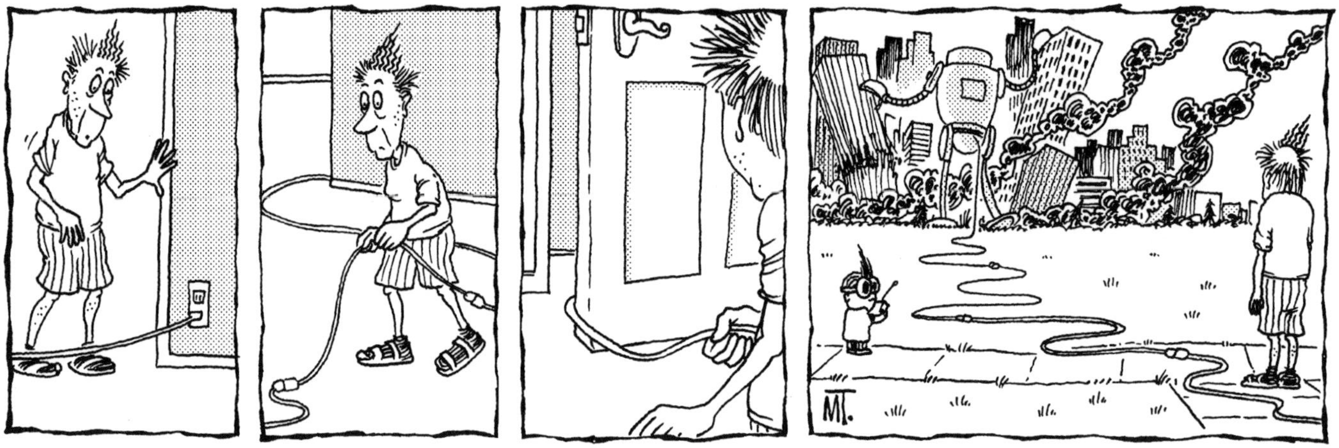

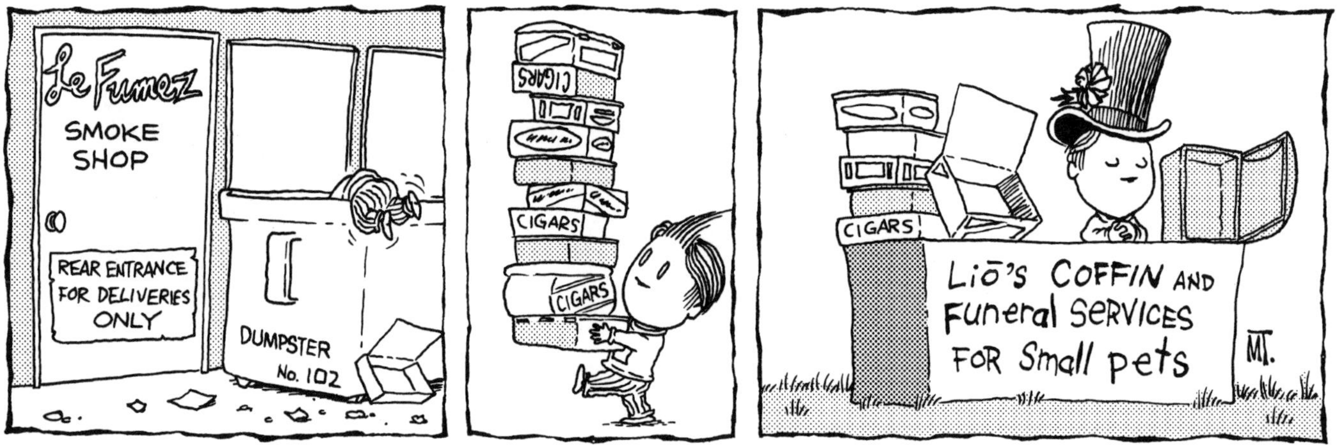
Le Fumez
SMOKE SHOP
REAR ENTRANCE FOR DELIVERIES ONLY
DUMPSTER No. 102
CIGARS
CIGARS
CIGARS
CIGARS
Liō's COFFIN AND Funeral SERVICES FOR Small pets

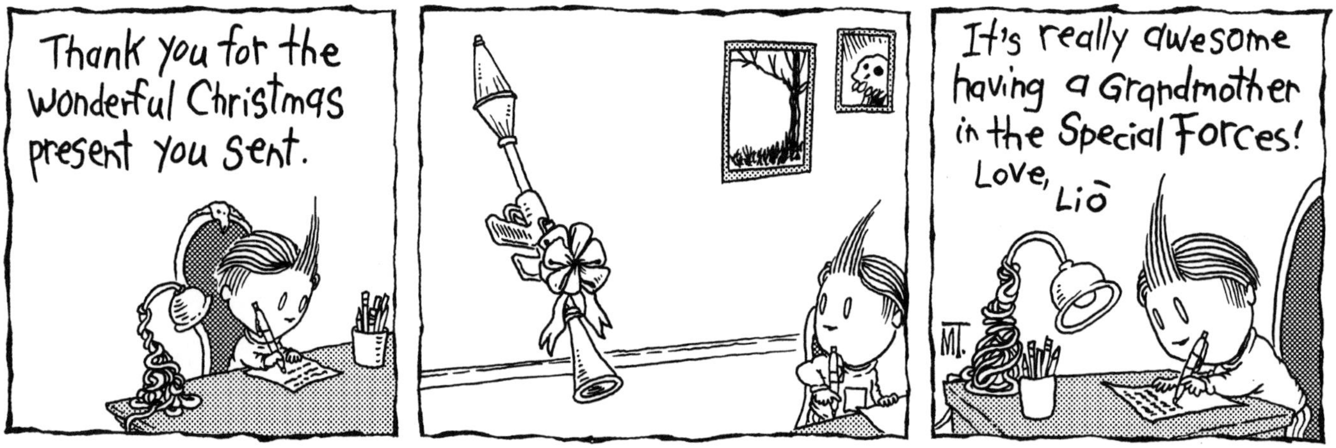
Thank you for the wonderful Christmas present you sent.
It's really awesome having a Grandmother in the Special Forces!
Love, Liō

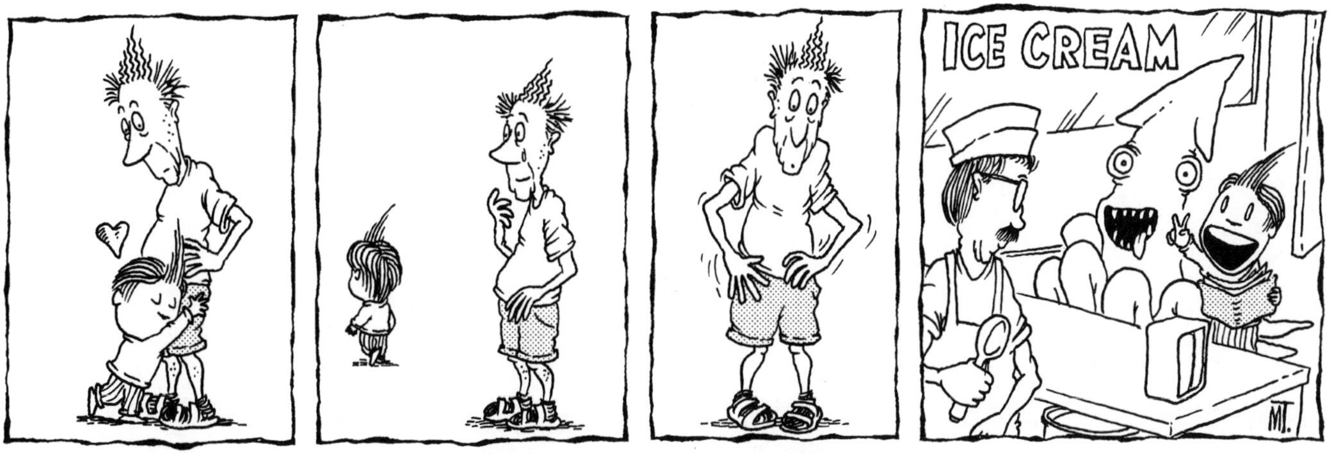
ICE CREAM
MT.

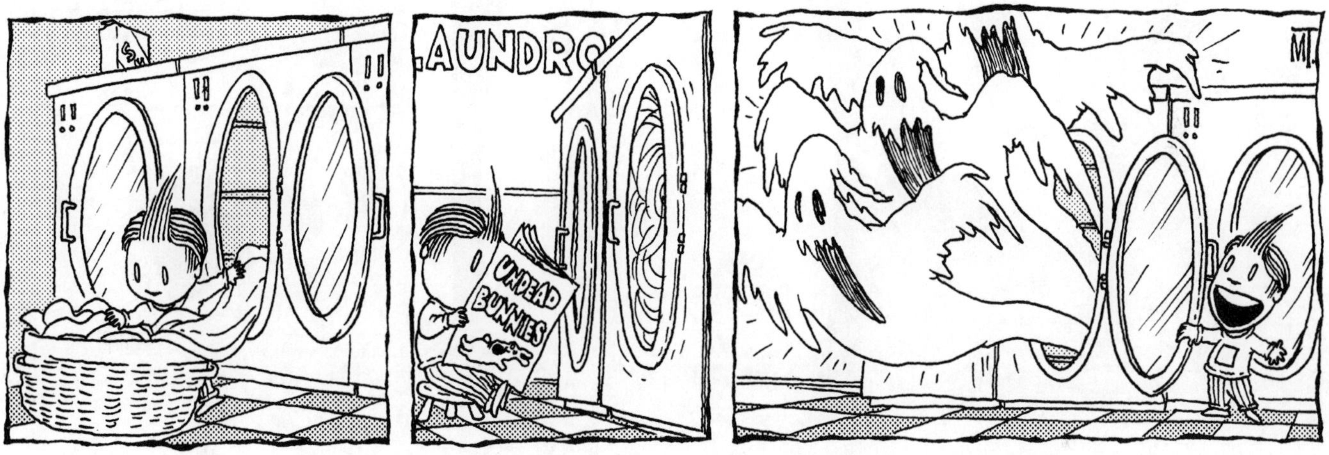
LAUNDRO
UNDEAD BUNNIES
MT.

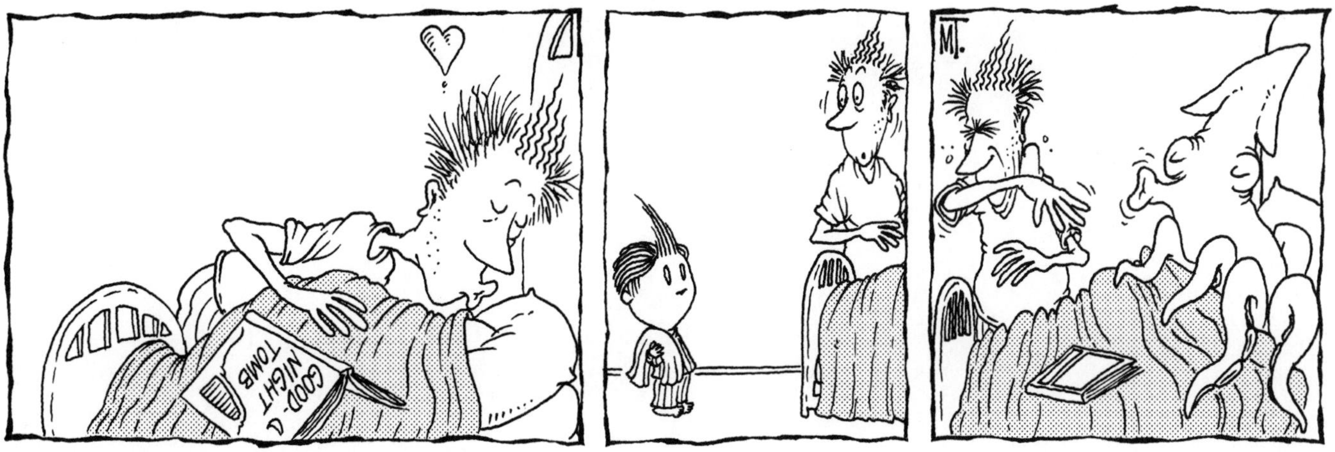
GOOD-NIGHT TOMB
MT.

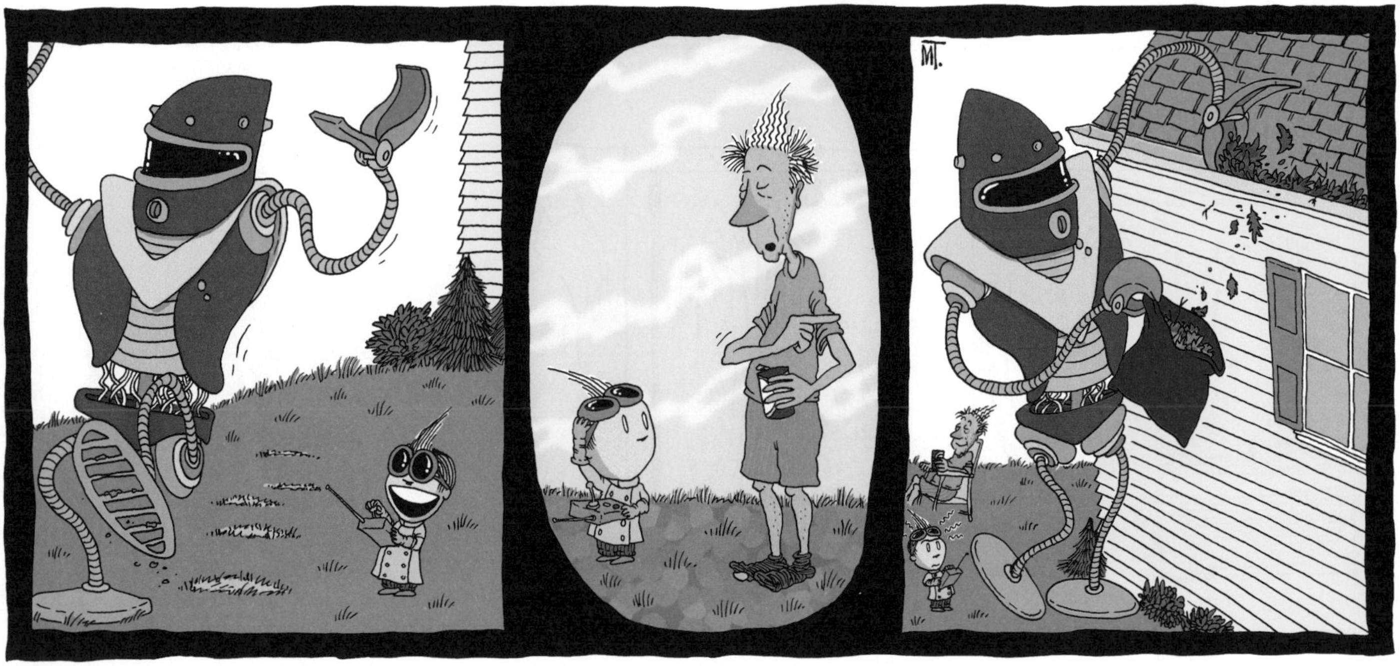
MT.

MT.
TOM CRUISE
MUSEUM OF THE JUST PLAIN WEIRD
MT.
SUPER·SQUIRT 9000
MT.

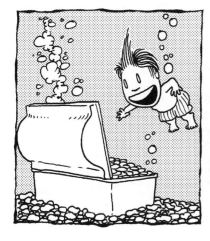

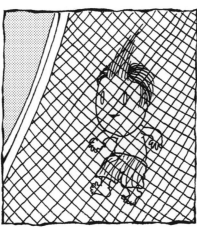

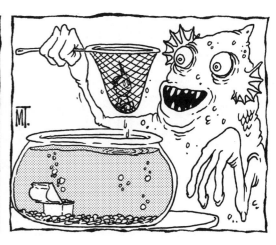

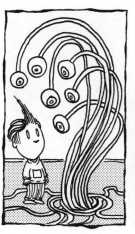

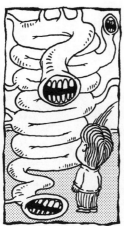

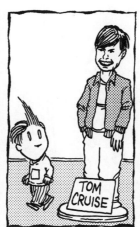

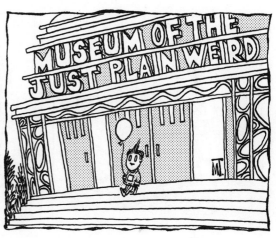

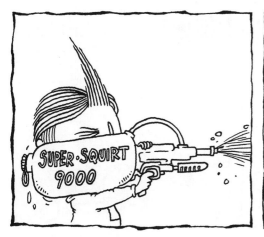

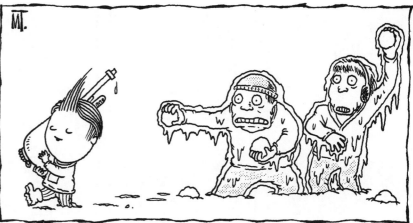

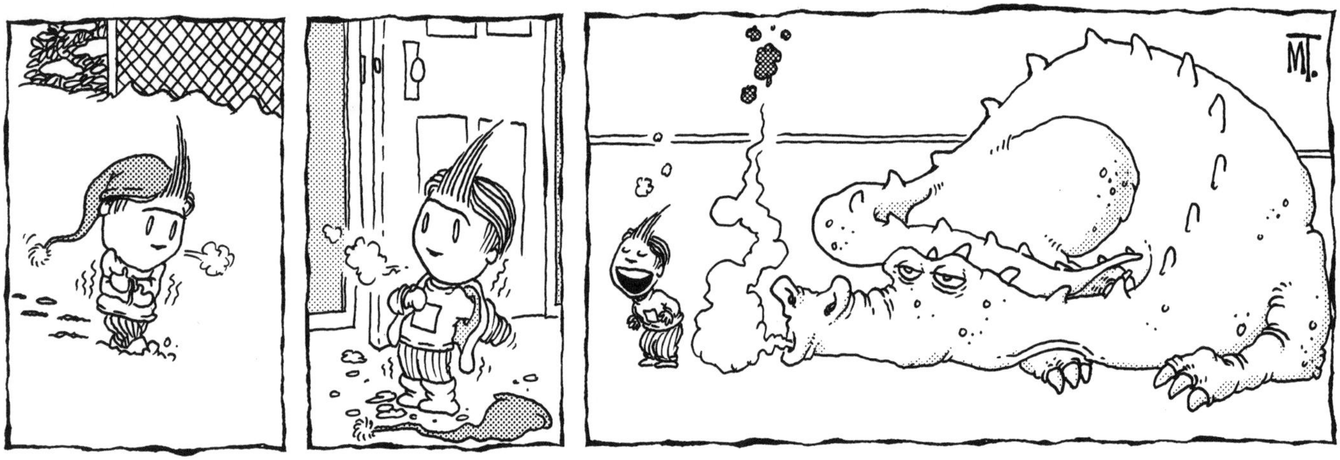

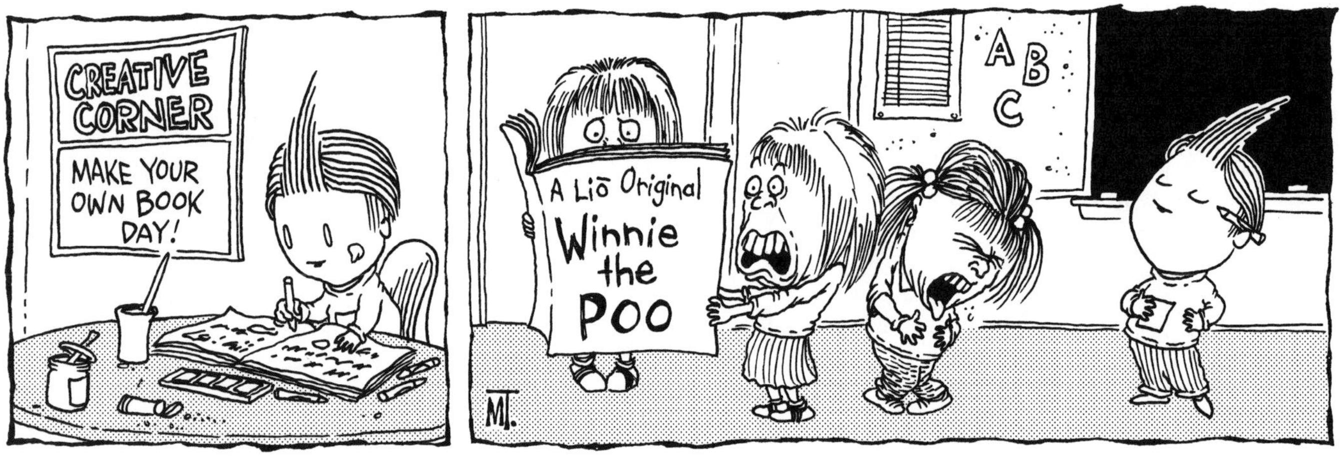
CREATIVE CORNER
MAKE YOUR OWN BOOK DAY!
A Liō Original
Winnie the POO
A B C

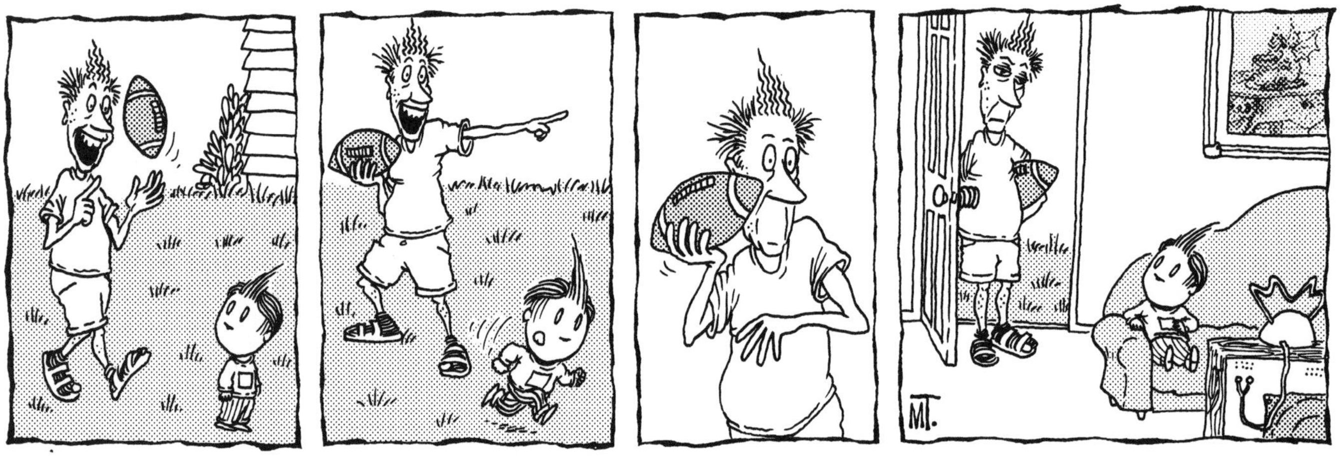

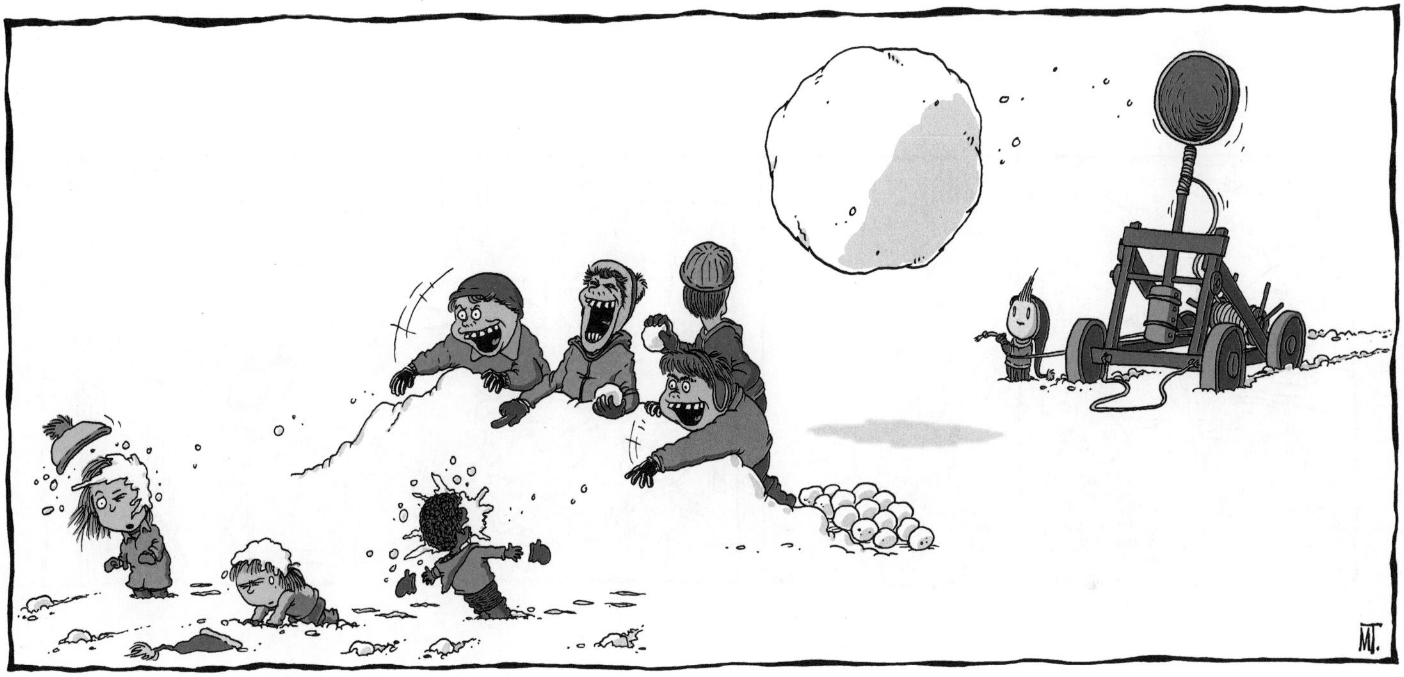
MT.

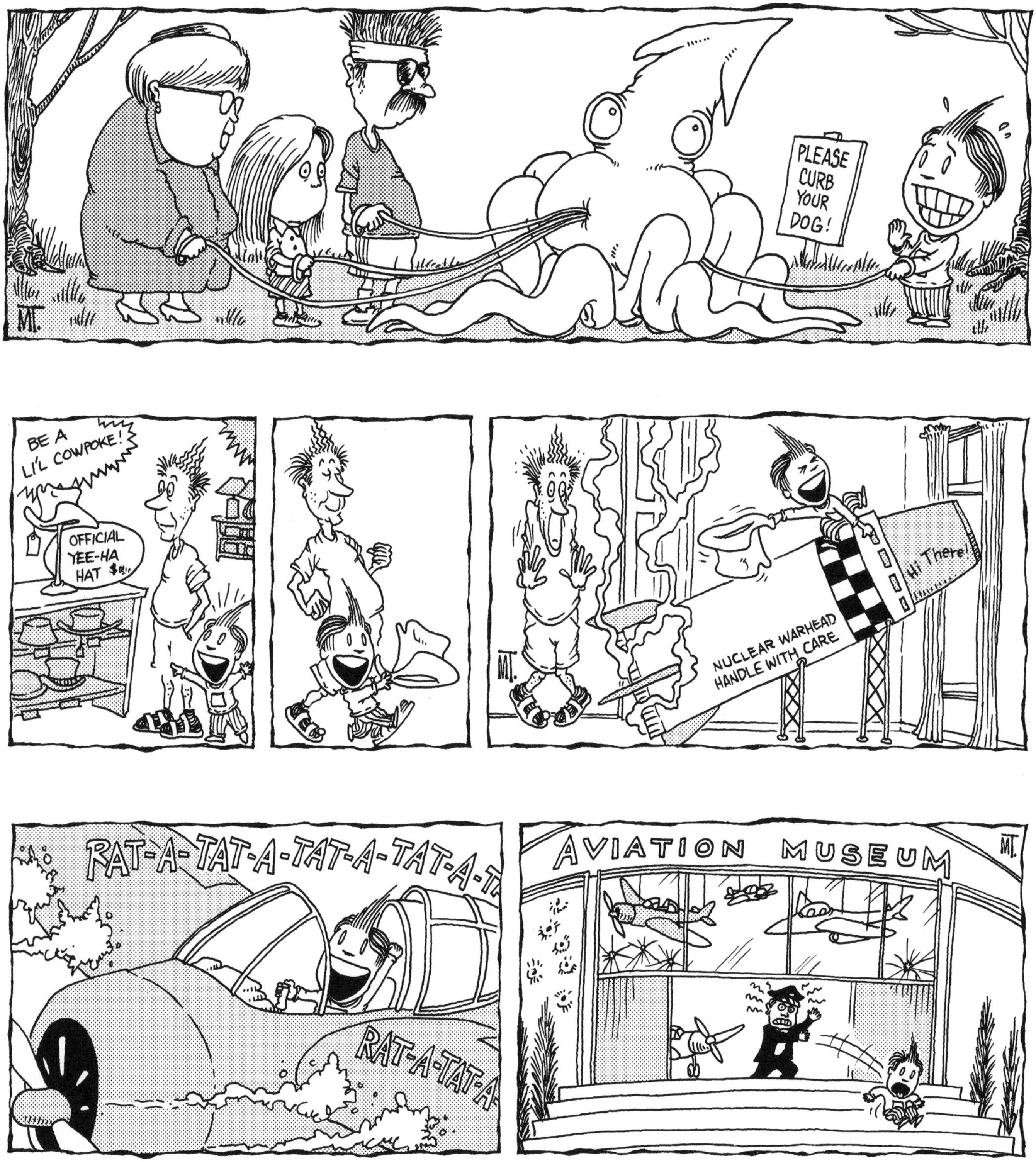
PLEASE CURB YOUR DOG!
BE A LI'L COWPOKE!
OFFICIAL YEE-HA HAT
NUCLEAR WARHEAD HANDLE WITH CARE
Hi There!
RAT-A-TAT-A-TAT-A-TAT-A-
RAT-A-TAT-A
AVIATION MUSEUM

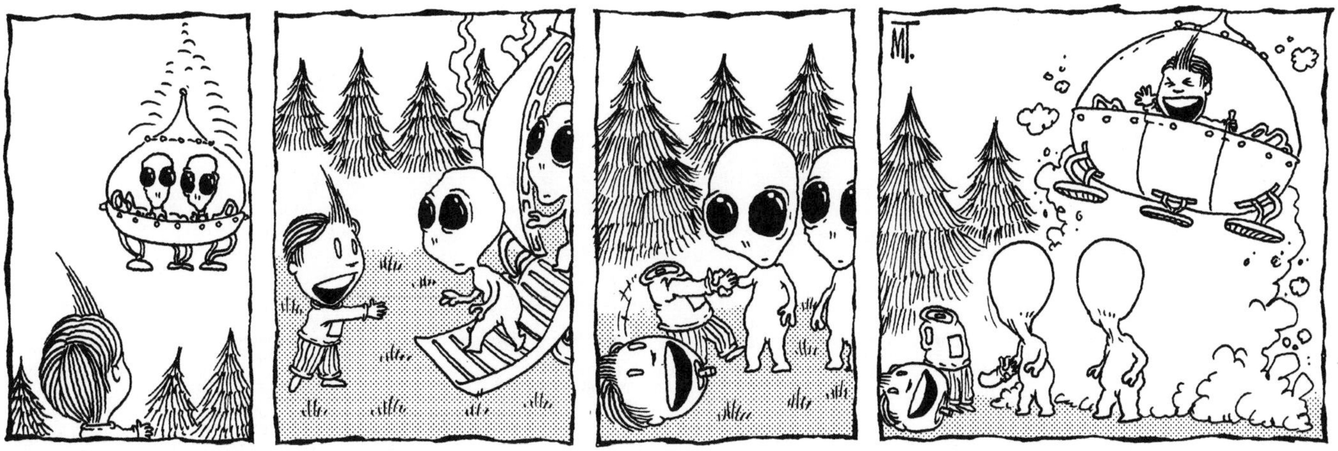

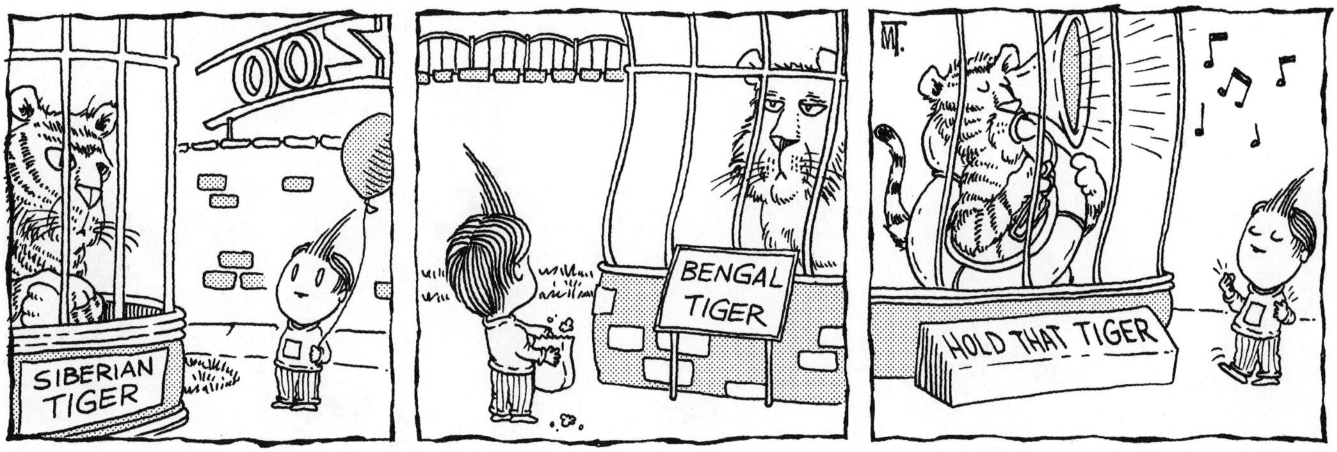
SIBERIAN TIGER
BENGAL TIGER
HOLD THAT TIGER

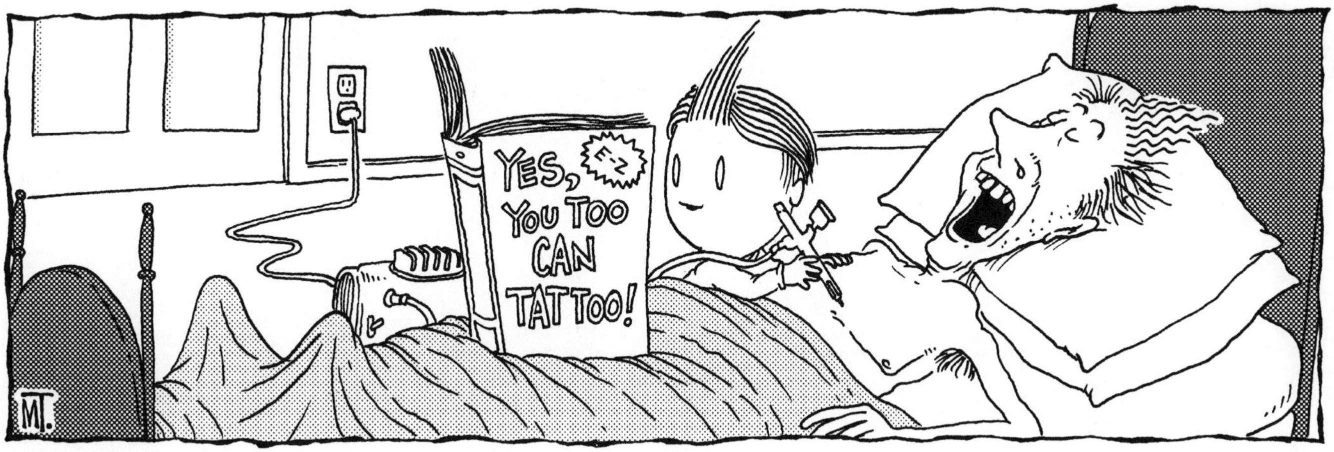
YES, E-Z YOU TOO CAN TATTOO!

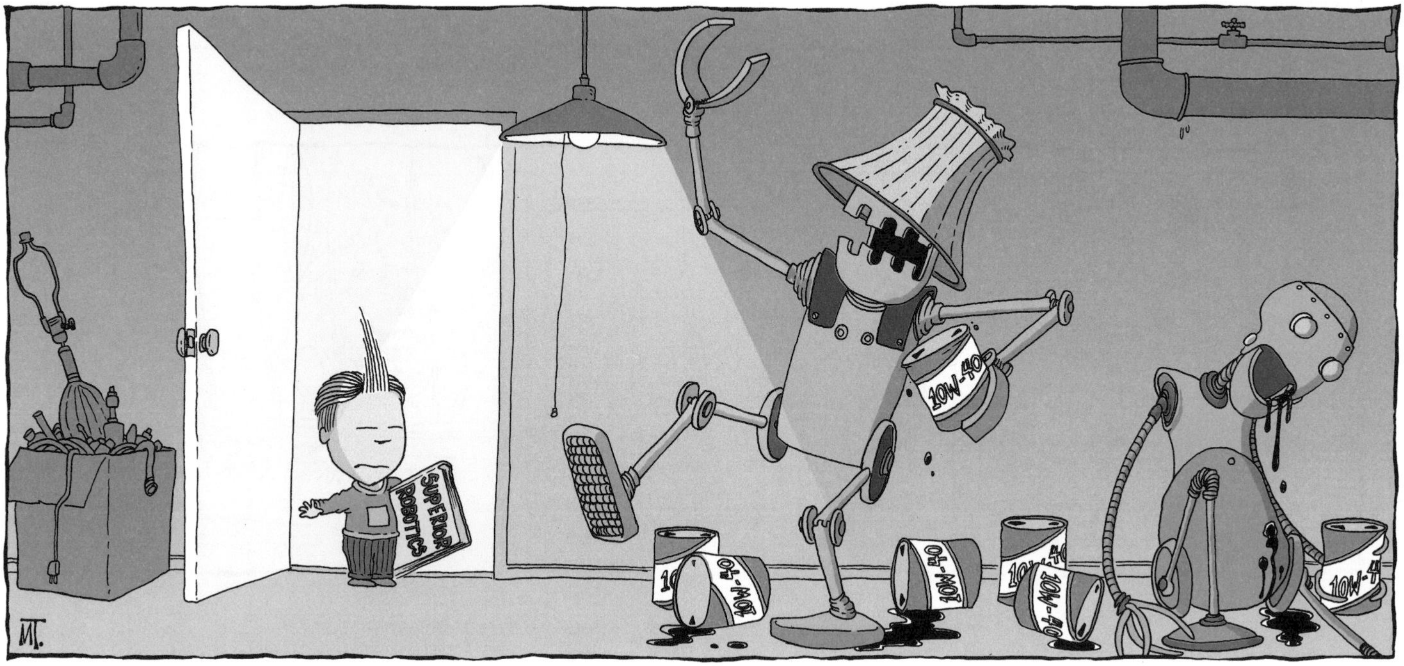
SUPERIOR ROBOTICS
10W-40

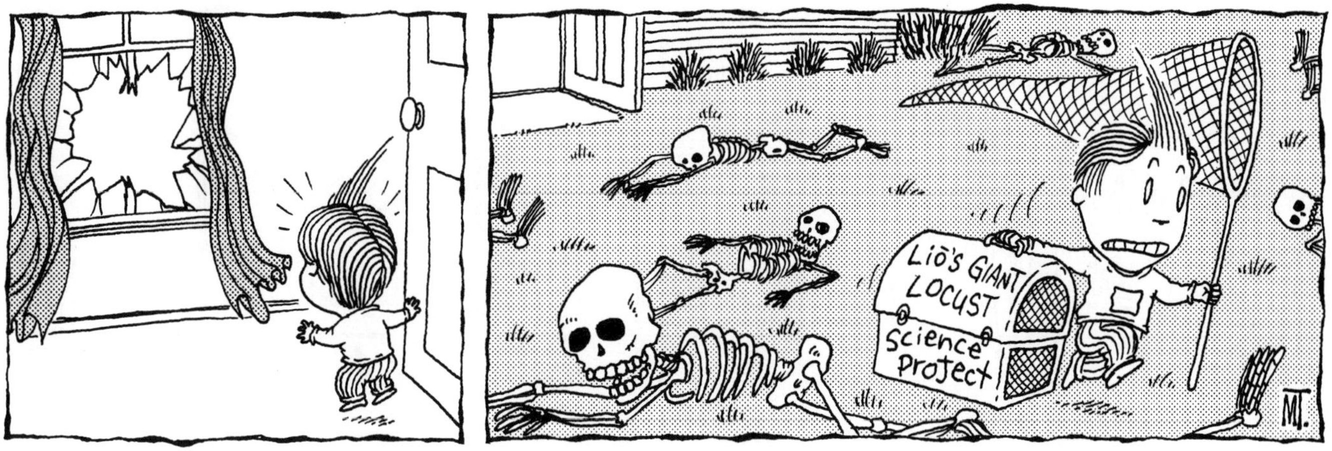
Liō's GIANT LOCUST Science Project
MT.

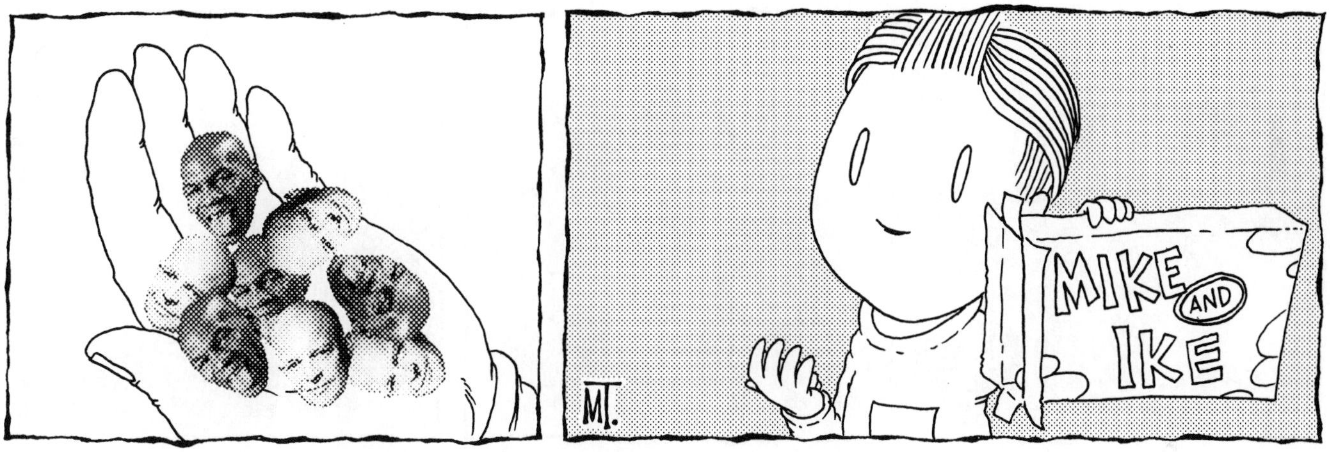
MIKE AND IKE
MT.

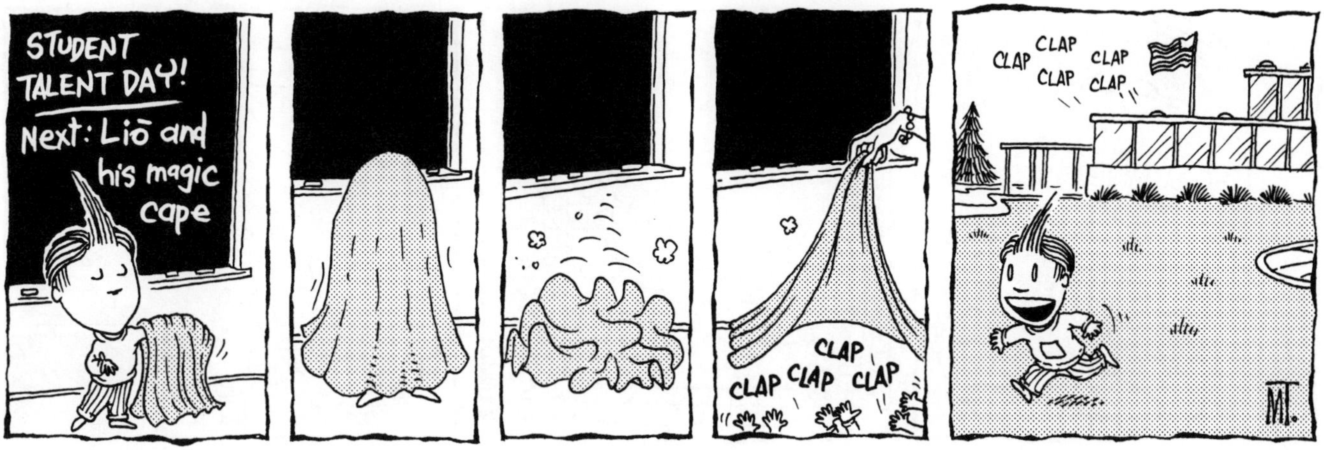
STUDENT TALENT DAY!
Next: Liō and his magic cape
CLAP CLAP CLAP CLAP
CLAP CLAP CLAP CLAP CLAP
MT.

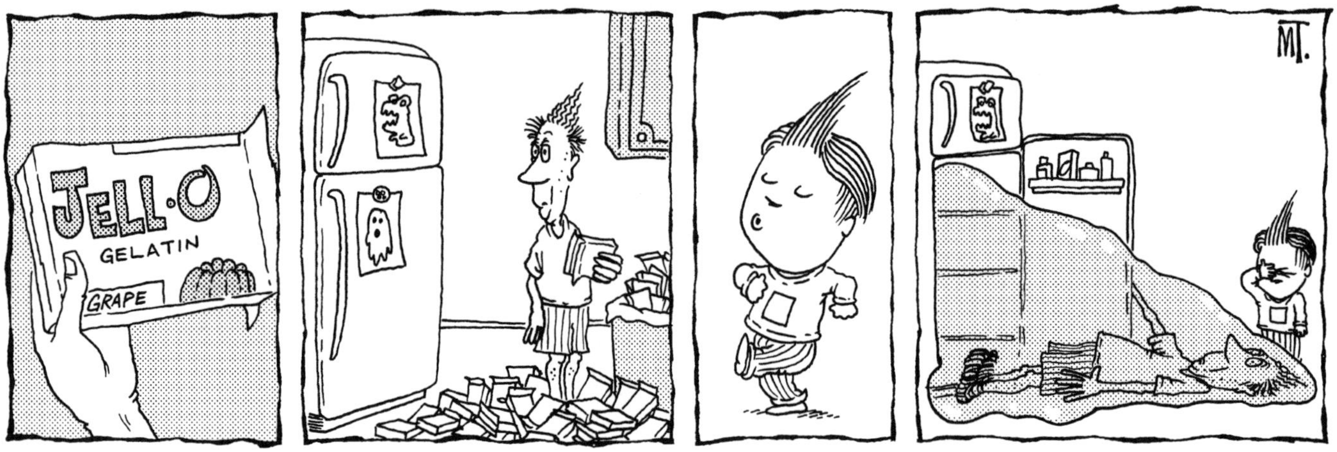
JELL-O
GELATIN
GRAPE
MT.

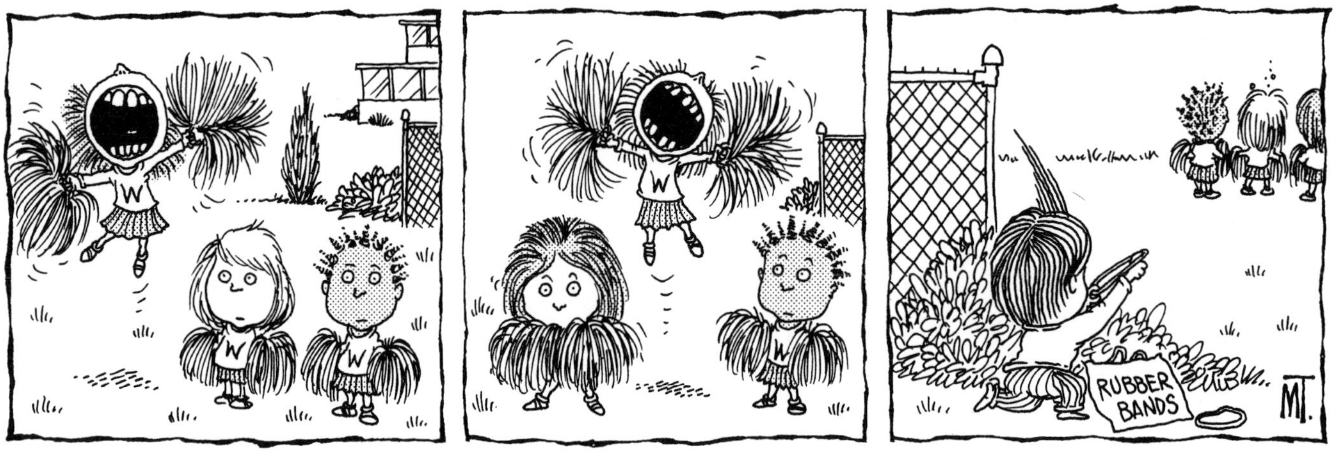
W
W
W
W
W
W
RUBBER BANDS
MT.

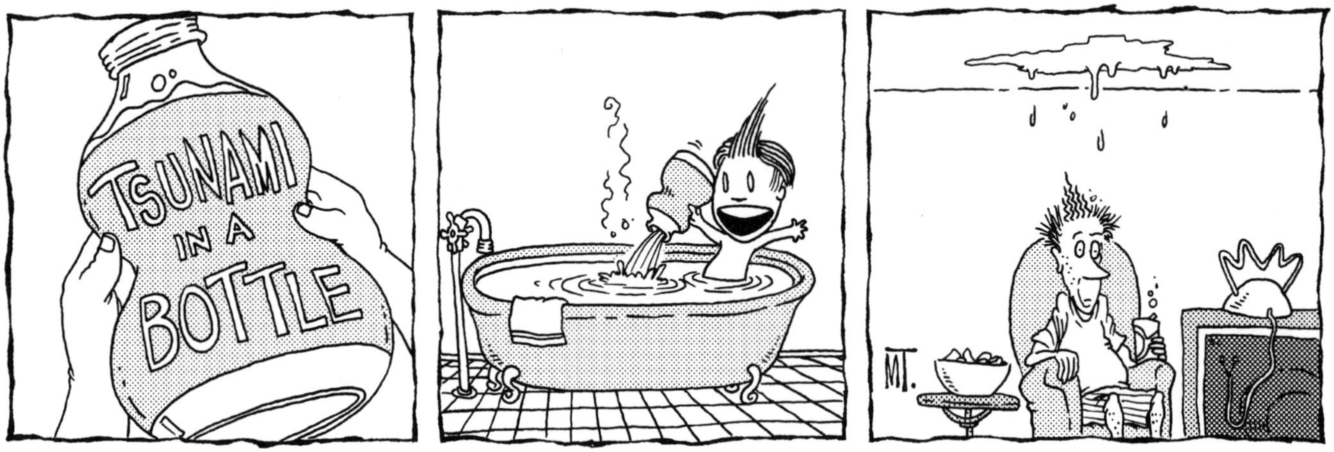
TSUNAMI IN A BOTTLE
MT.

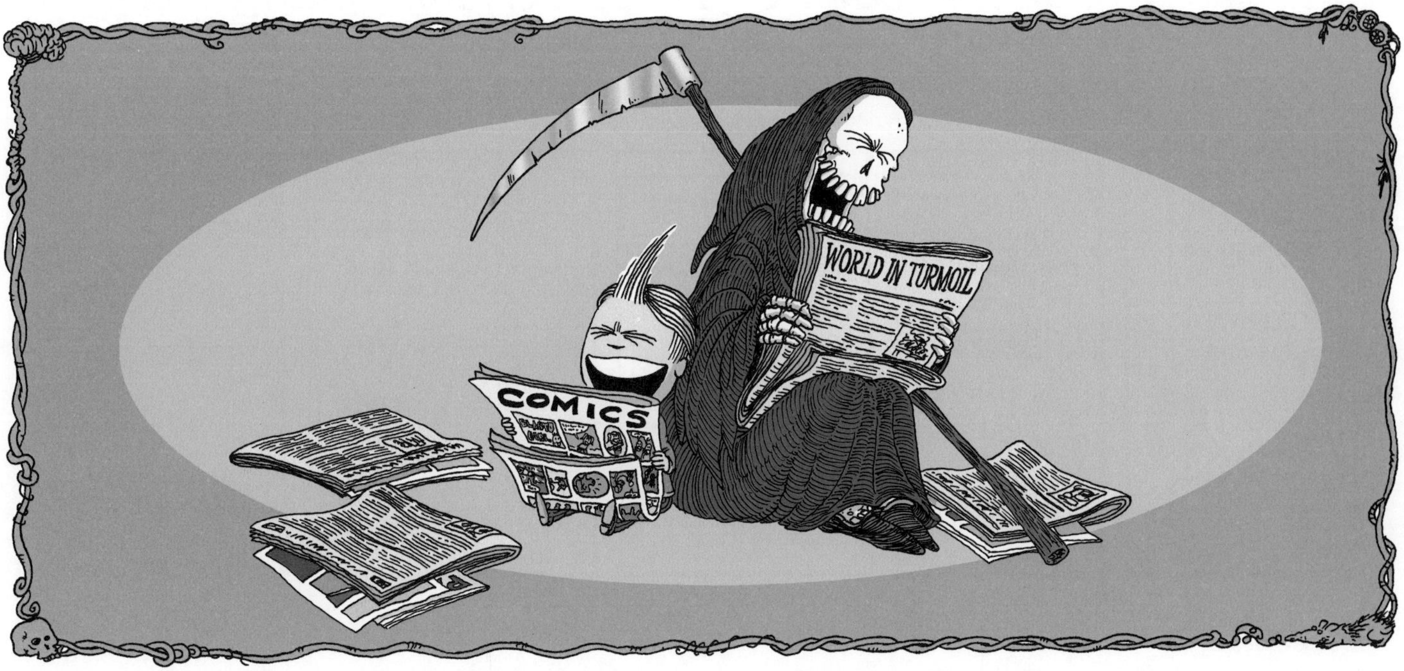
WORLD IN TURMOIL
COMICS

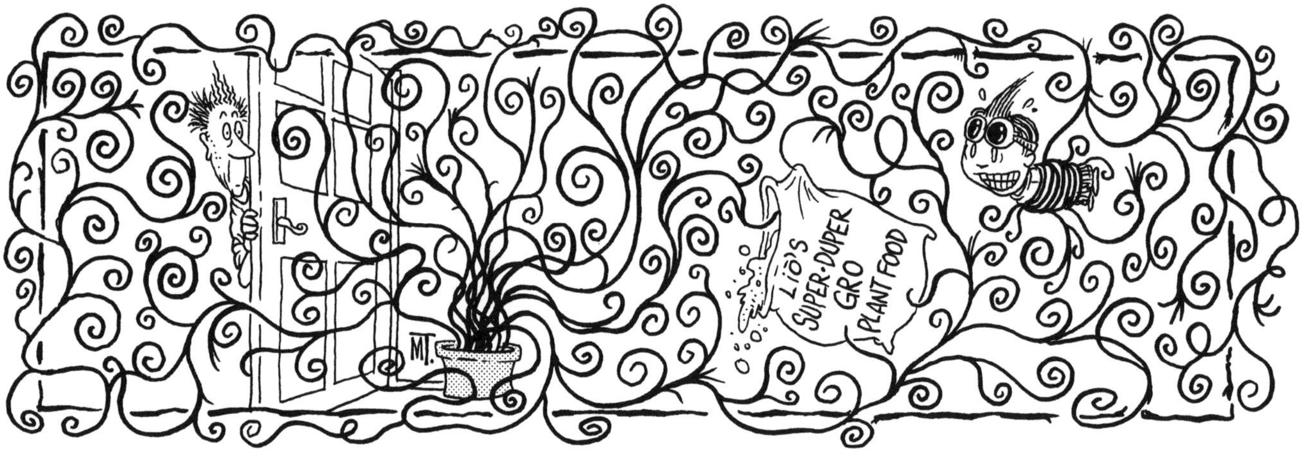
LIO'S SUPER-DUPER GRO PLANT FOOD
MT.

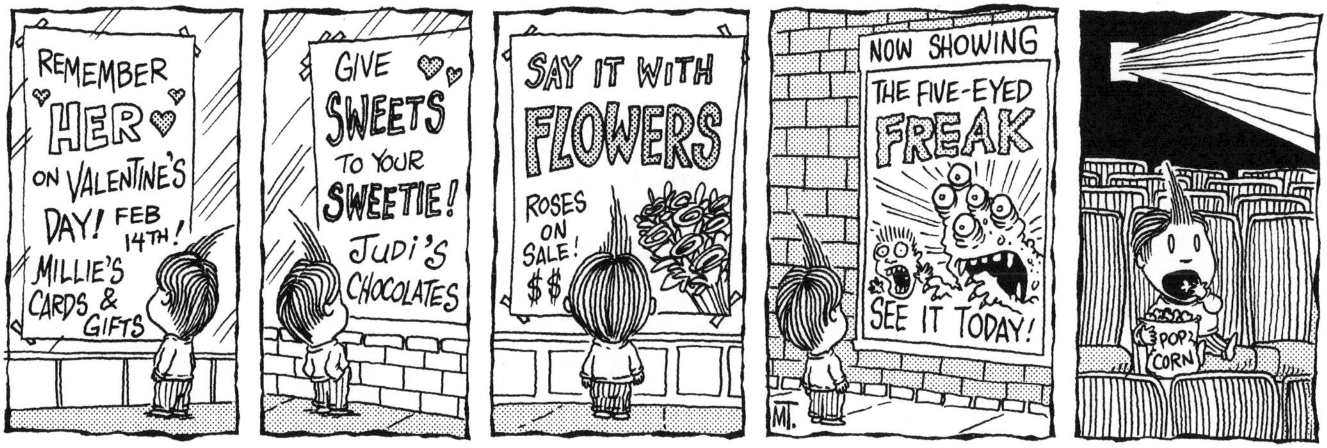
REMEMBER HER ON VALENTINE'S DAY! FEB 14TH! MILLIE'S CARDS & GIFTS
GIVE SWEETS TO YOUR SWEETIE! JUDI'S CHOCOLATES
SAY IT WITH FLOWERS ROSES ON SALE! $$
NOW SHOWING THE FIVE-EYED FREAK SEE IT TODAY!
MT.
POPCORN

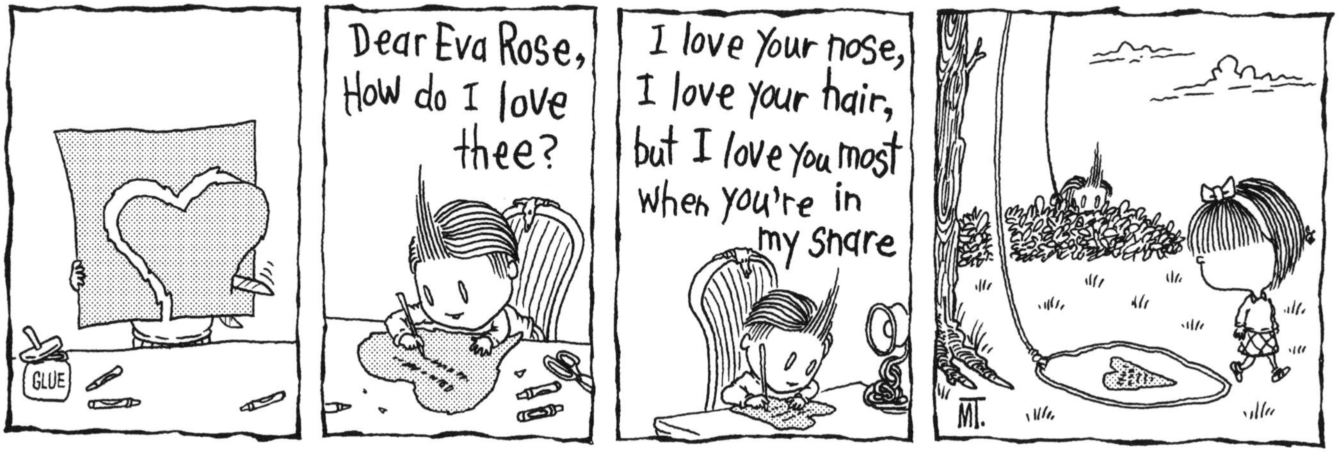
GLUE
Dear Eva Rose, How do I love thee?
I love your nose, I love your hair, but I love you most when you're in my snare
MT.

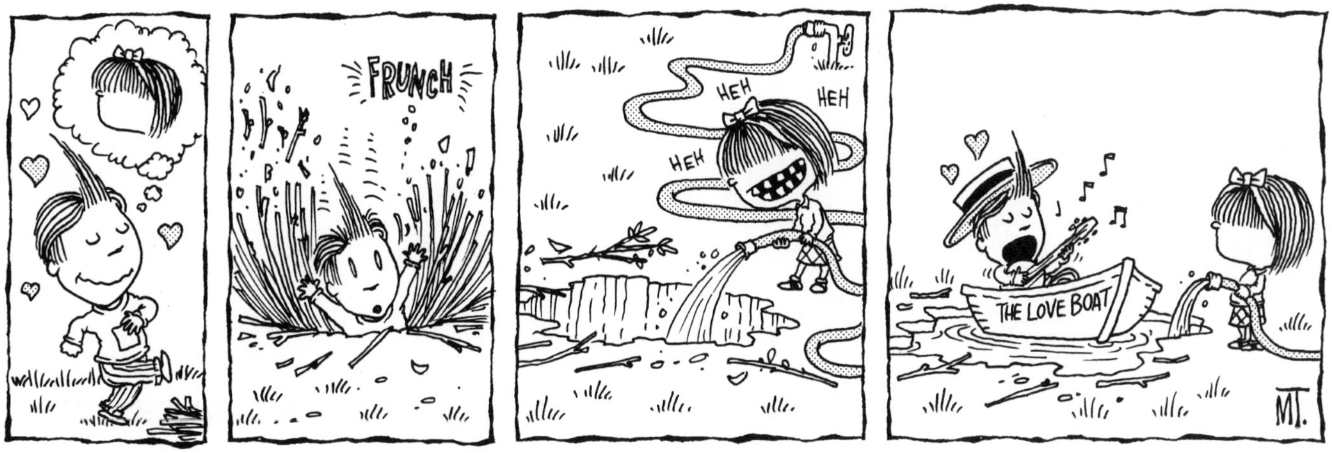
FRUNCH
HEH
HEH
HEH
THE LOVE BOAT
MT.

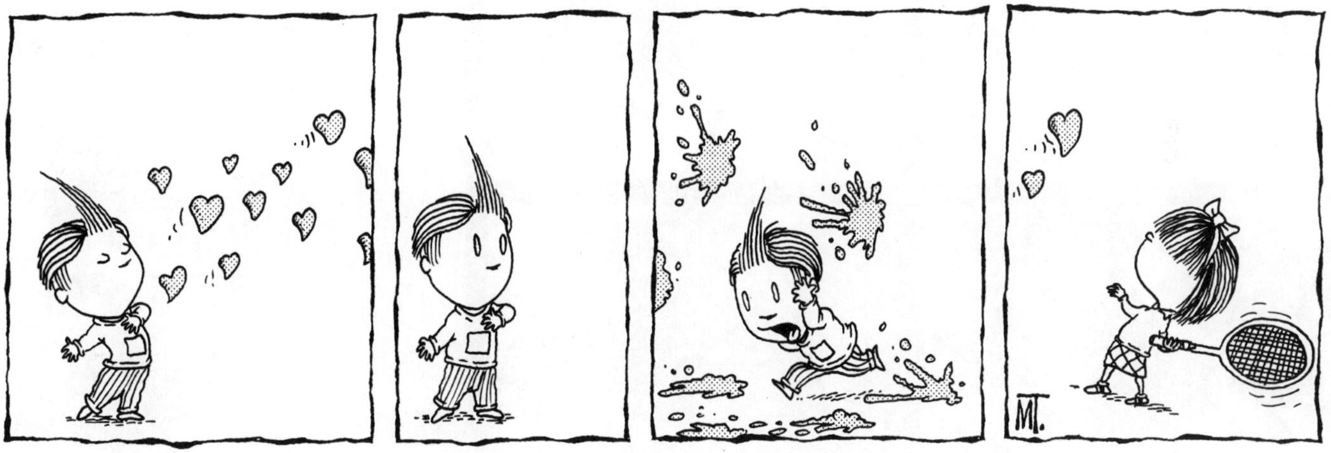
MT.

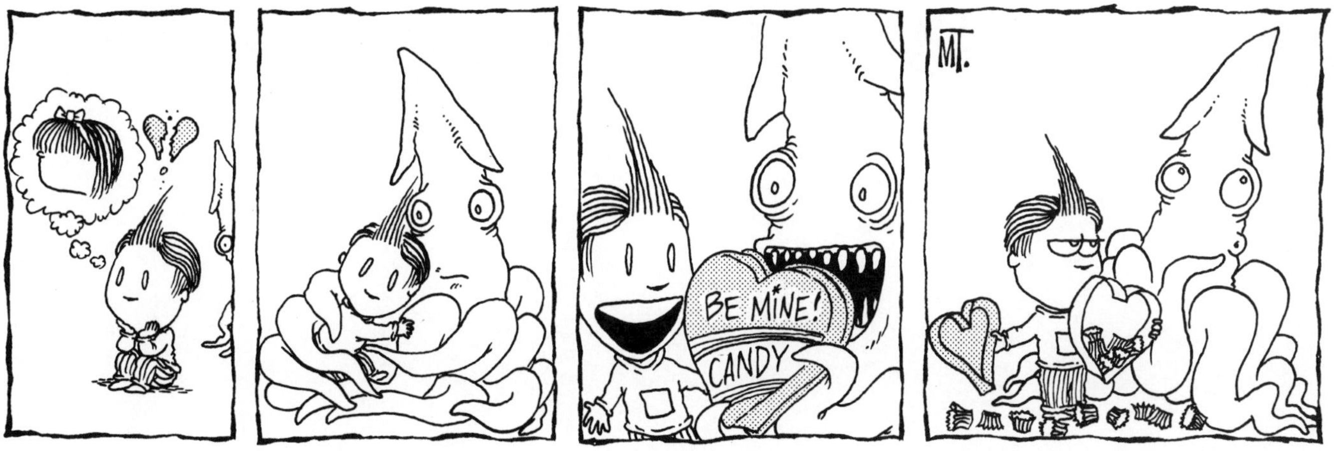
BE MINE!
CANDY
MT.

Zitmore Furs co.
SALE!
ALL RED FOX
COATS 20% OFF
MT.

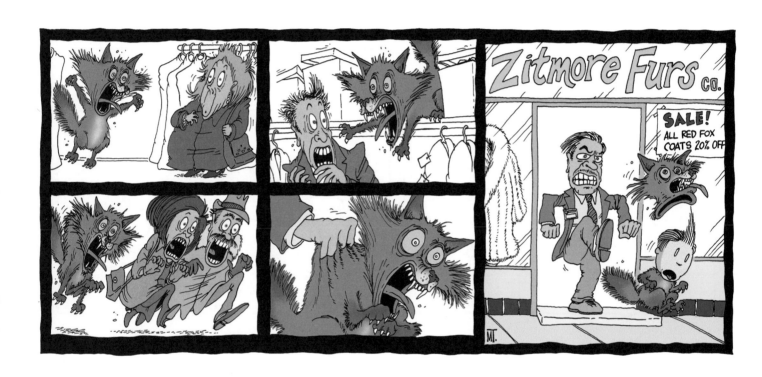

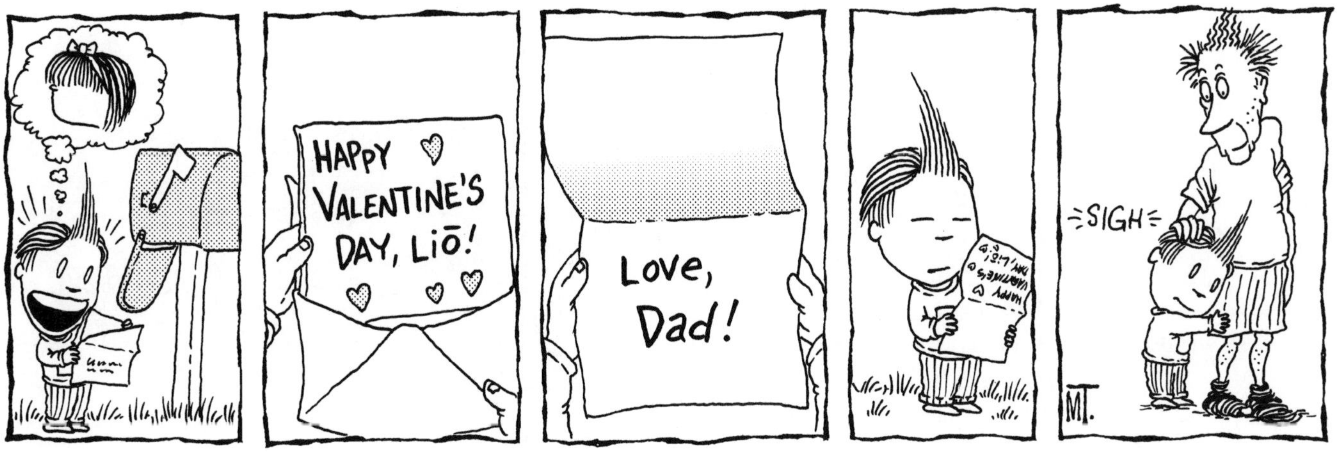
HAPPY VALENTINE'S DAY, LIŌ!
Love, Dad!
SIGH
MT.

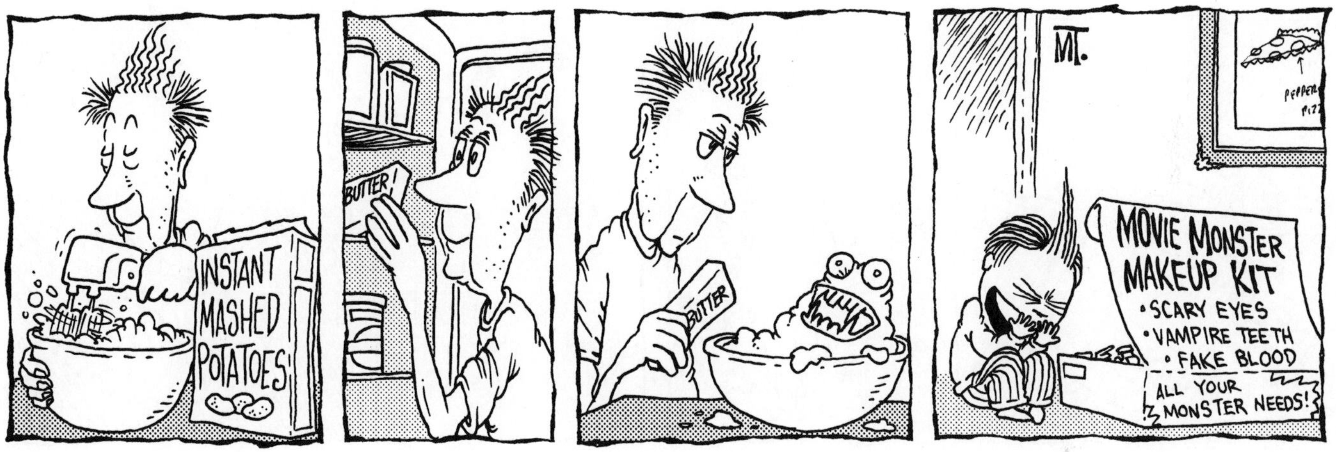
INSTANT MASHED POTATOES
BUTTER!
BUTTER
MT.
MOVIE MONSTER MAKEUP KIT
• SCARY EYES
• VAMPIRE TEETH
• FAKE BLOOD
ALL YOUR MONSTER NEEDS!

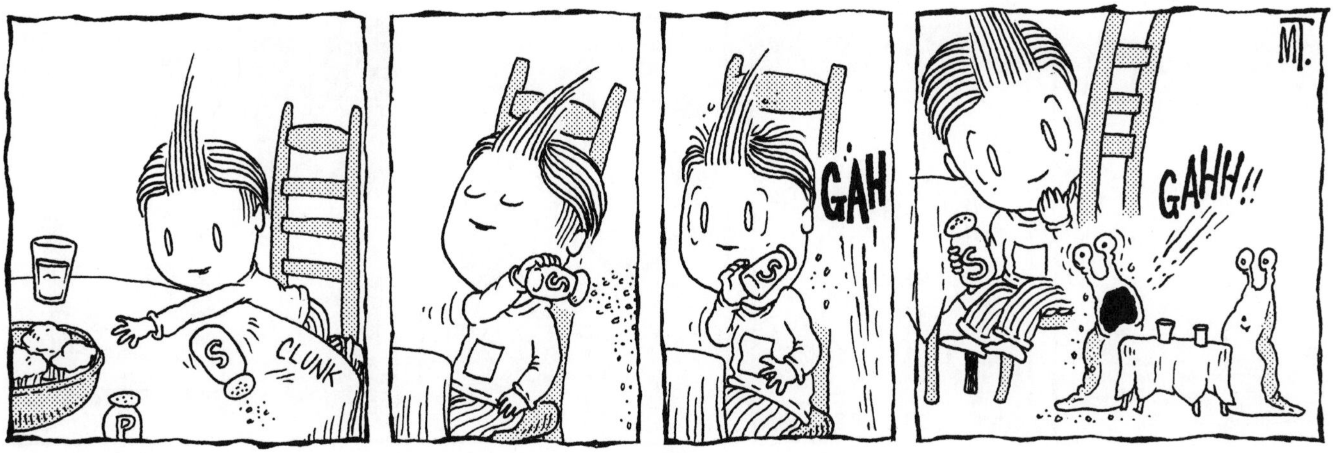
S
P
CLUNK
GAH
GAHH!!
MT.

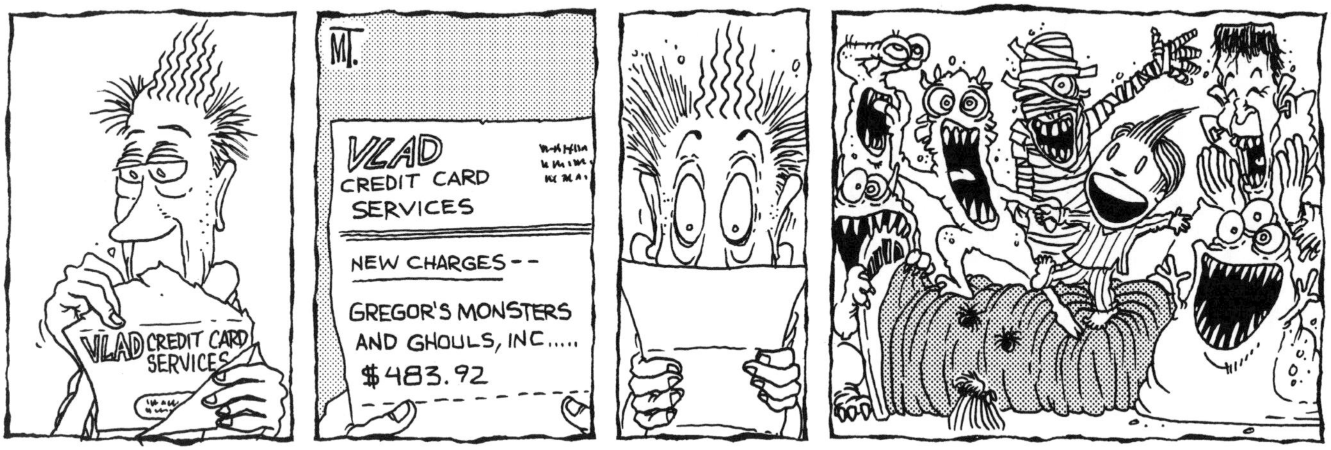
VLAD CREDIT CARD SERVICES
VLAD CREDIT CARD SERVICES
NEW CHARGES--
GREGOR'S MONSTERS AND GHOULS, INC.....
$483.92

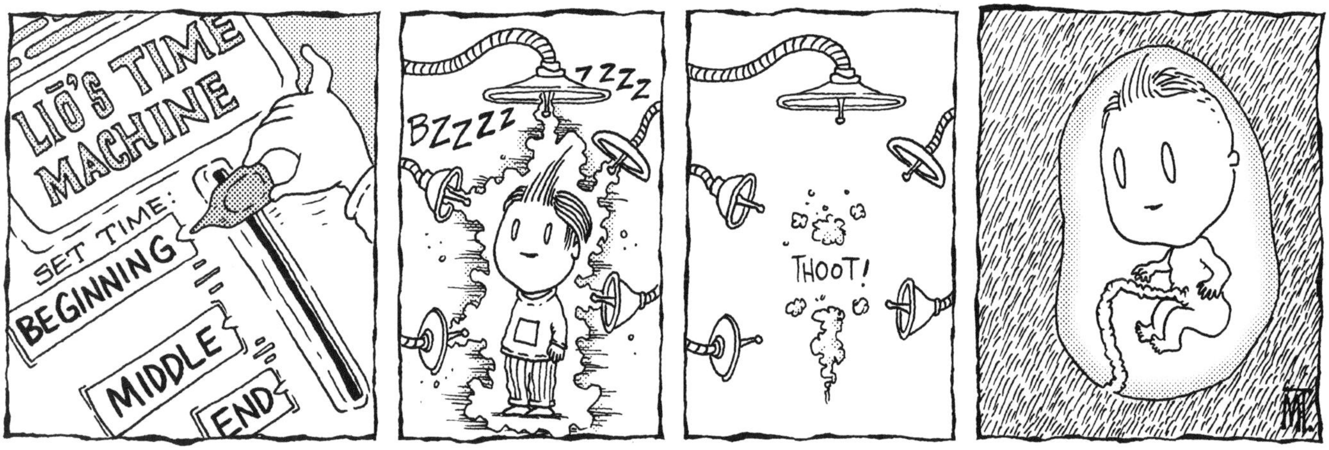
LIŌ'S TIME MACHINE
SET TIME:
BEGINNING
MIDDLE
END
BZZZZ
ZZZZ
THOOT!

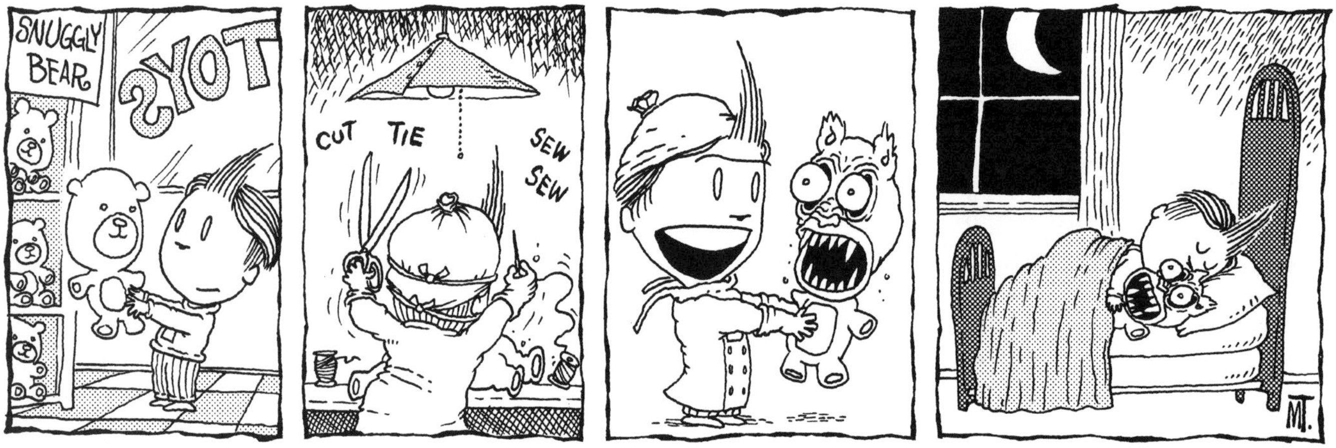
SNUGGLY BEAR
TOYS
CUT
TIE
SEW
SEW

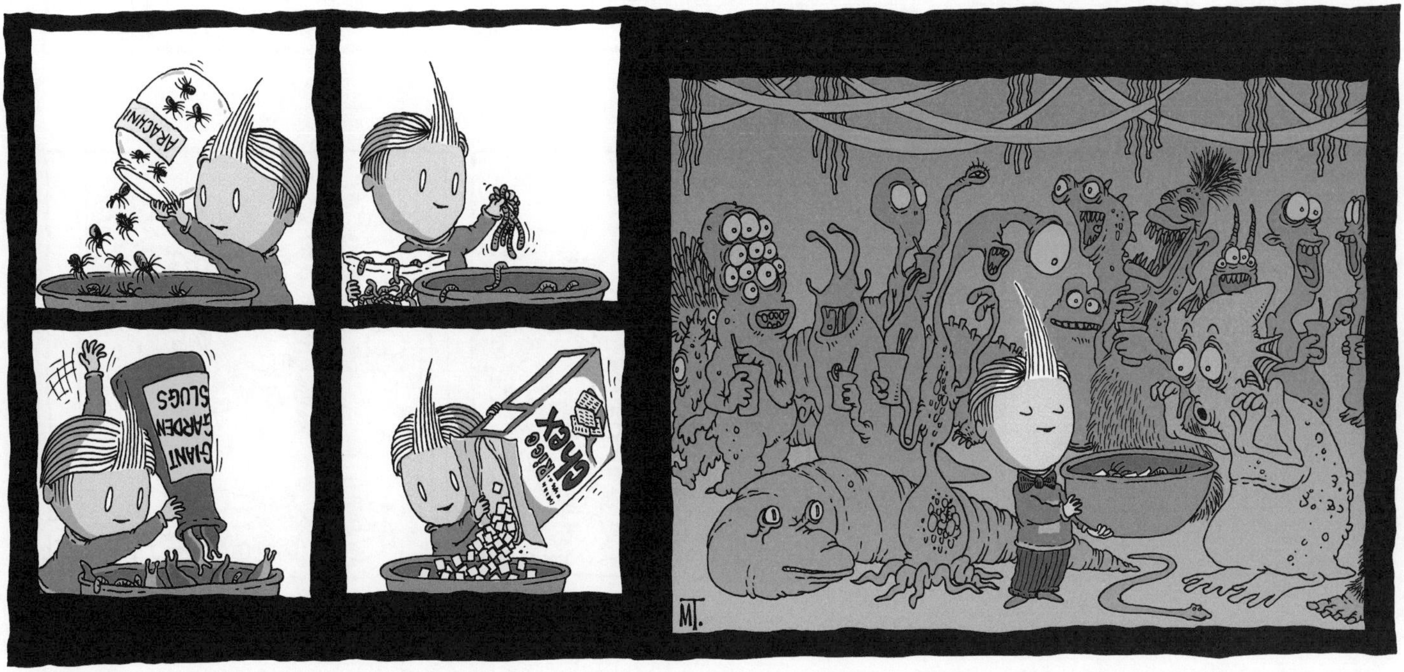
ARACHNI
GIANT GARDEN SLUGS
Rice Chex
MT.

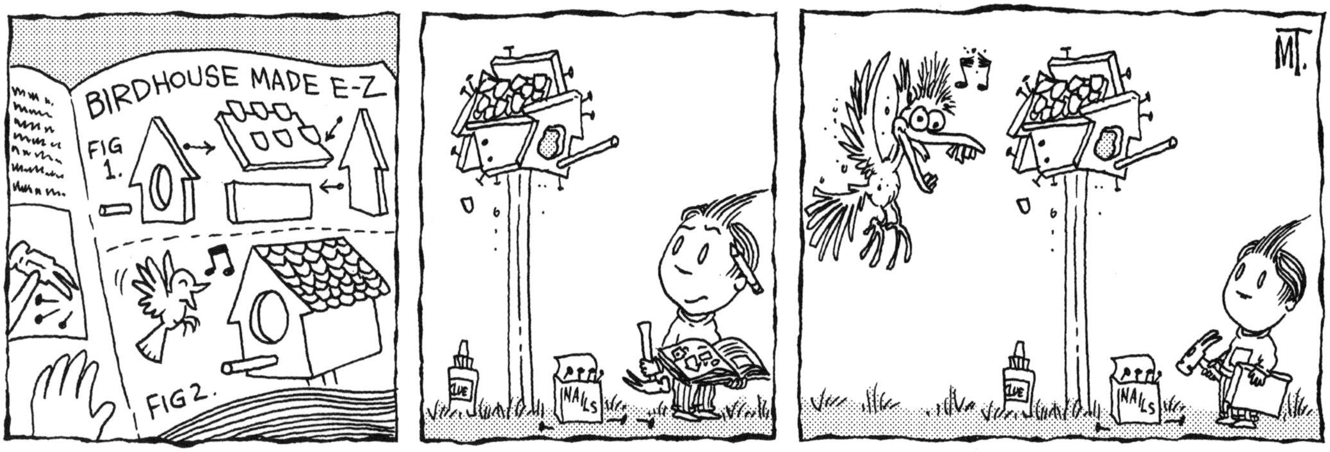
BIRDHOUSE MADE E-Z
FIG 1.
FIG 2.
GLUE
NAILS

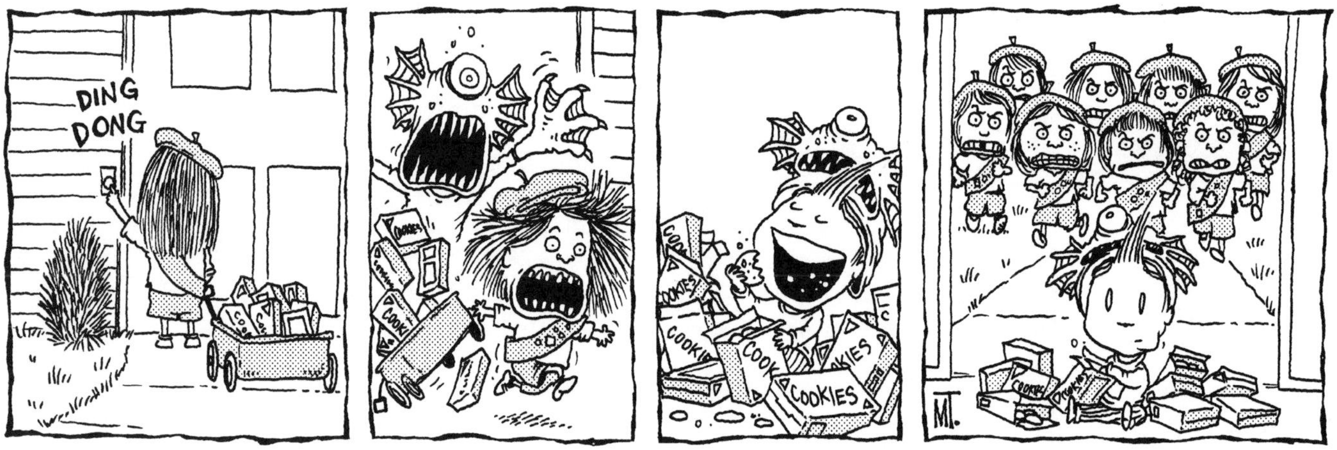
DING DONG
COOKIES

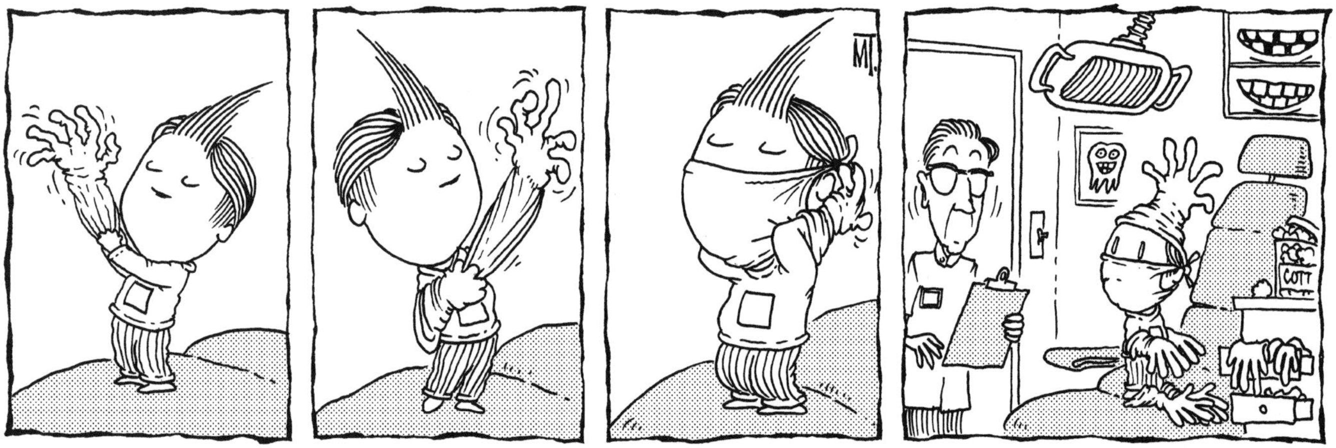

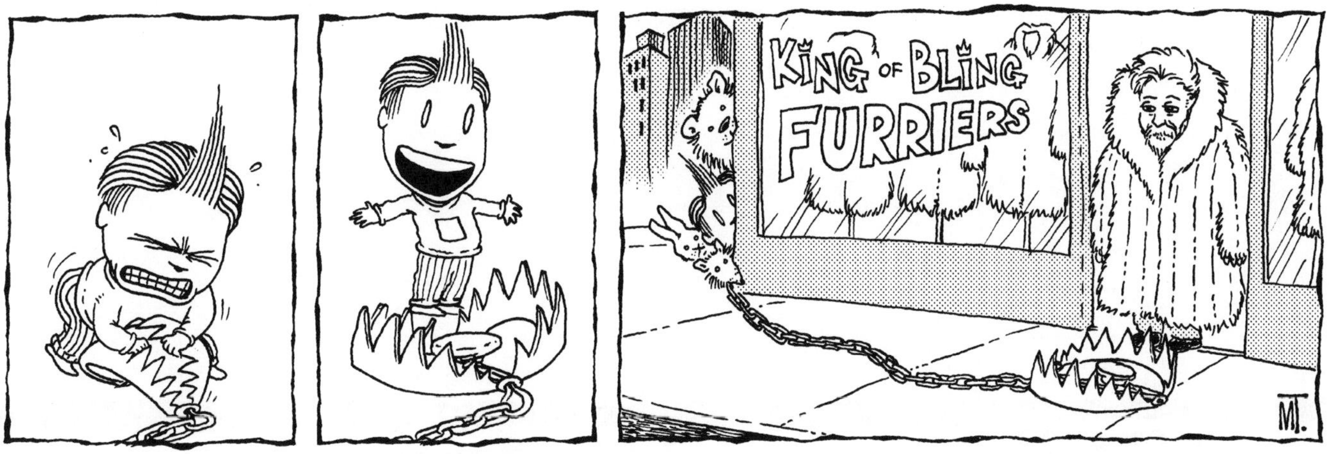
KING OF BLING
FURRIERS
MT.

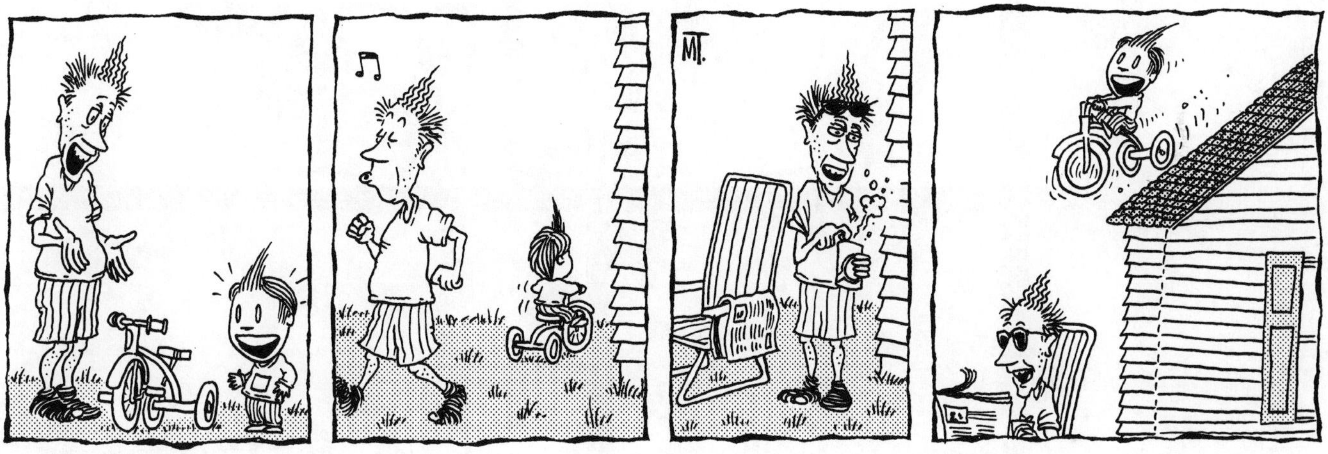
MT.

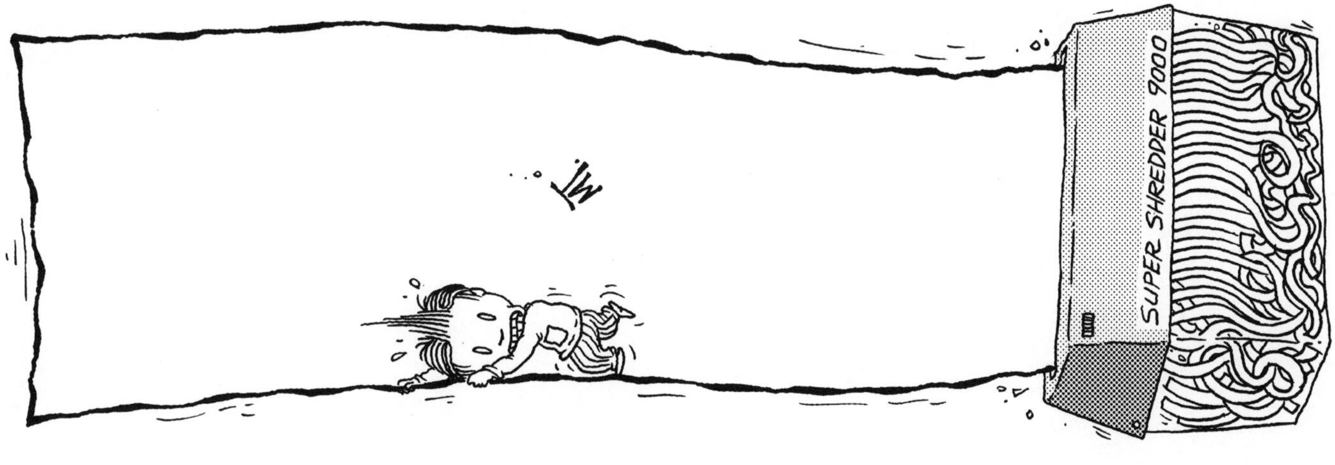
SUPER SHREDDER 9000

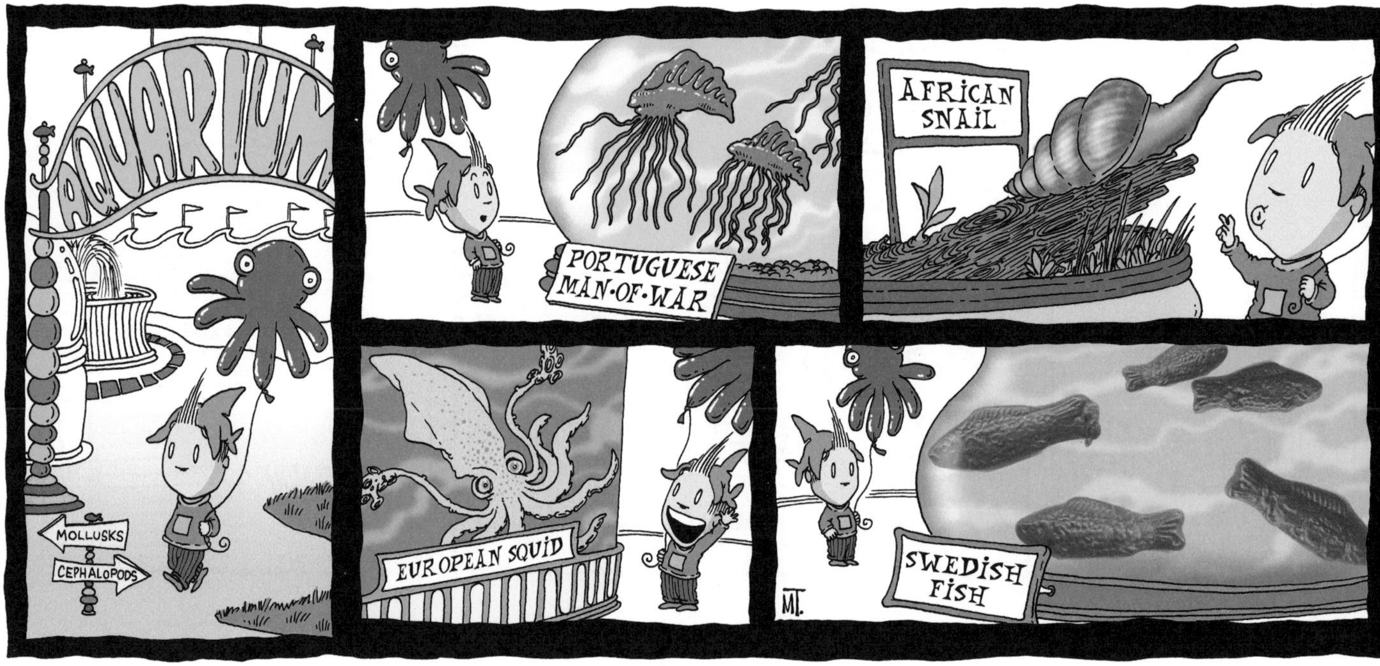
AQUARIUM
MOLLUSKS
CEPHALOPODS
PORTUGUESE MAN-OF-WAR
AFRICAN SNAIL
EUROPEAN SQUID
SWEDISH FISH
MT.

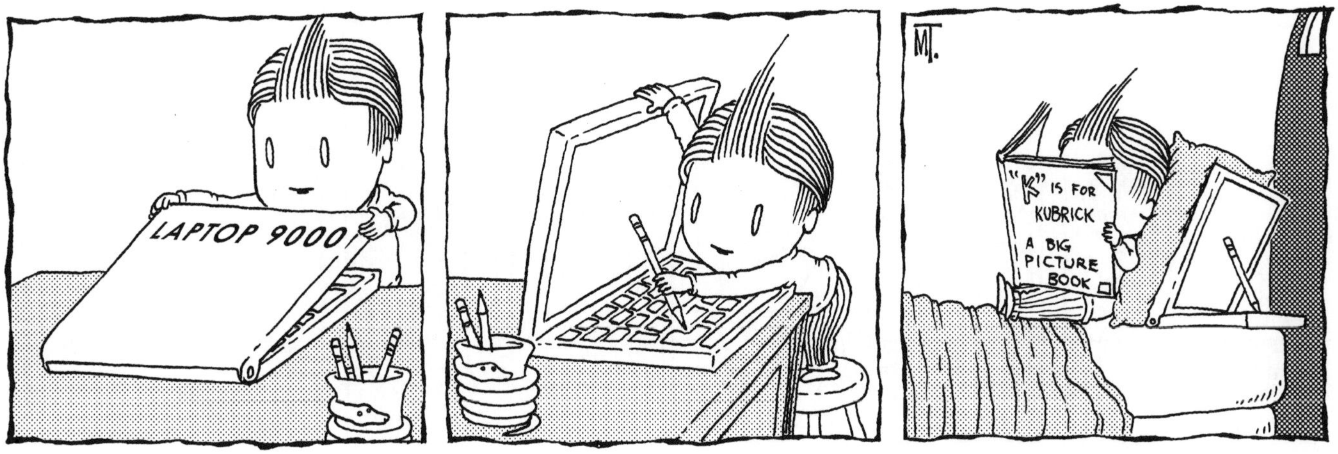
LAPTOP 9000
MT.
"K" IS FOR KUBRICK
A BIG PICTURE BOOK

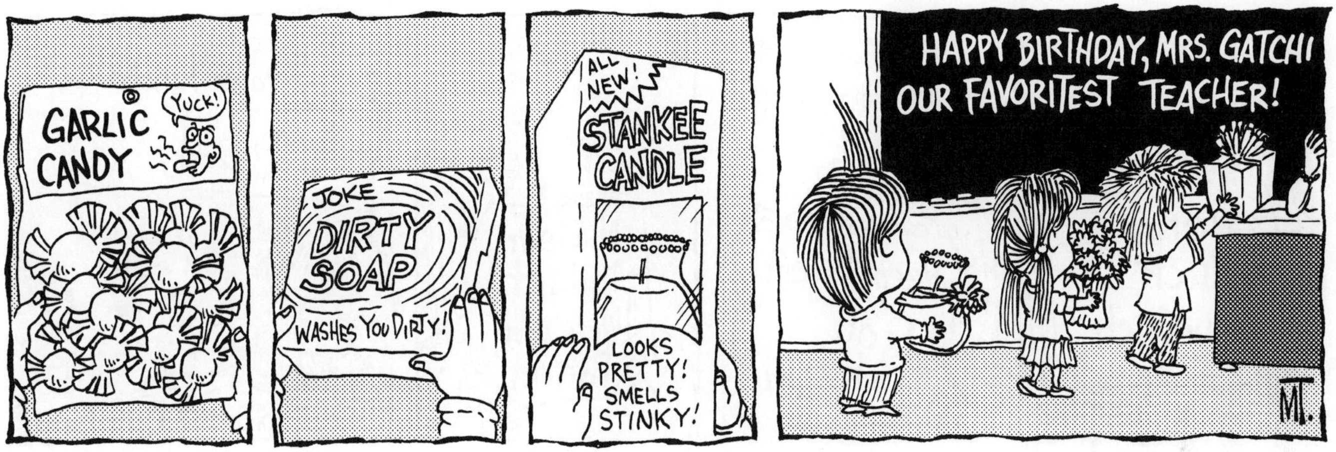
GARLIC CANDY
YUCK!
JOKE
DIRTY SOAP
WASHES YOU DIRTY!
ALL NEW!
STANKEE CANDLE
LOOKS PRETTY! SMELLS STINKY!
HAPPY BIRTHDAY, MRS. GATCHI
OUR FAVORITEST TEACHER!
MT.

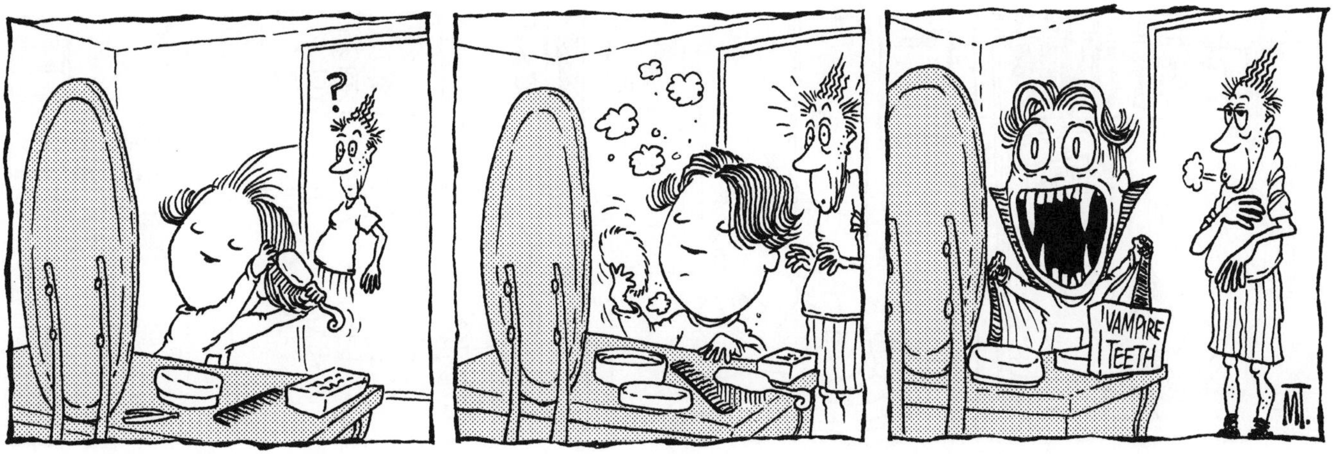
?
VAMPIRE TEETH
MT.

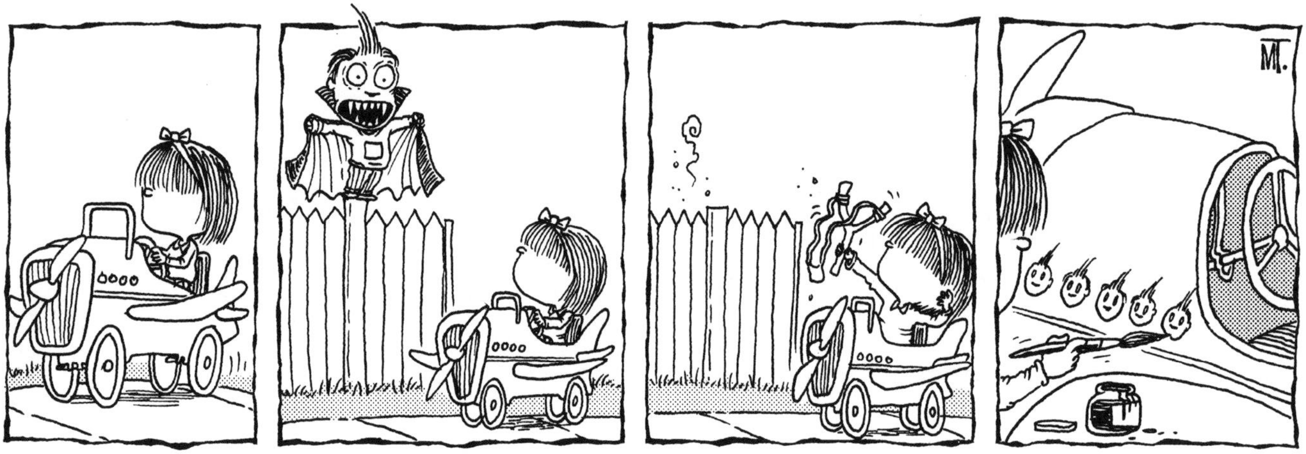

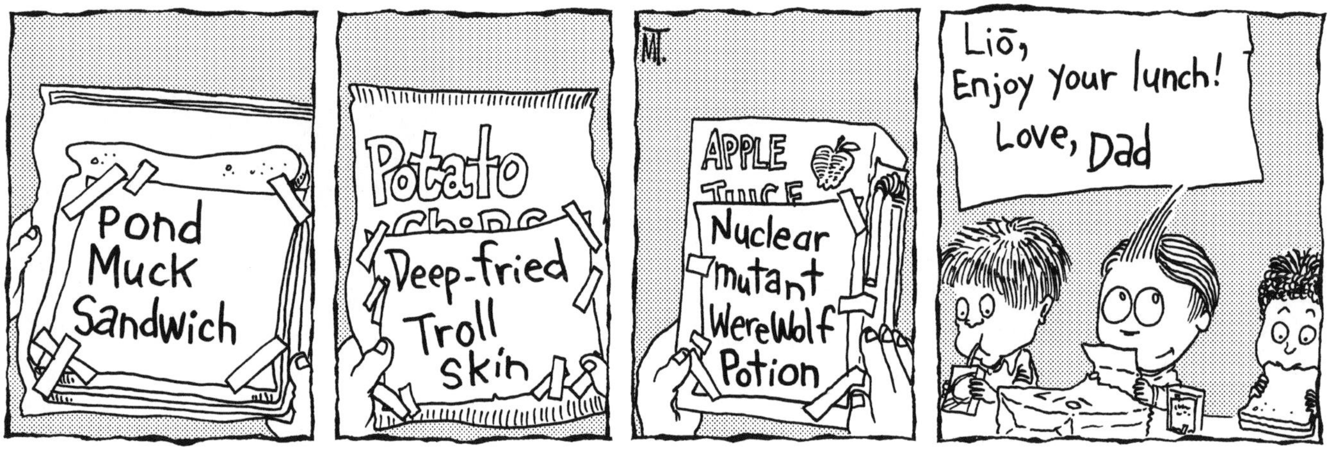
Pond Muck Sandwich
Potato
Deep-fried Troll skin
APPLE
Nuclear mutant WereWolf Potion
Lio,
Enjoy your lunch!
Love, Dad

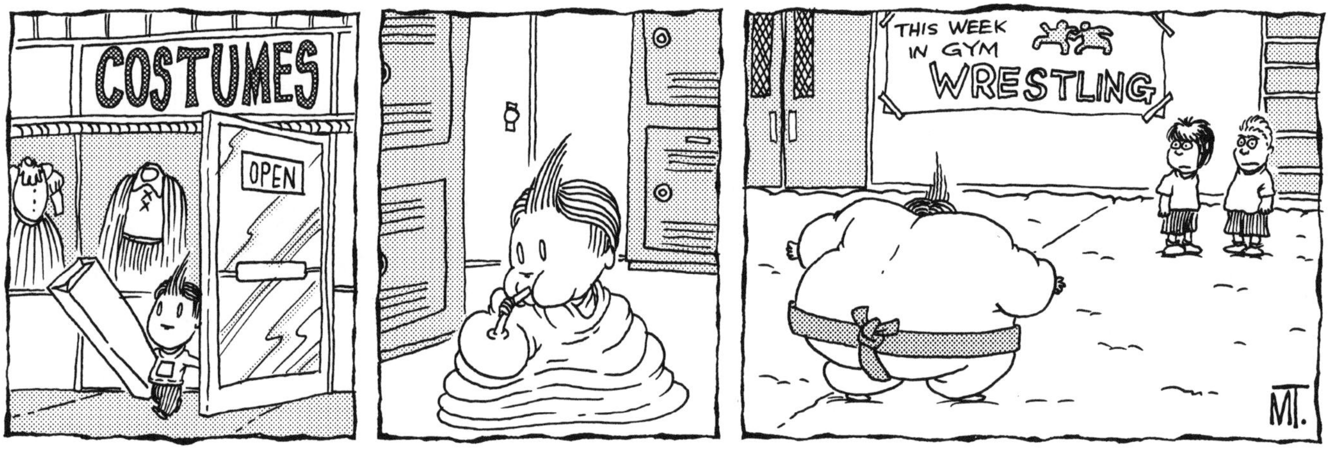
COSTUMES
OPEN
THIS WEEK IN GYM
WRESTLING

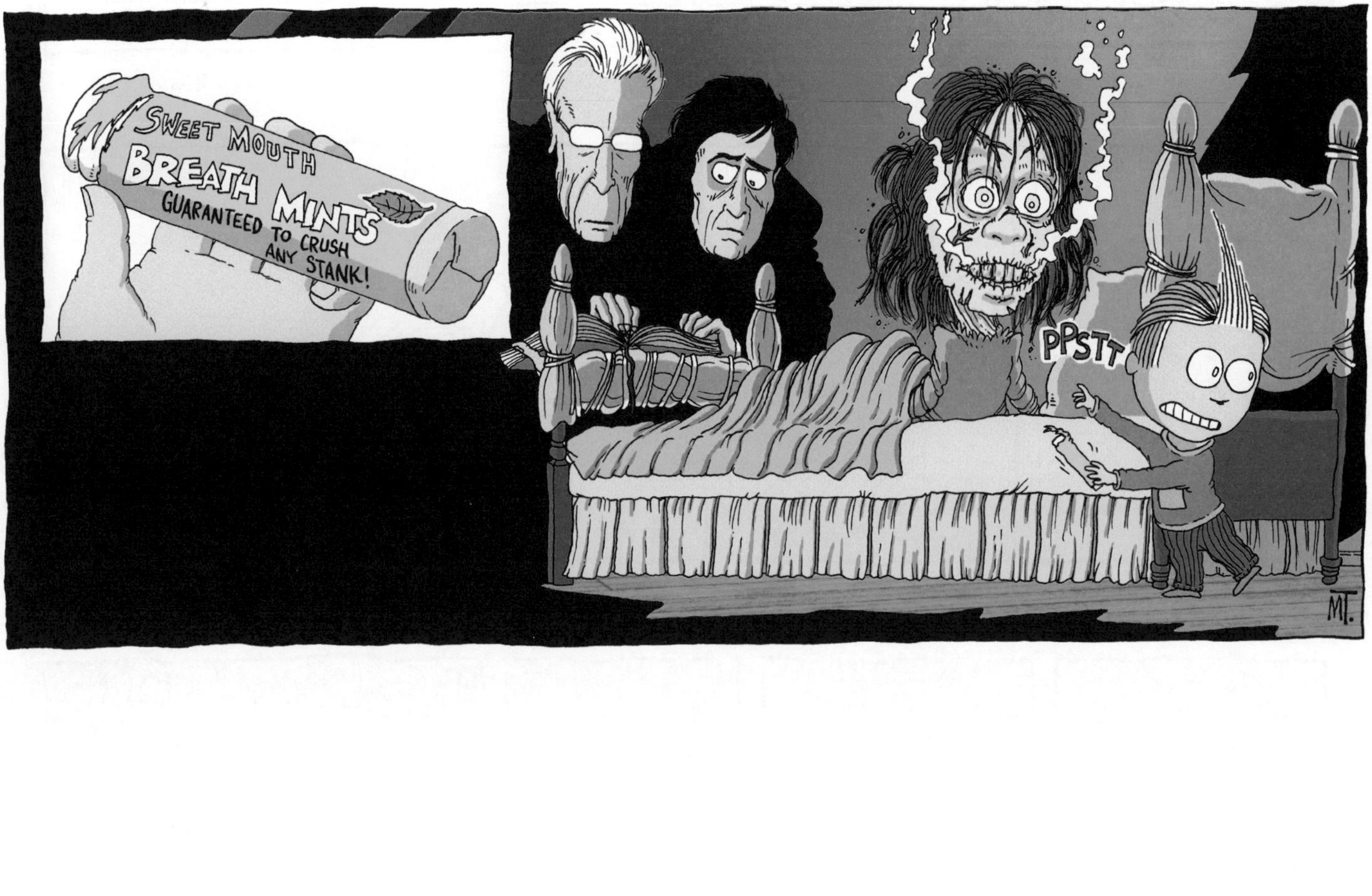
SWEET MOUTH
BREATH MINTS
GUARANTEED TO CRUSH ANY STANK!
PPSTT
MT.

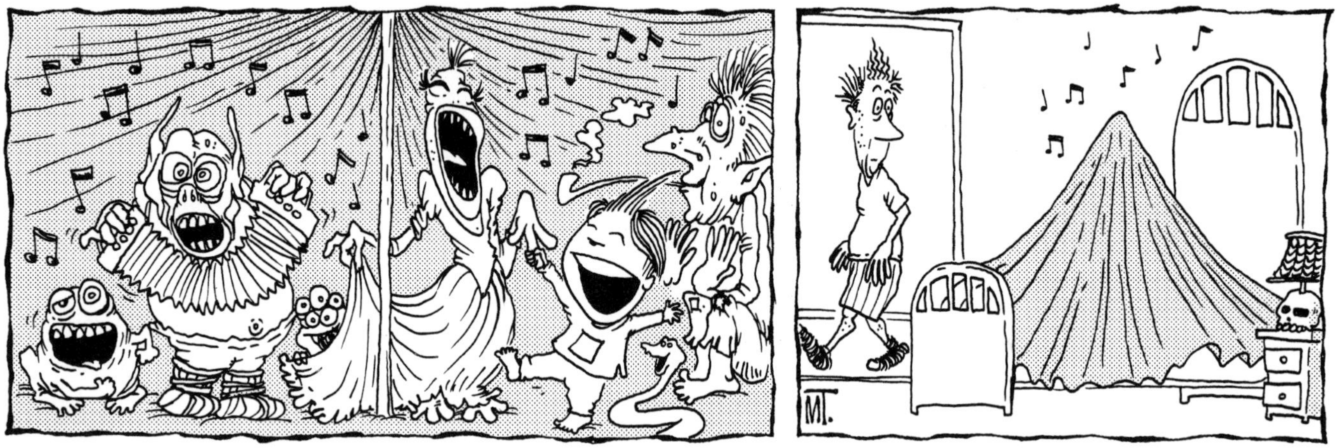

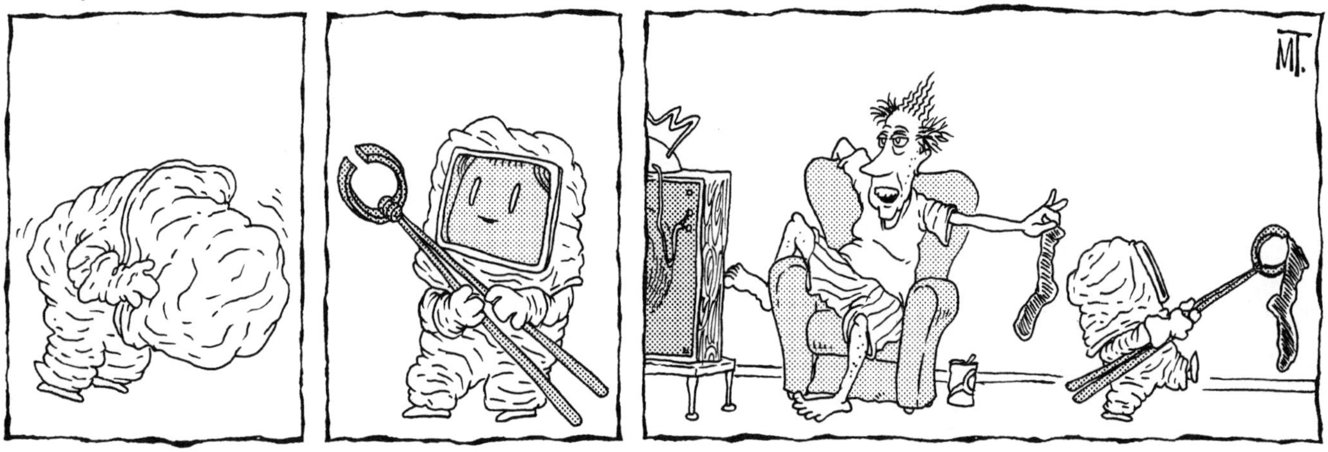

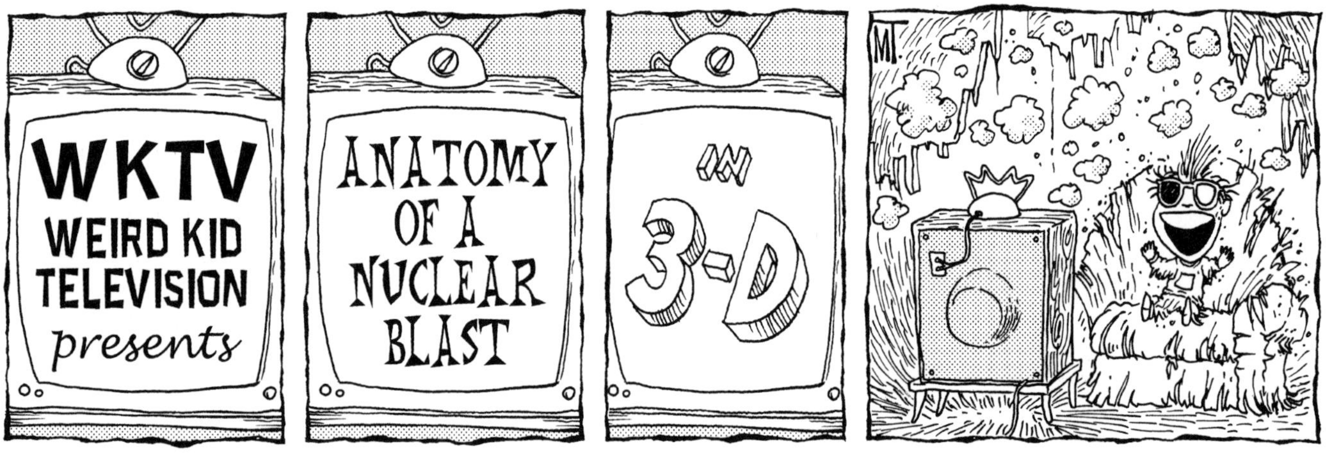
WKTV
WEIRD KID
TELEVISION
presents
ANATOMY
OF A
NUCLEAR
BLAST
IN
3-D

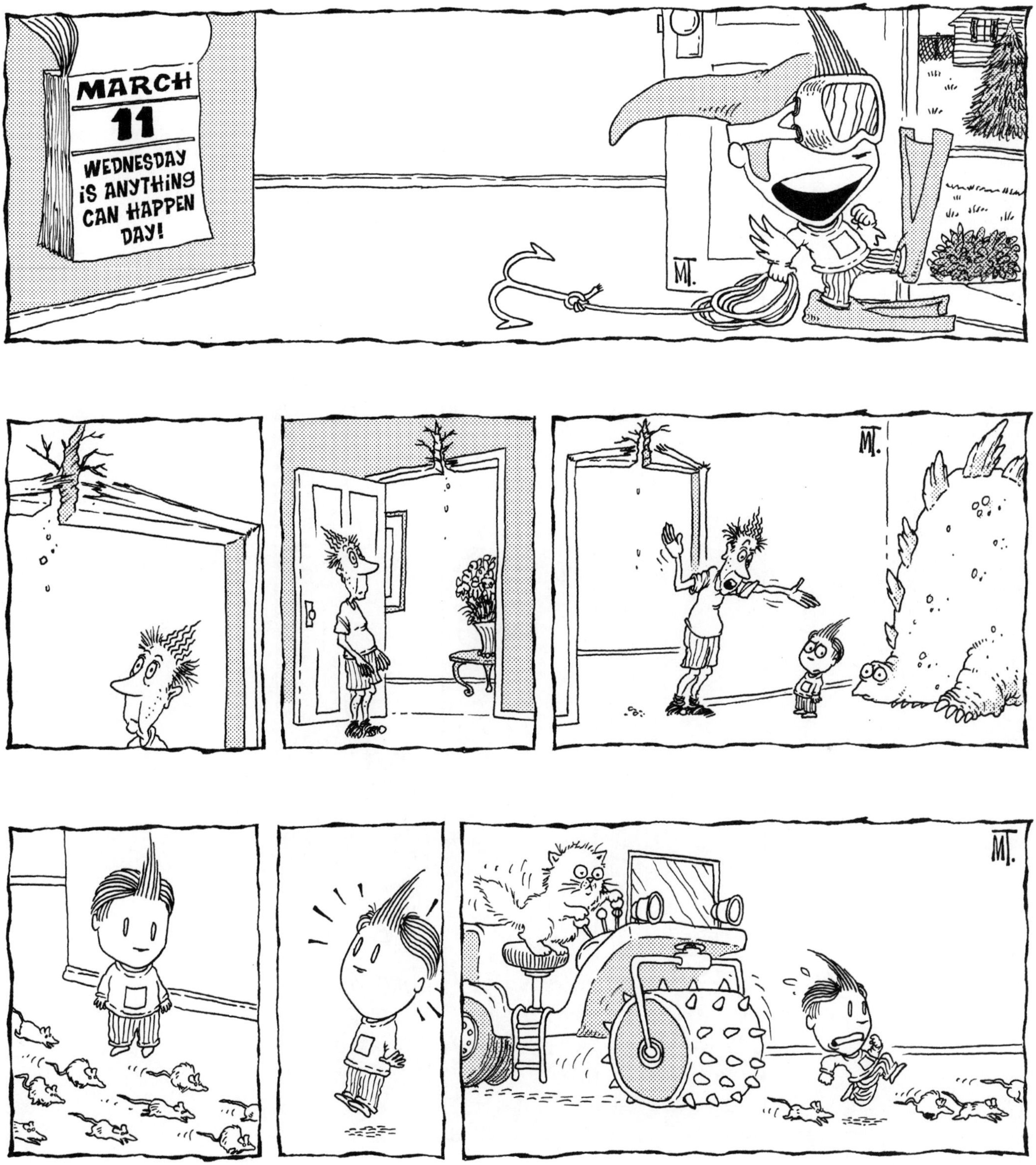
MARCH
11
WEDNESDAY IS ANYTHING CAN HAPPEN DAY!

ARE YOU SAVED?

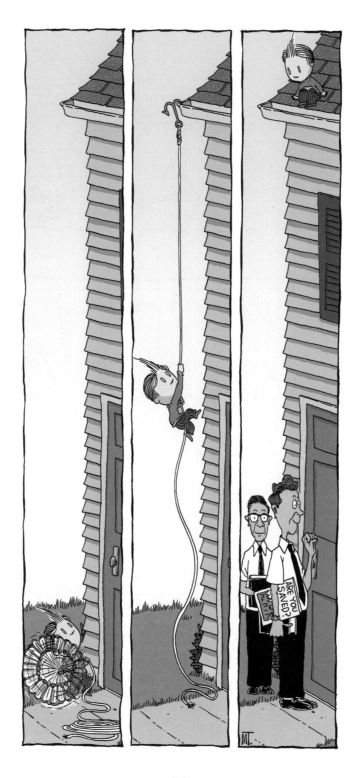

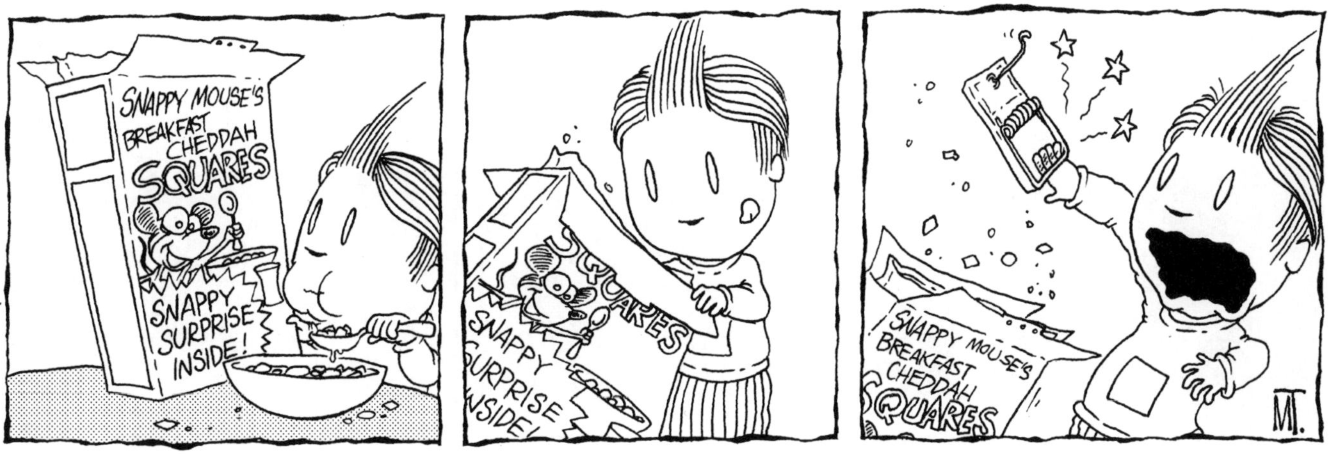
SNAPPY MOUSE'S BREAKFAST CHEDDAH SQUARES
SNAPPY SURPRISE INSIDE!
SQUARES
SNAPPY SURPRISE INSIDE!
SNAPPY MOUSE'S BREAKFAST CHEDDAH SQUARES
MT.

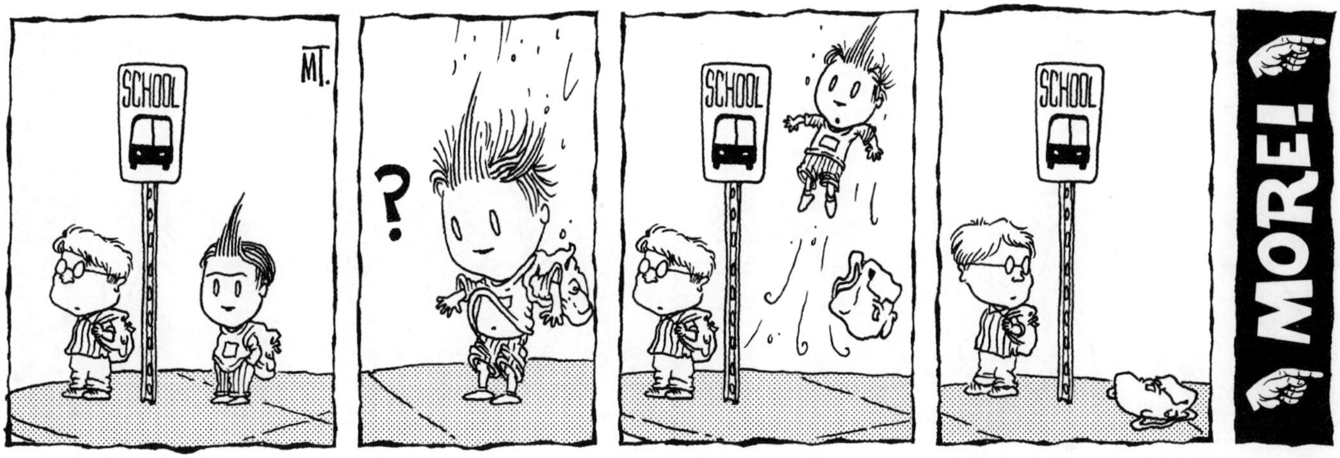
SCHOOL
MT.
?
SCHOOL
SCHOOL
MORE!

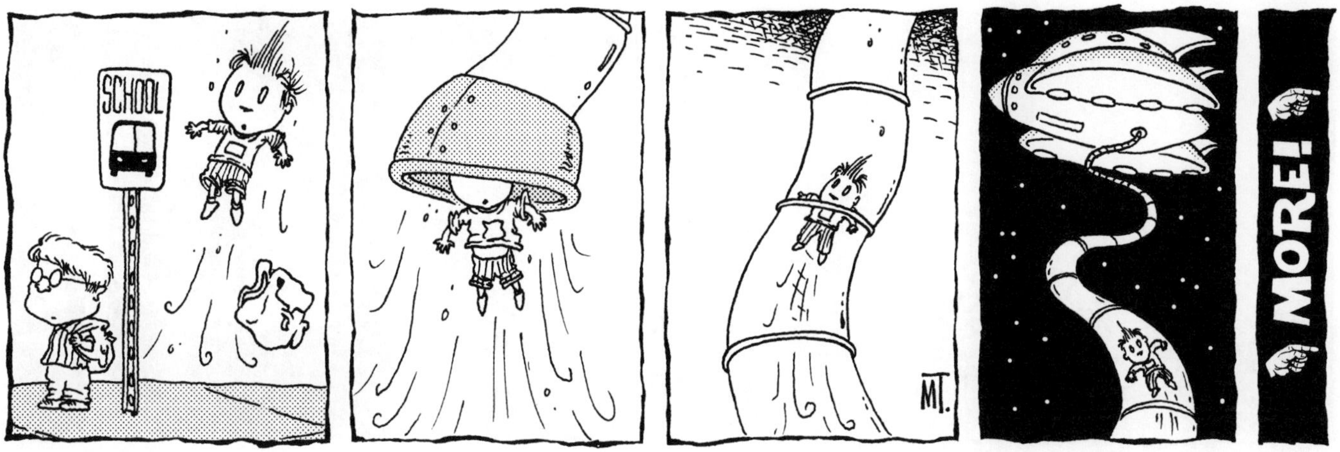
SCHOOL
MT.
MORE!

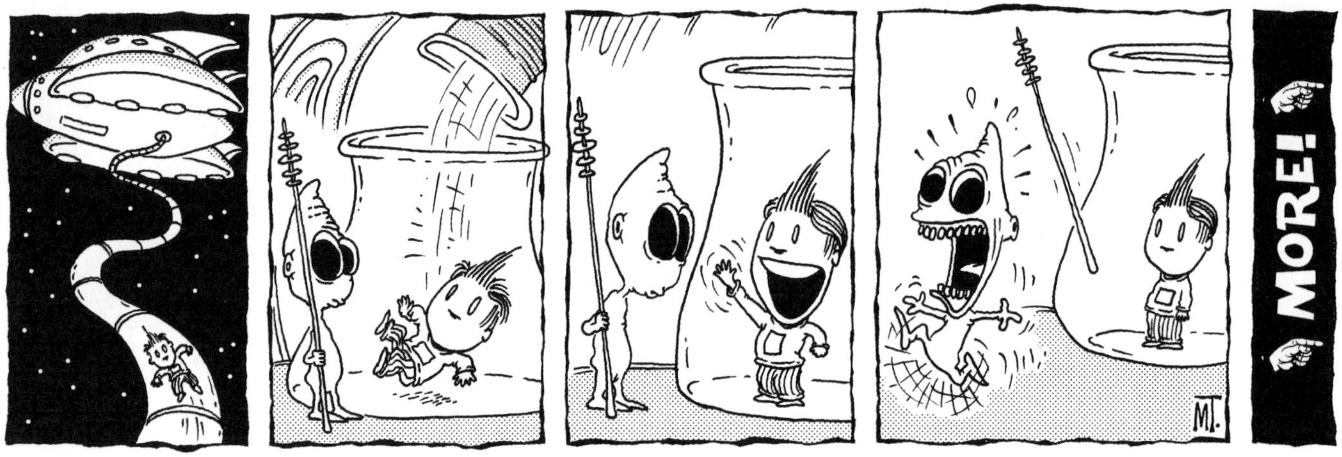
MORE!

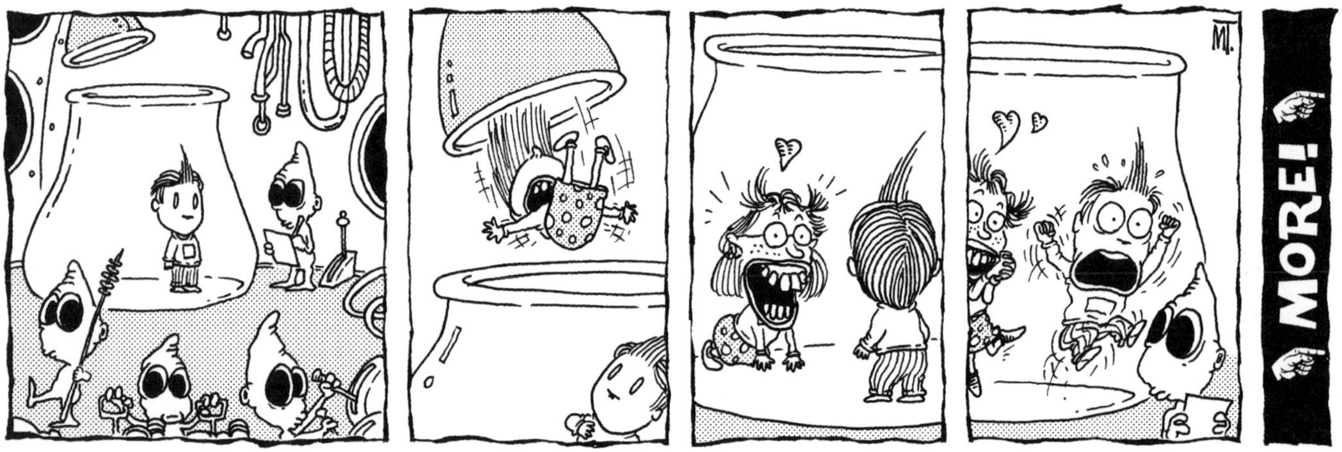
MORE!

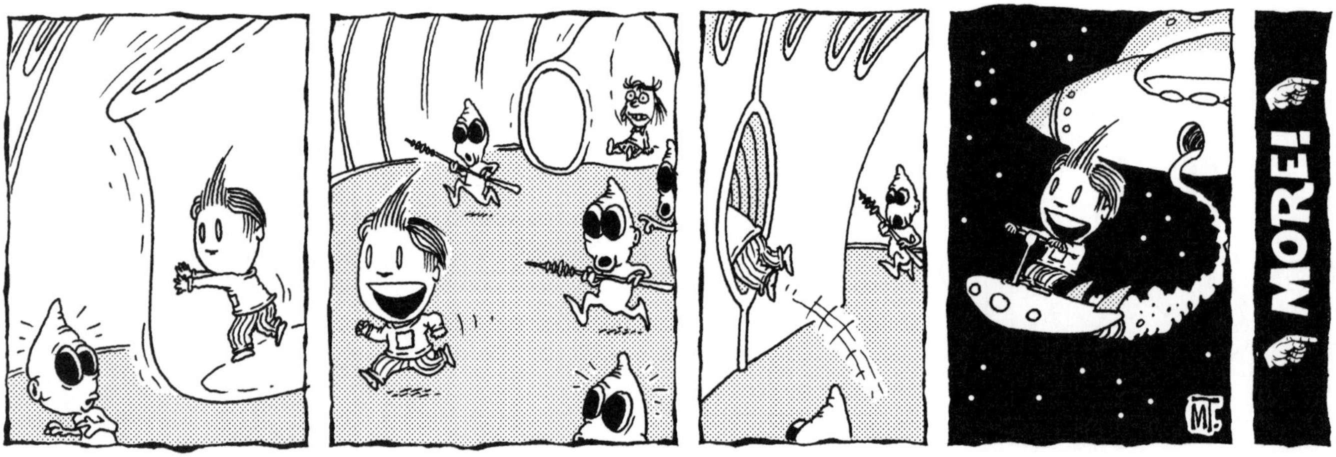
MORE!

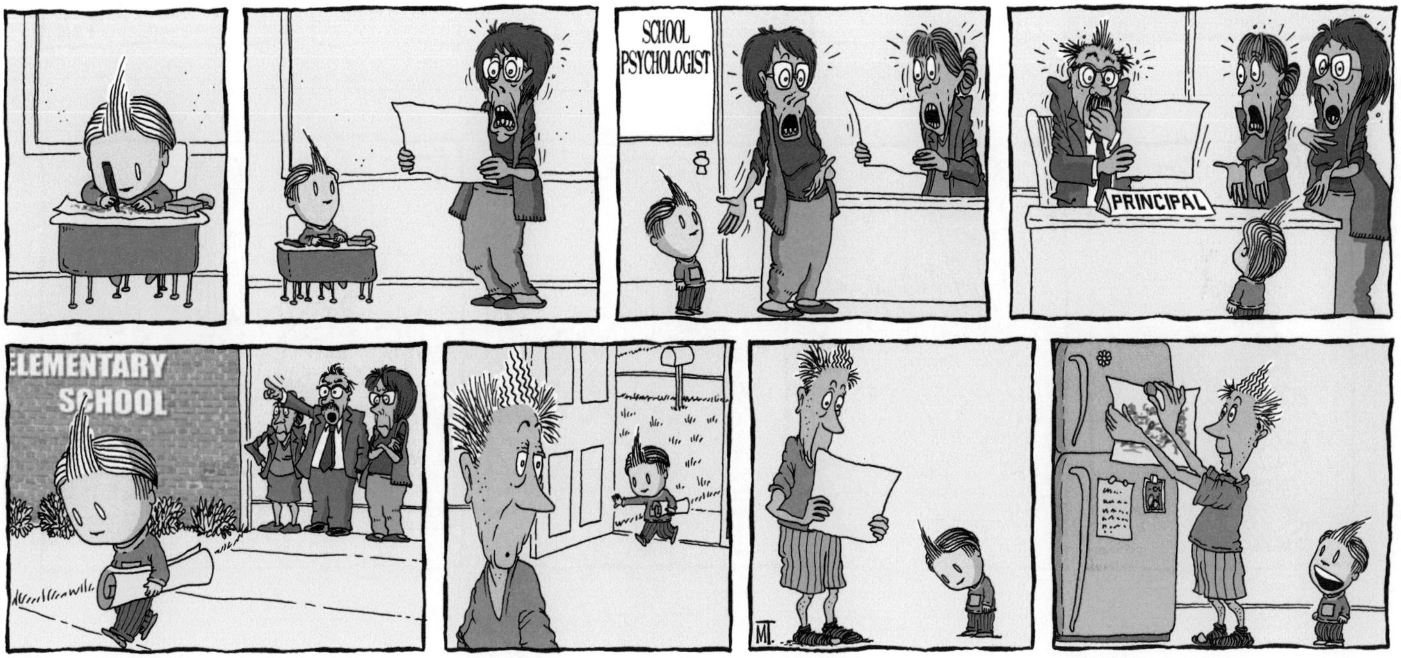
SCHOOL PSYCHOLOGIST
PRINCIPAL
ELEMENTARY SCHOOL
MT.

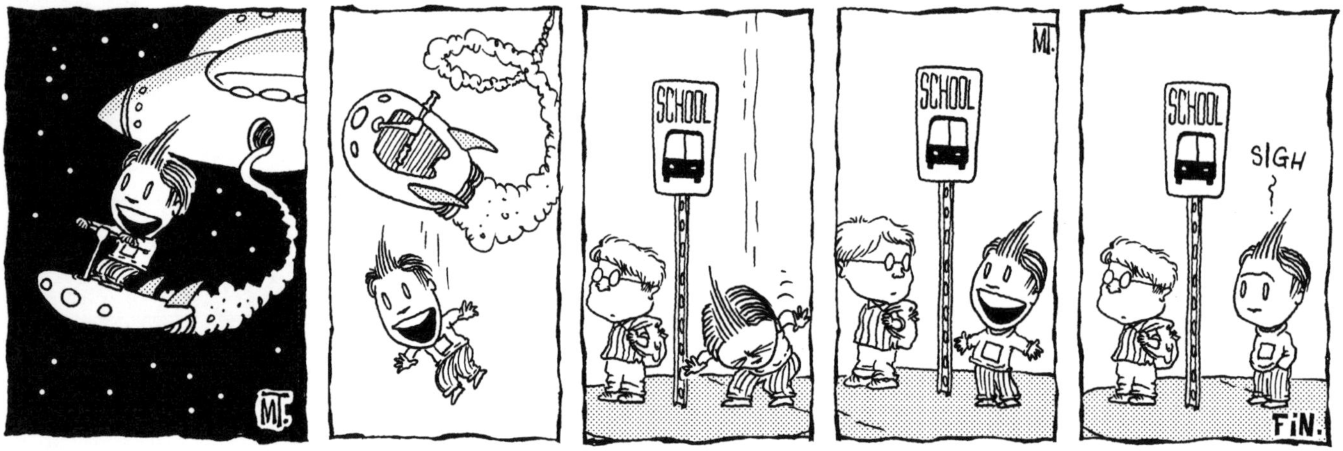
MT.
SCHOOL
SCHOOL
MT.
SCHOOL
SIGH
FIN.

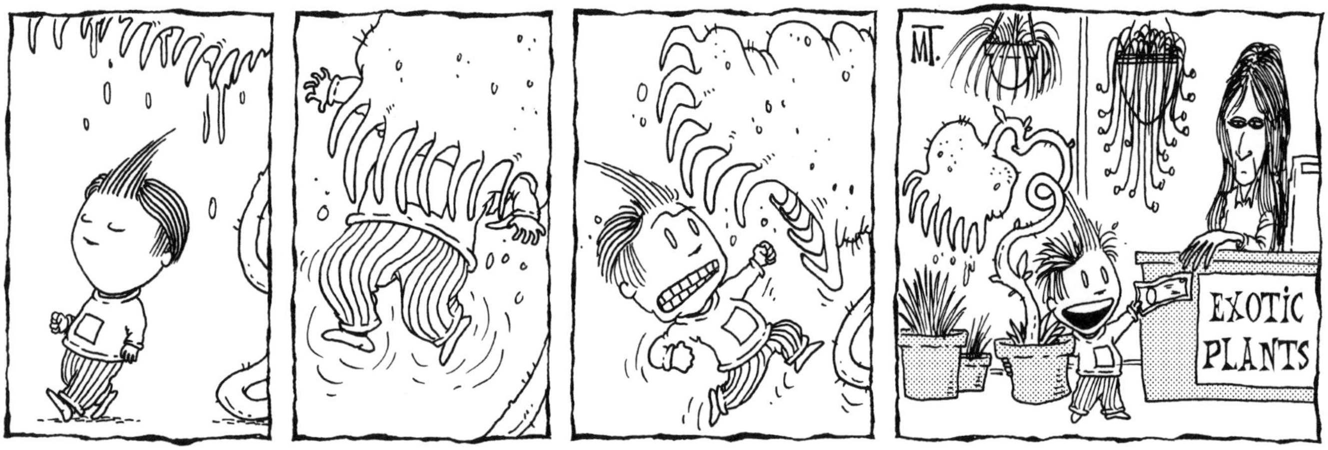
MT.
EXOTIC PLANTS

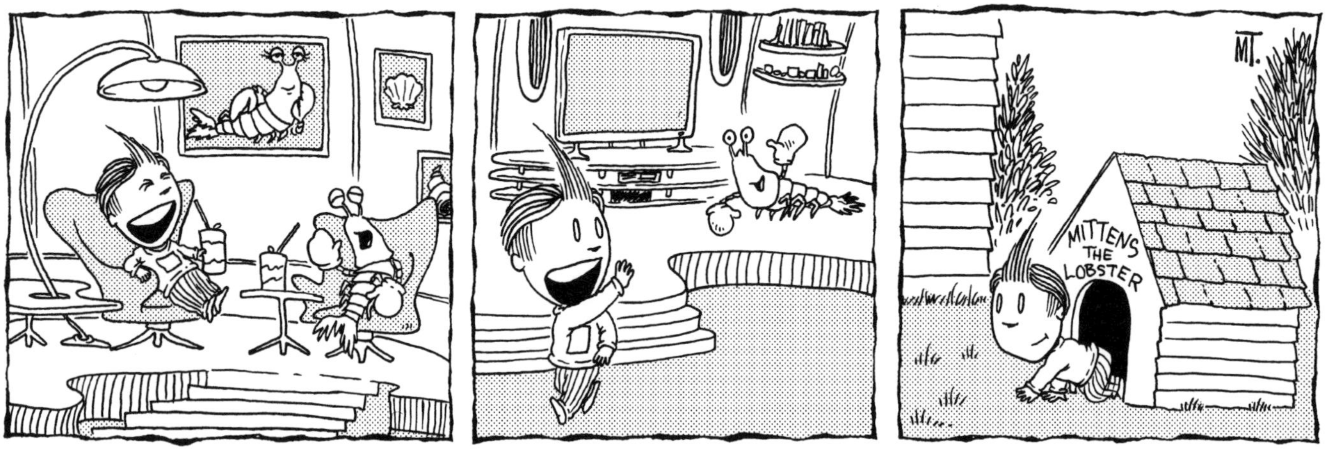
MT.
MITTENS THE LOBSTER

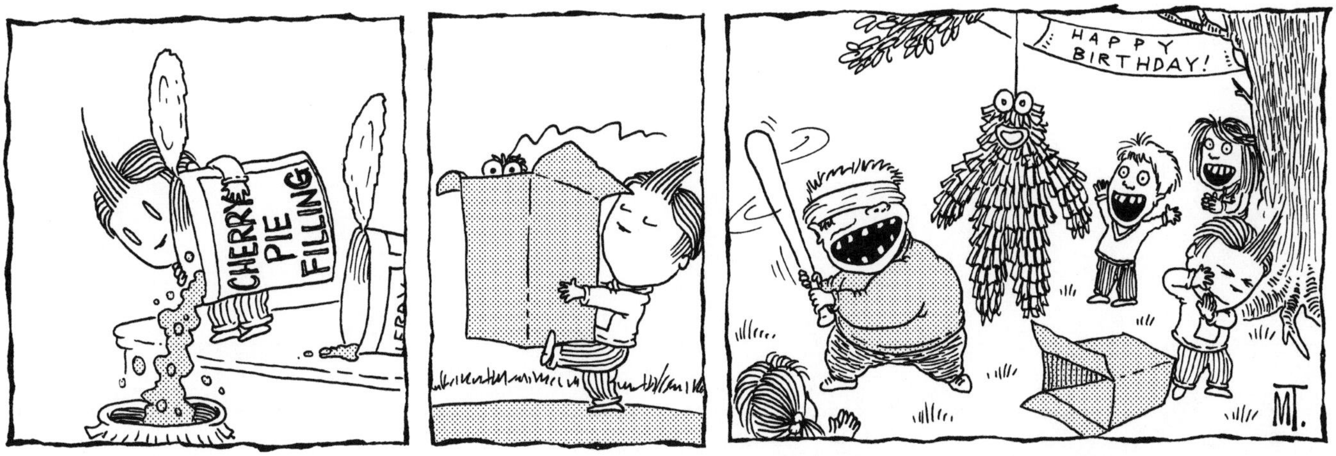
CHERRY PIE FILLING
HAPPY BIRTHDAY!
MT.

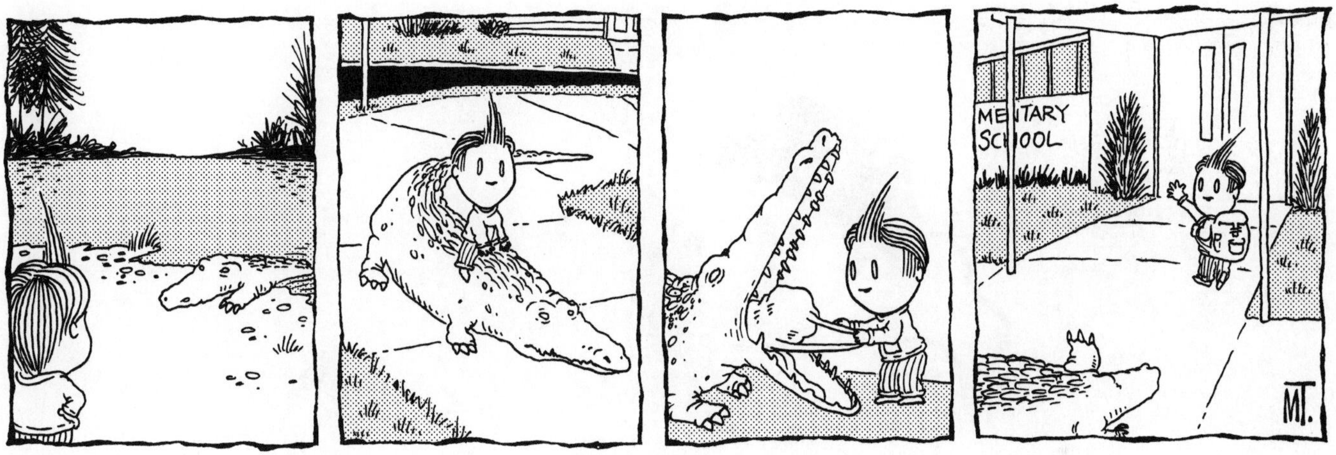
MENTARY SCHOOL
MT.

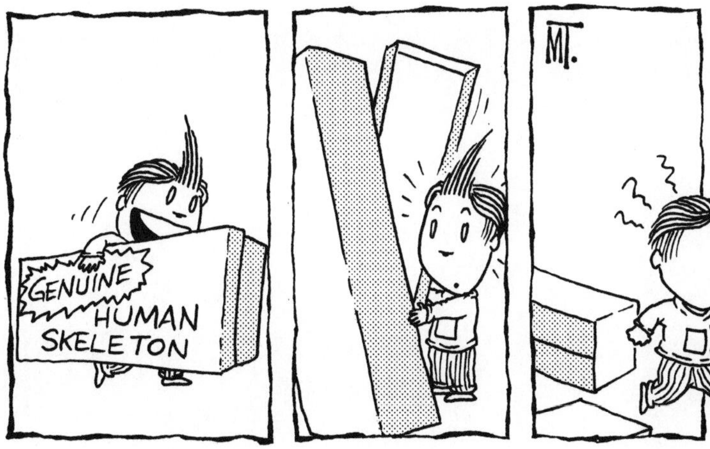
GENUINE HUMAN SKELETON
MT.

MARMADUKE

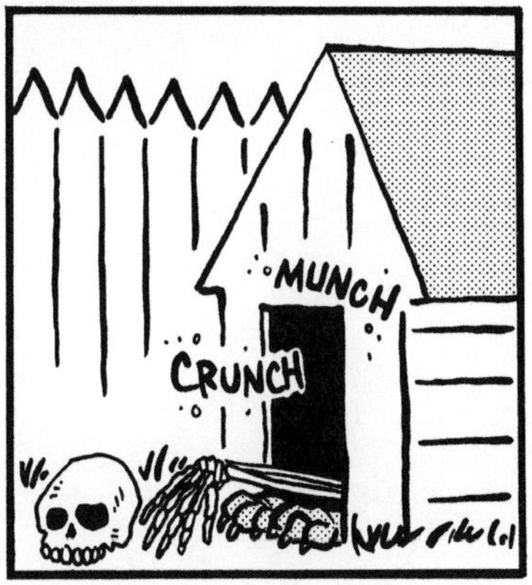
MUNCH
CRUNCH

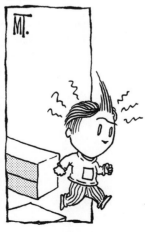

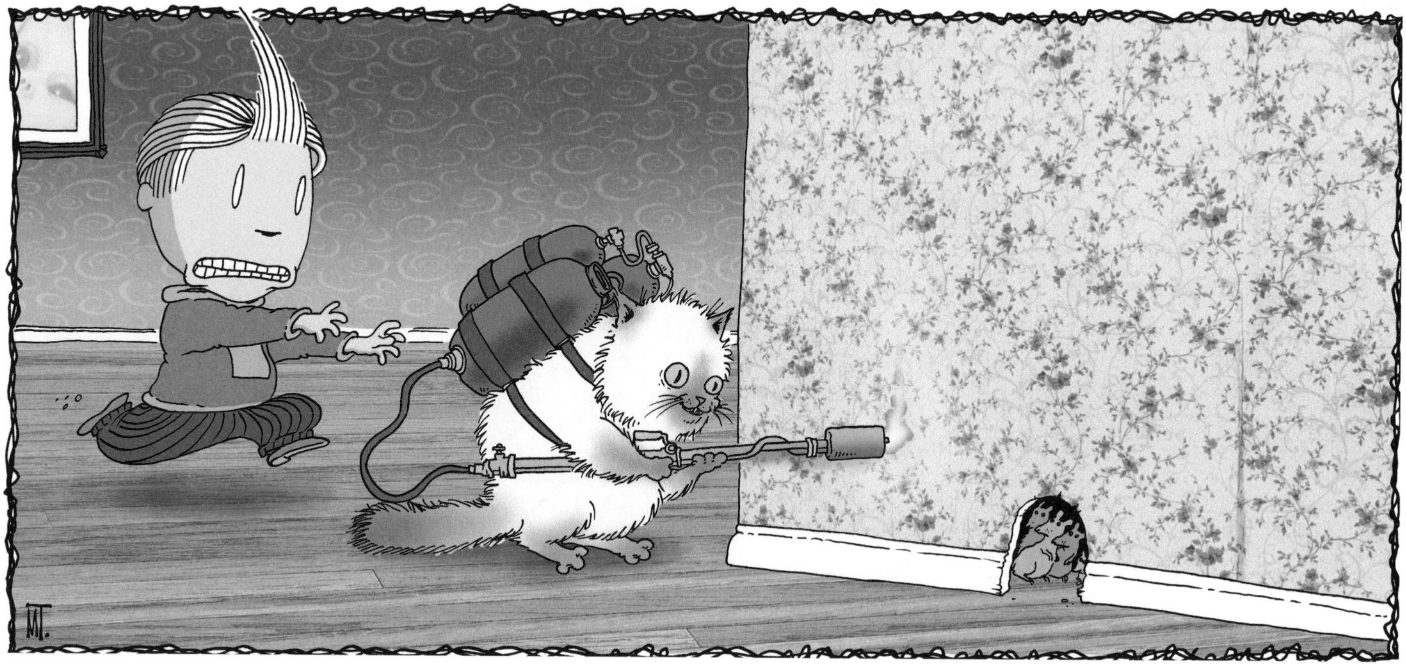
MT.

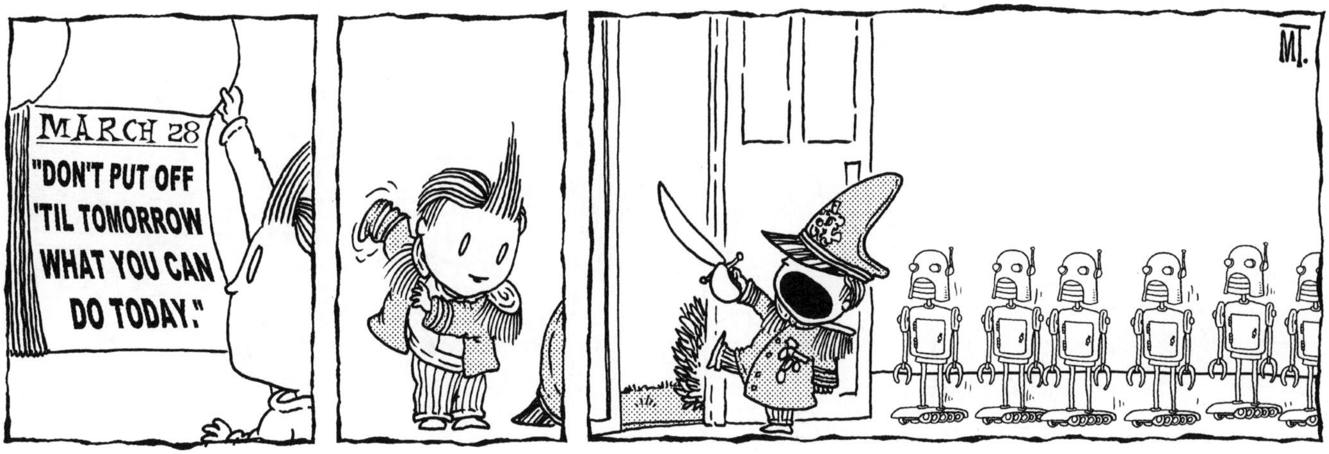
MARCH 28
"DON'T PUT OFF 'TIL TOMORROW WHAT YOU CAN DO TODAY."

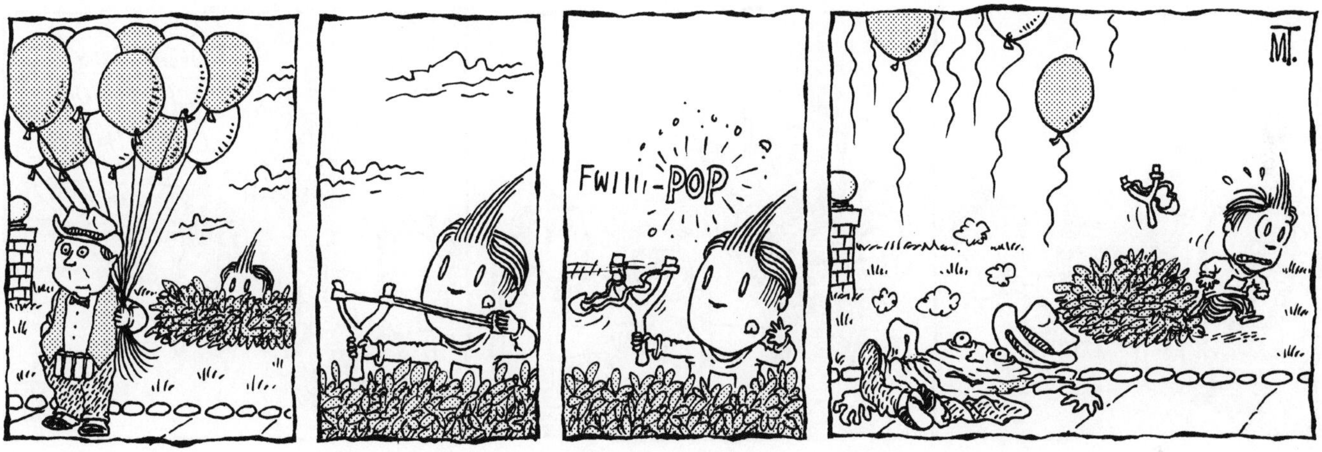
FWIIII
POP

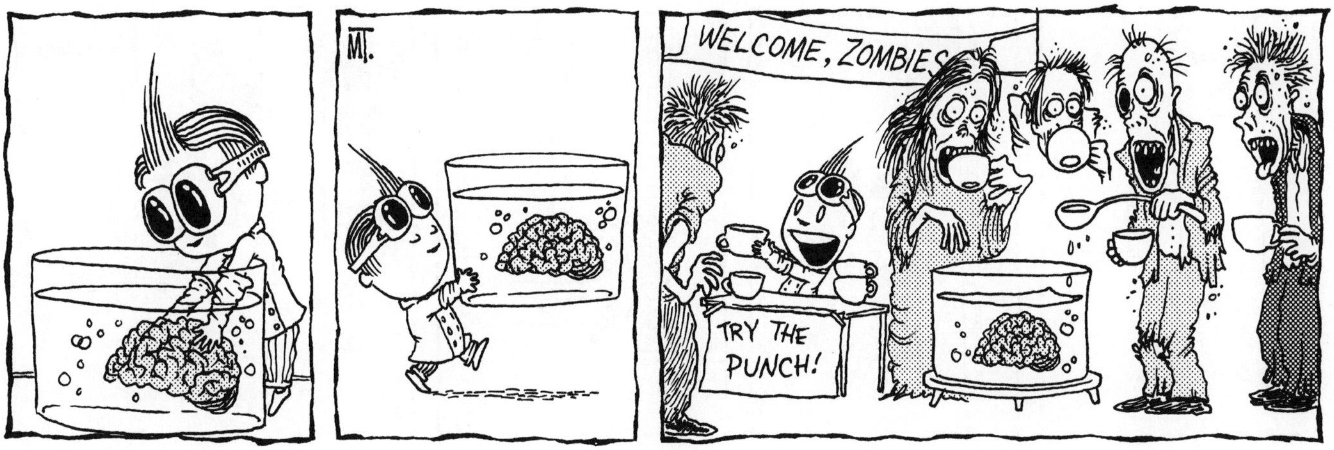
WELCOME, ZOMBIES
TRY THE PUNCH!

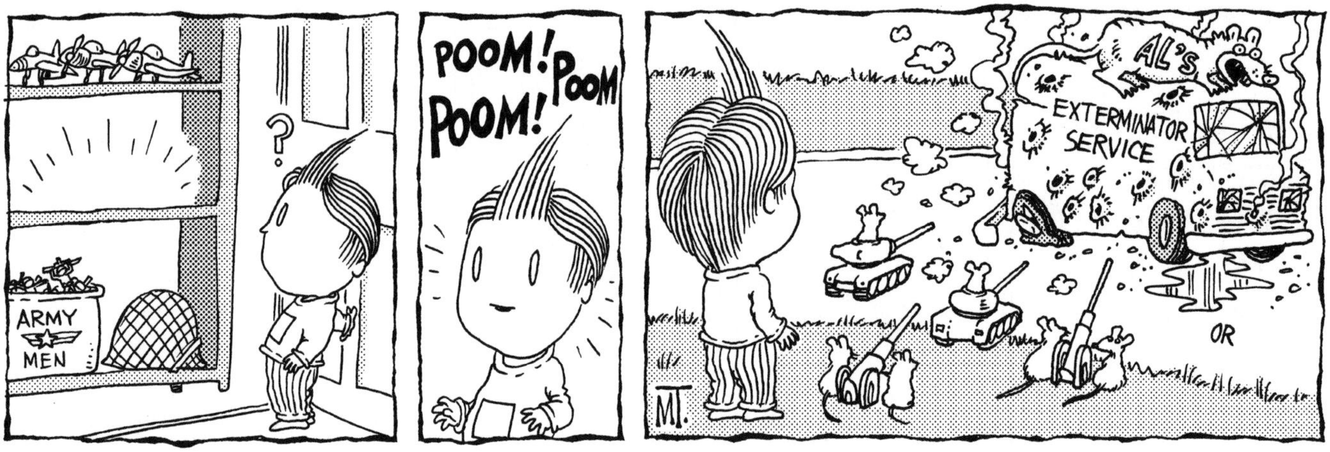
ARMY MEN
?
POOM! POOM! POOM
AL'S
EXTERMINATOR SERVICE
OR
MT.

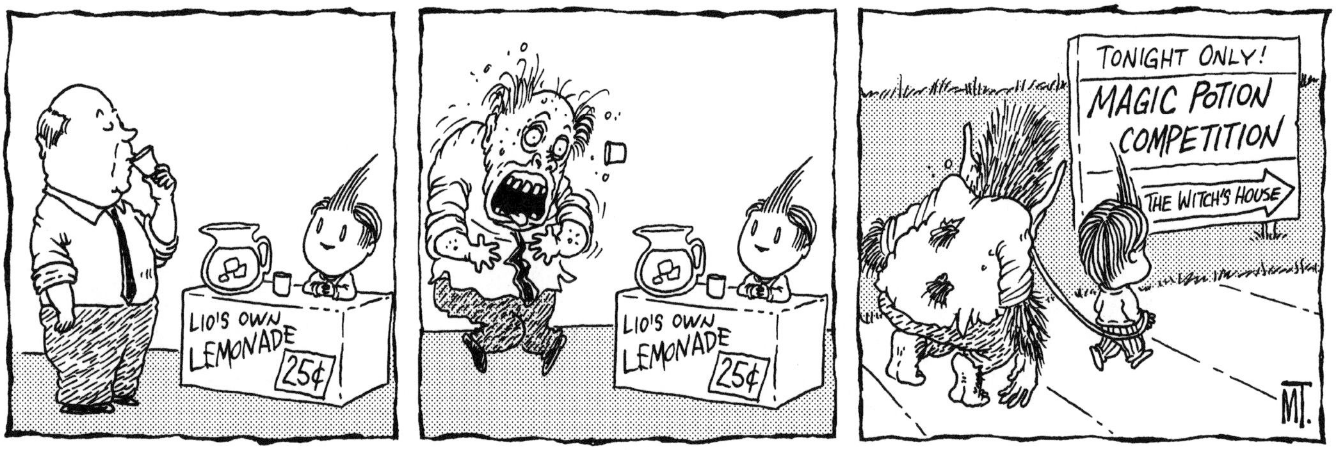
LIO'S OWN LEMONADE
25¢
TONIGHT ONLY!
MAGIC POTION COMPETITION
THE WITCH'S HOUSE
MT.

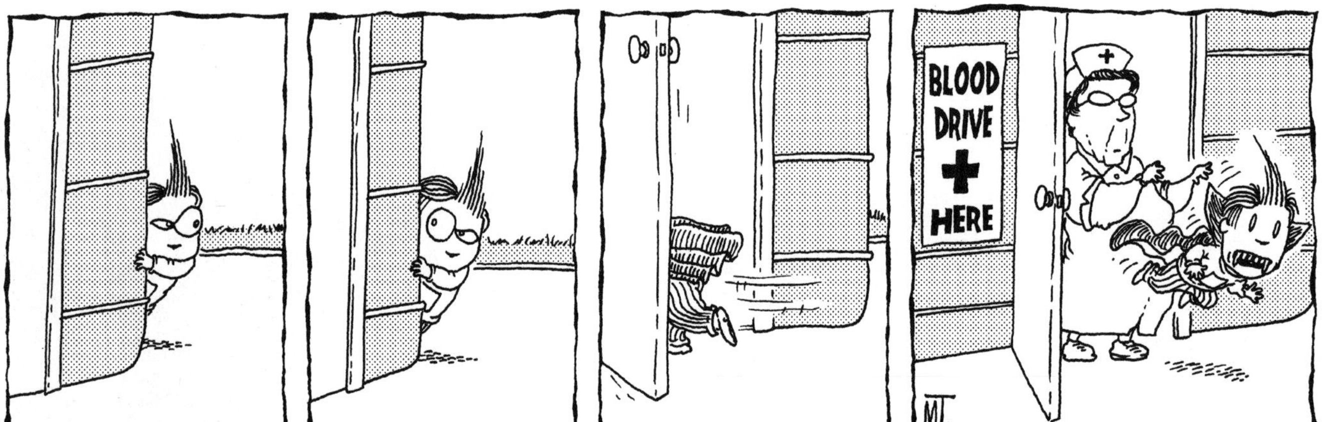
BLOOD DRIVE HERE
MT.

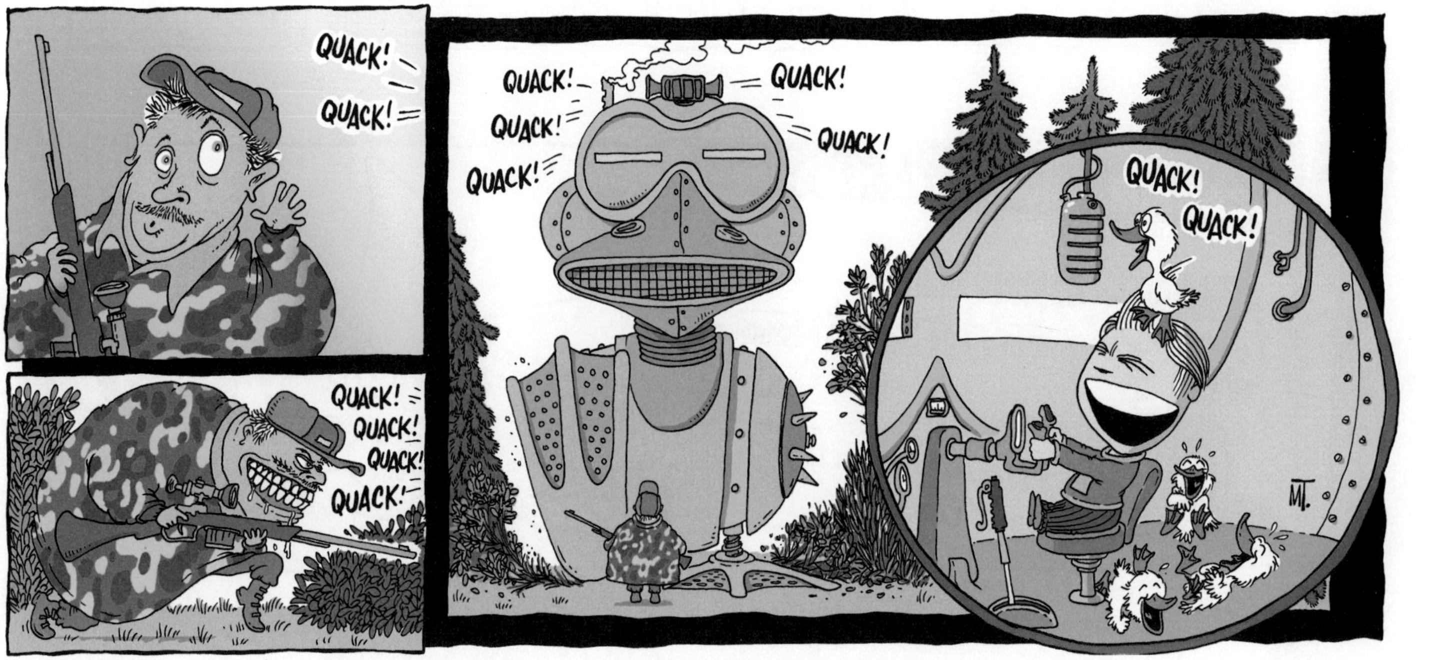
QUACK!
QUACK!
QUACK!
QUACK!
QUACK!
QUACK!
QUACK!
QUACK!
QUACK!
QUACK!
QUACK!
QUACK!
QUACK!
MT.

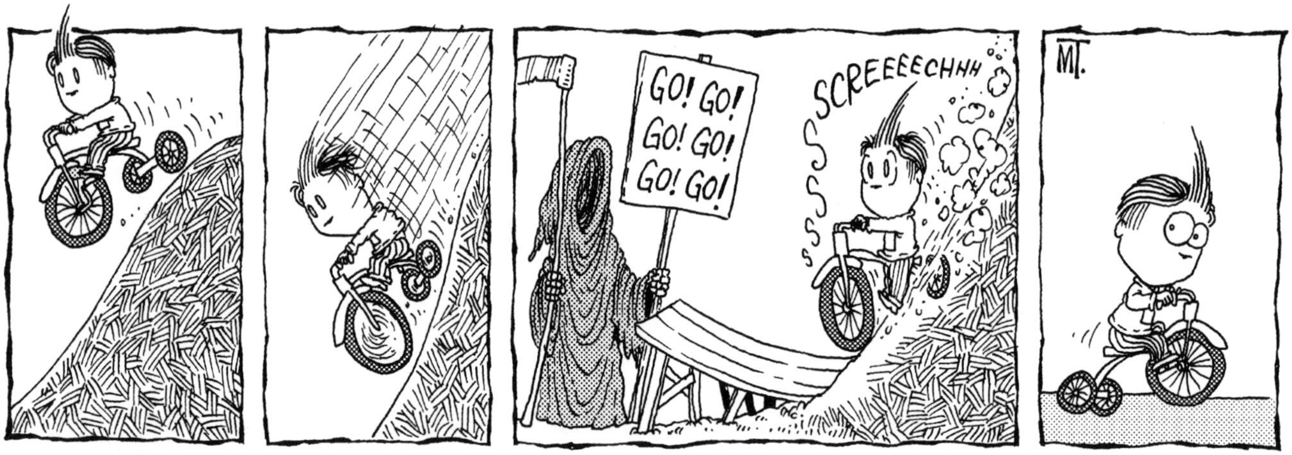
GO! GO!
GO! GO!
GO! GO!
SCREEEEECHHH

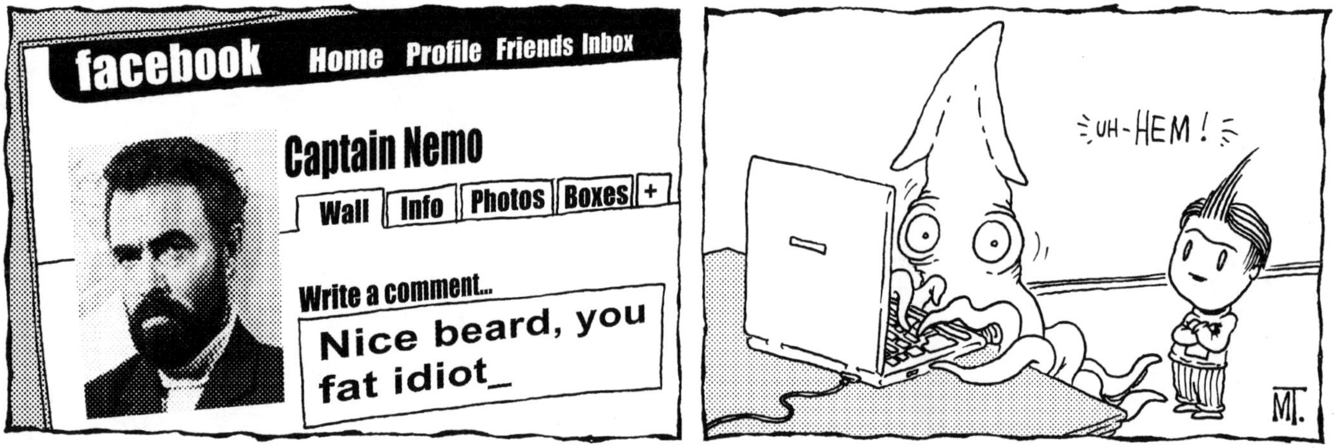
facebook
Home Profile Friends Inbox
Captain Nemo
Wall Info Photos Boxes +
Write a comment...
Nice beard, you fat idiot_
UH-HEM!

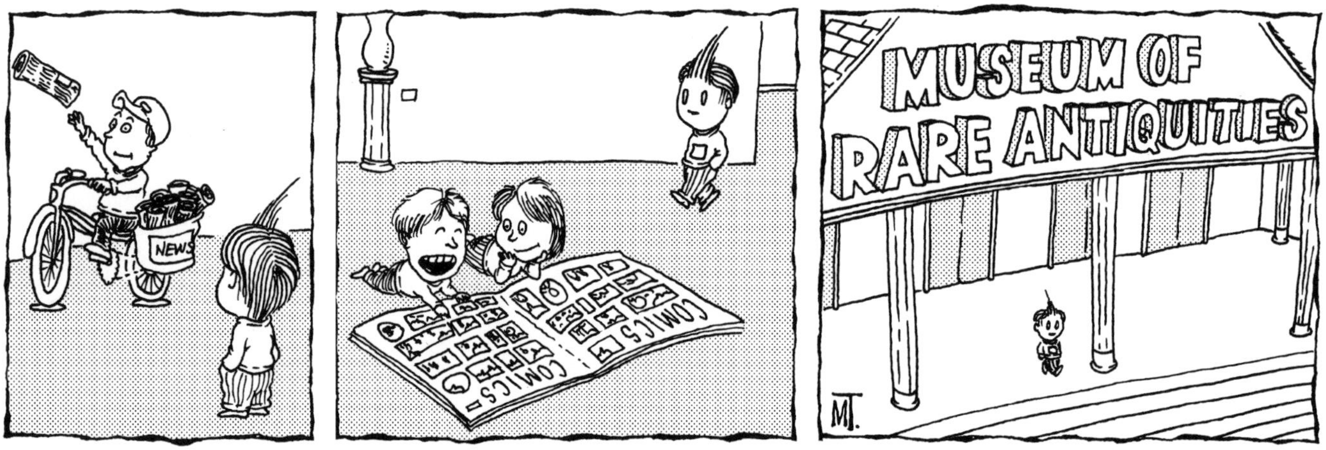
NEWS
COMICS
COMICS
MUSEUM OF
RARE ANTIQUITIES

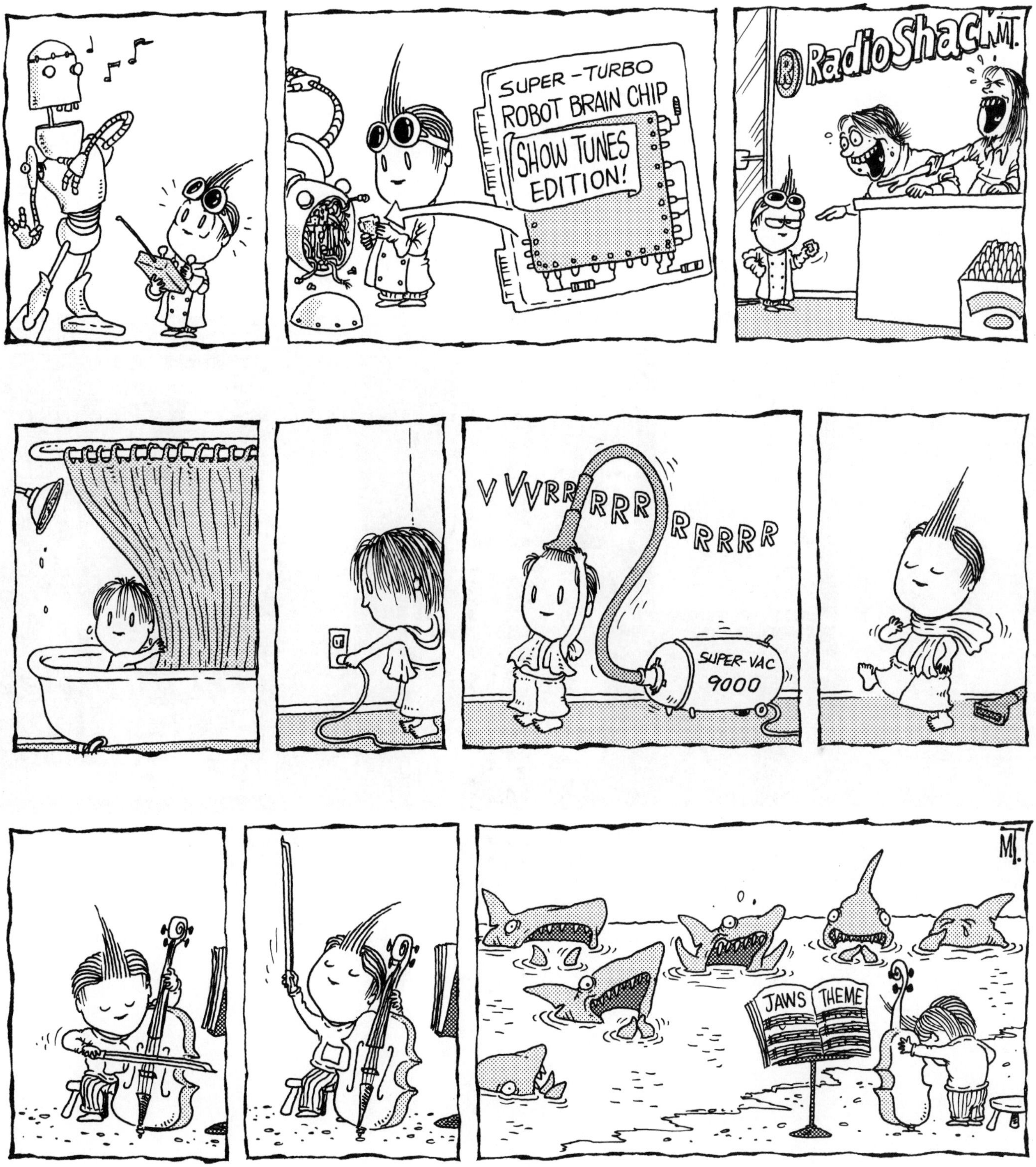
SUPER-TURBO
ROBOT BRAIN CHIP
SHOW TUNES EDITION!
RadioShack
M.T.
VVVRRRRRRRRRRR
SUPER-VAC 9000
M.T.
JAWS THEME

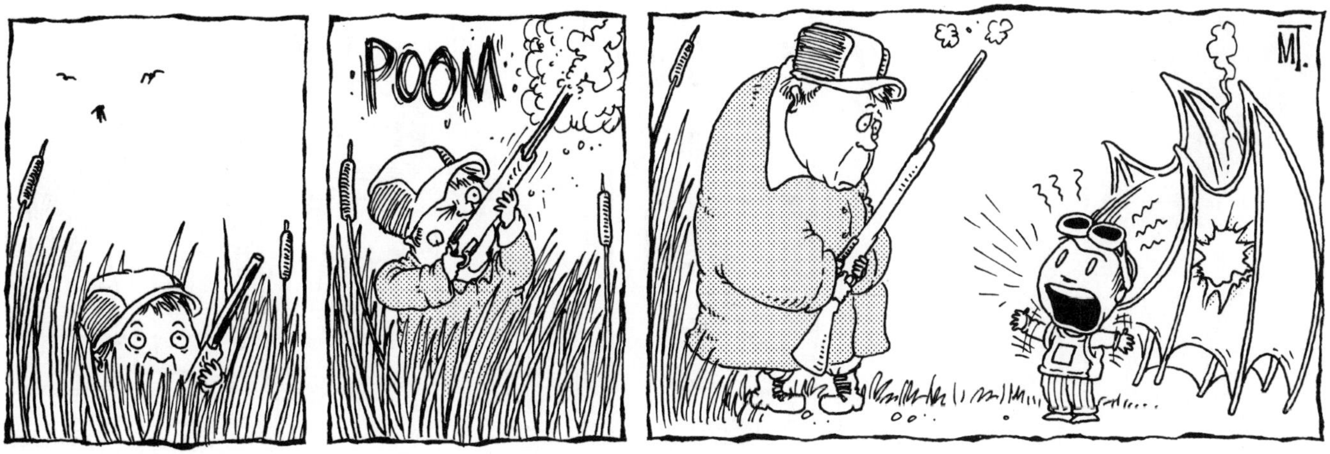
POOM

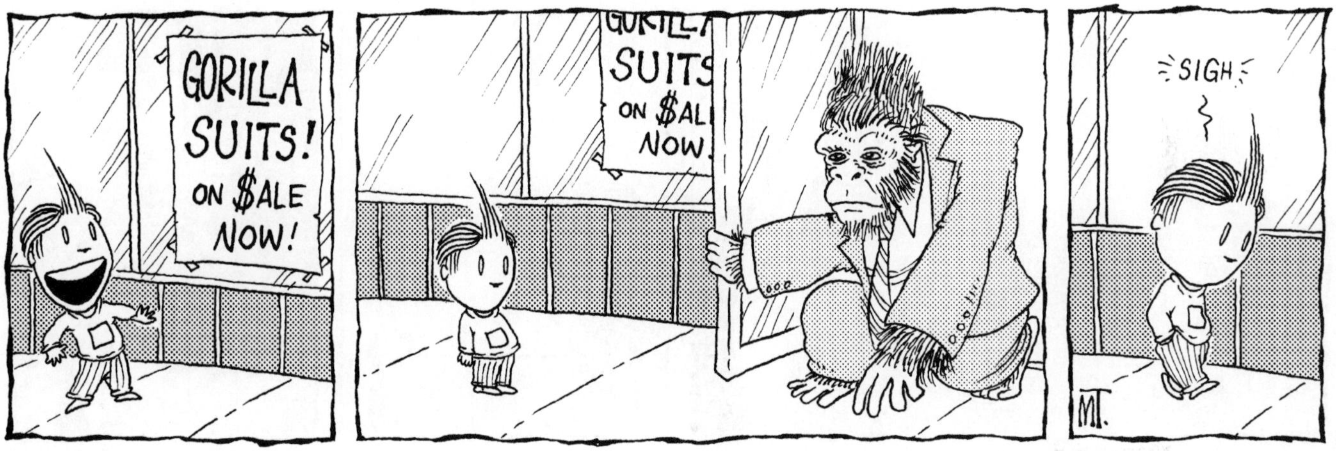
GORILLA SUITS! ON $ALE NOW!
SIGH

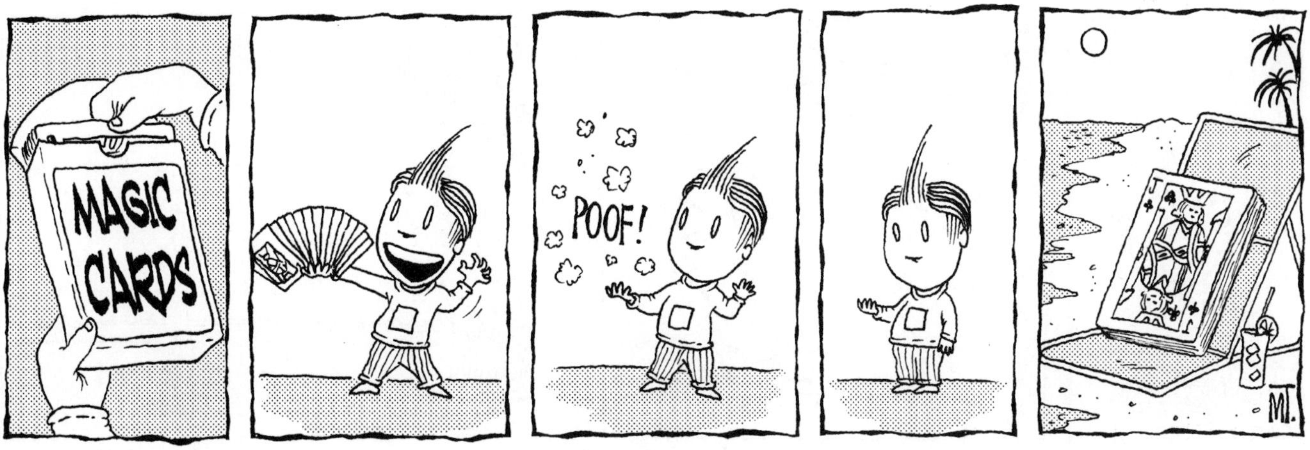
MAGIC CARDS
POOF!

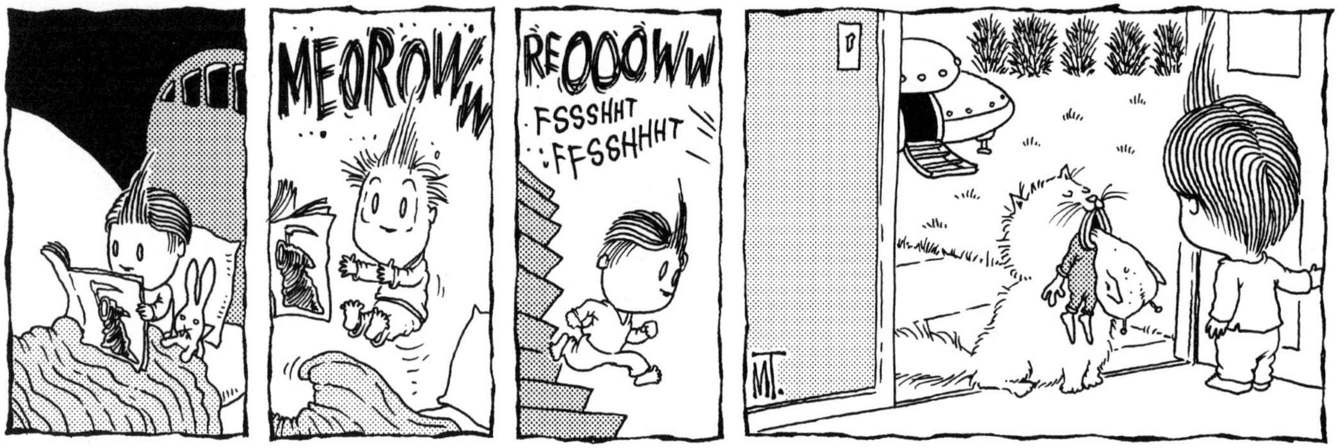
MEOROWW
REOOOWW
FSSSHHT
FFSSHHHT
MT.

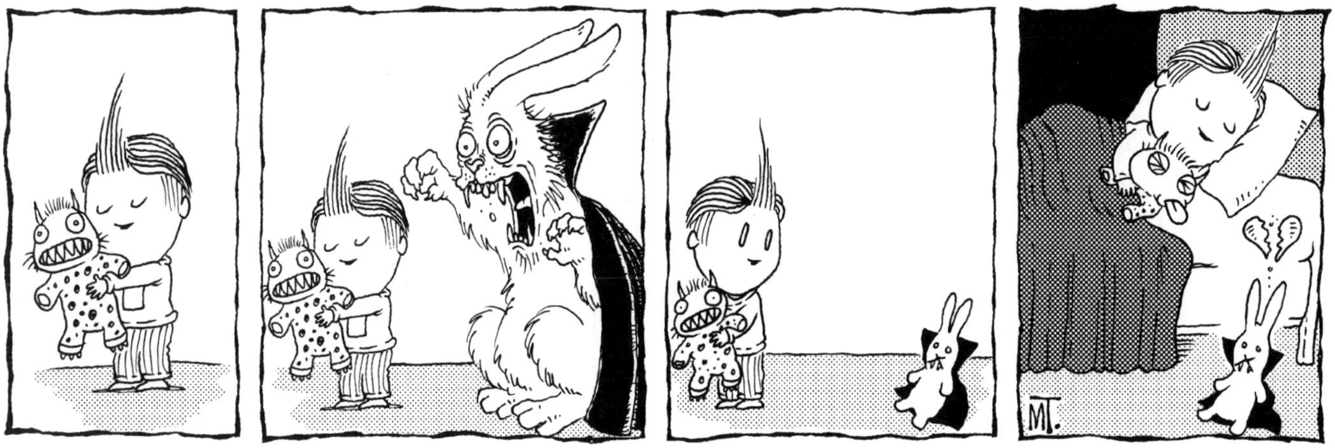
MT.

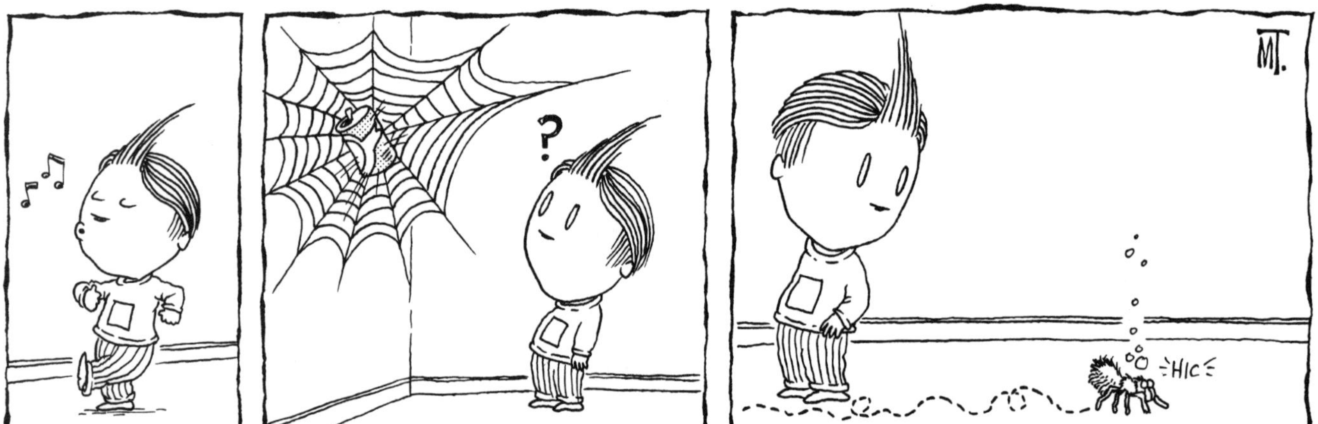
?
MT.
HIC

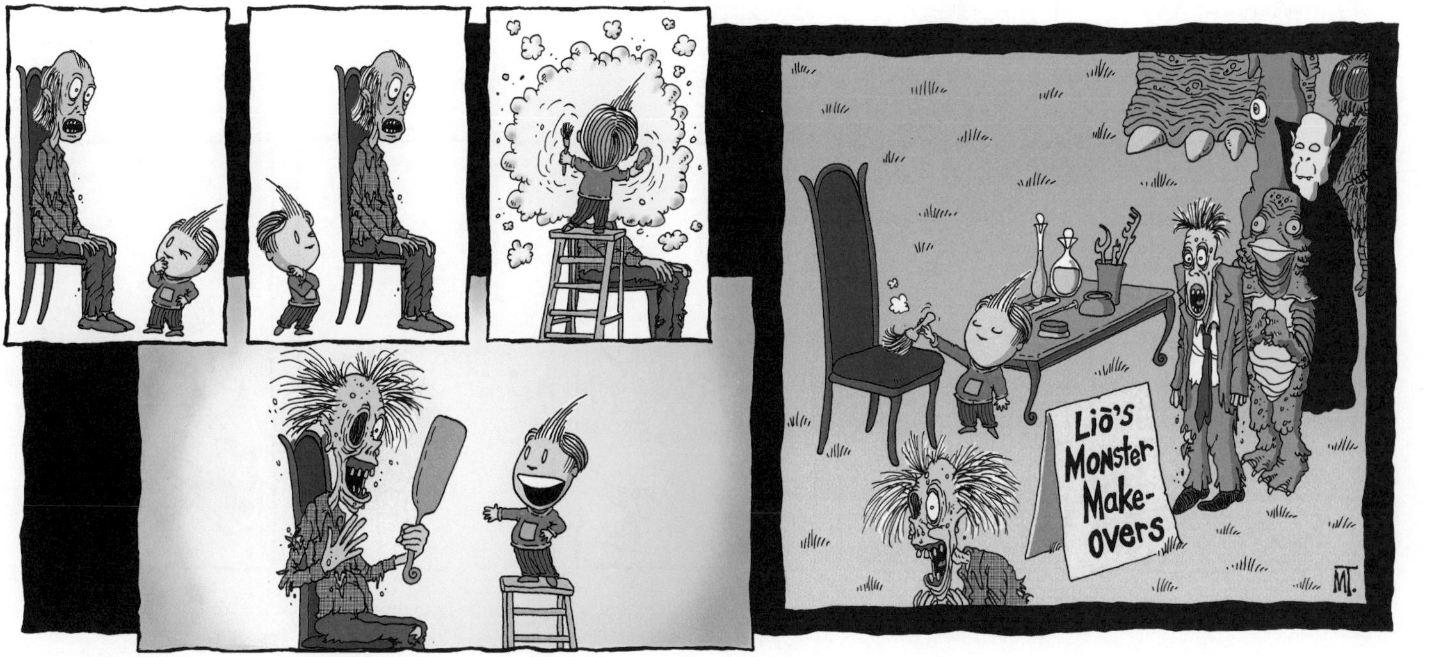
Liō's
Monster
Make-
overs
MT.

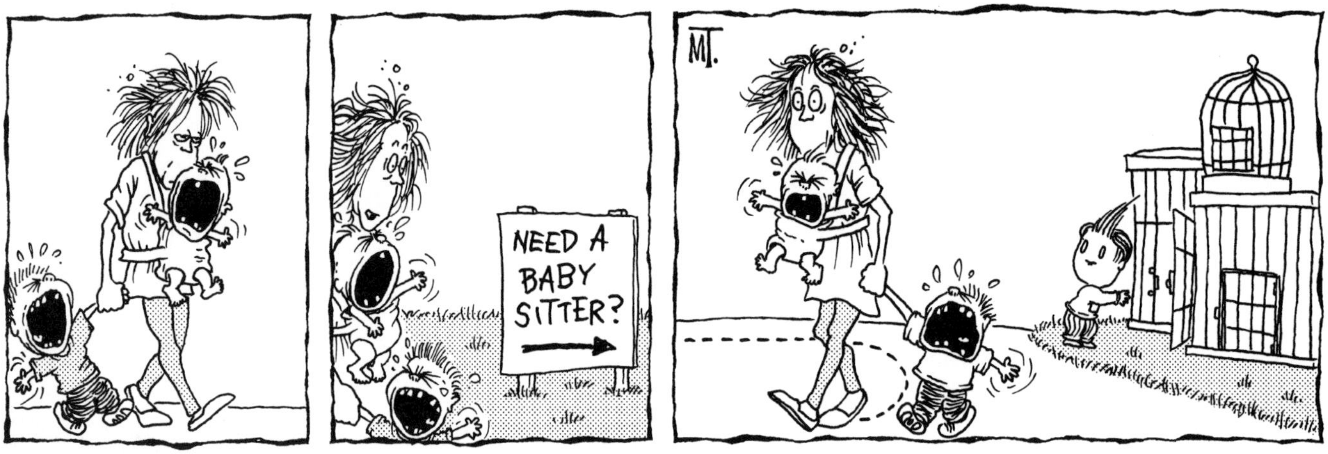
MT.
NEED A BABY SITTER?

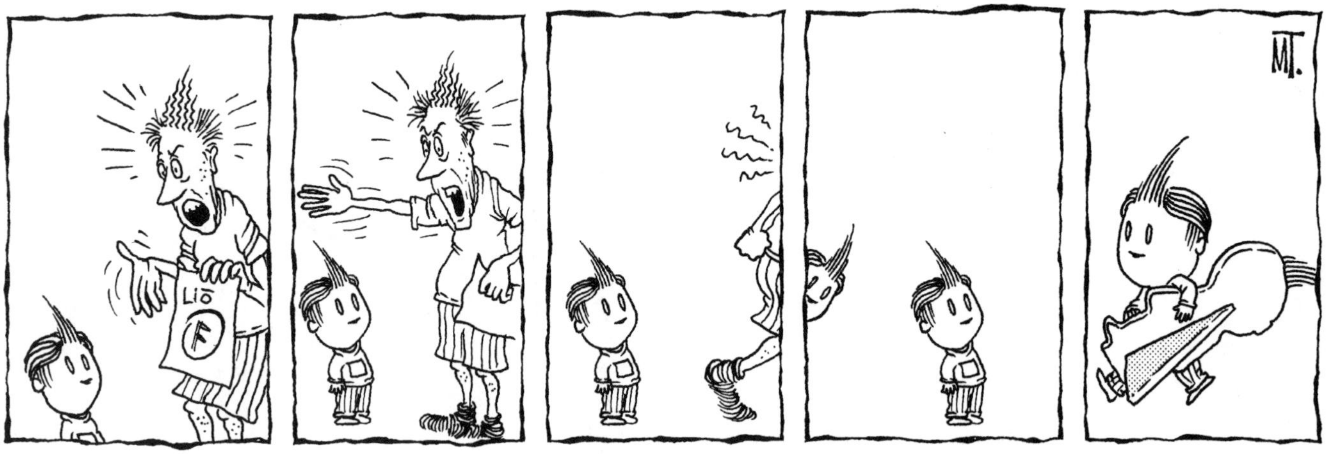
LIO
F
MT.

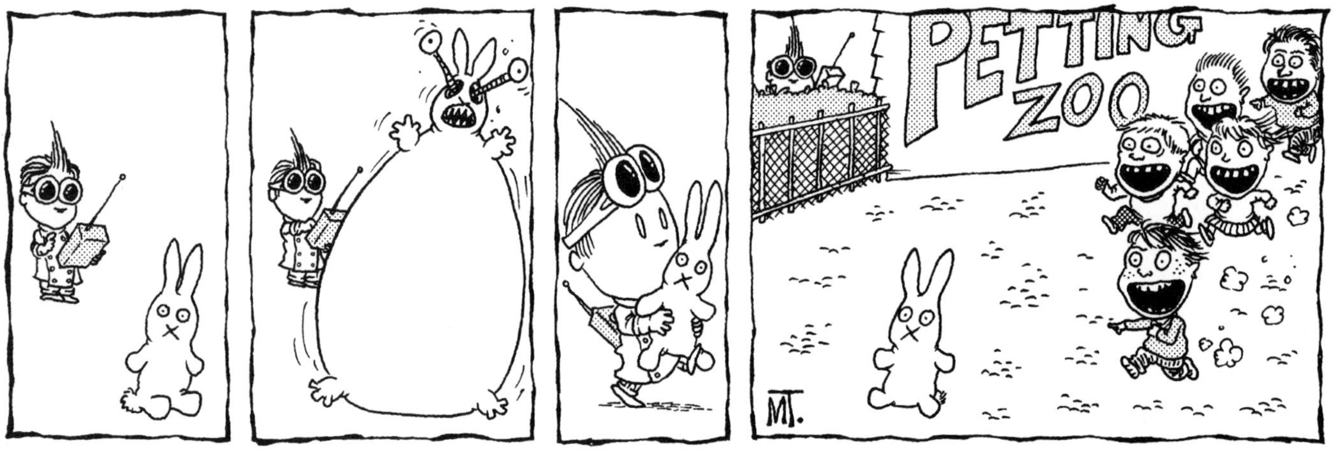
PETTING ZOO
MT.

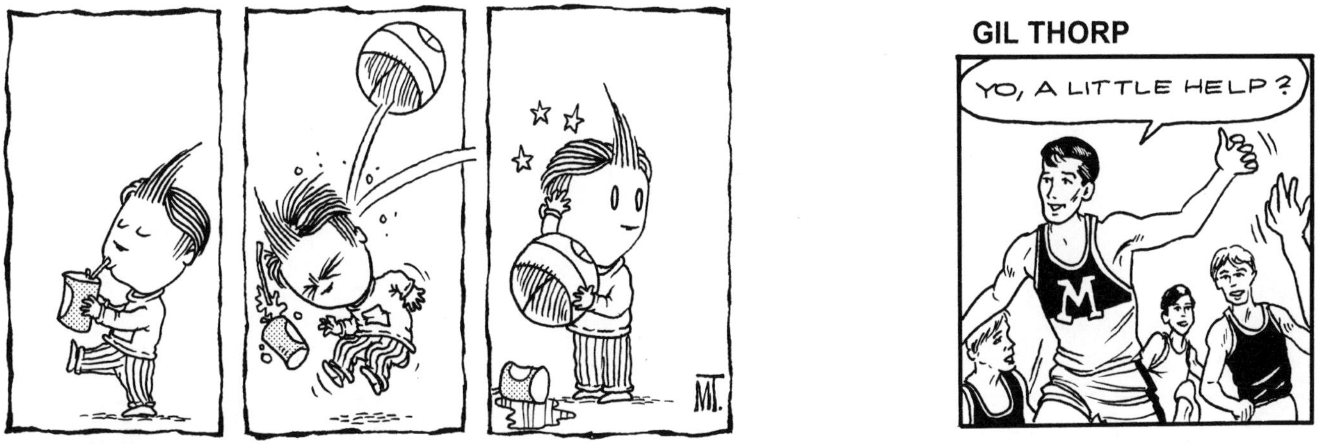
GIL THORP
YO, A LITTLE HELP ?

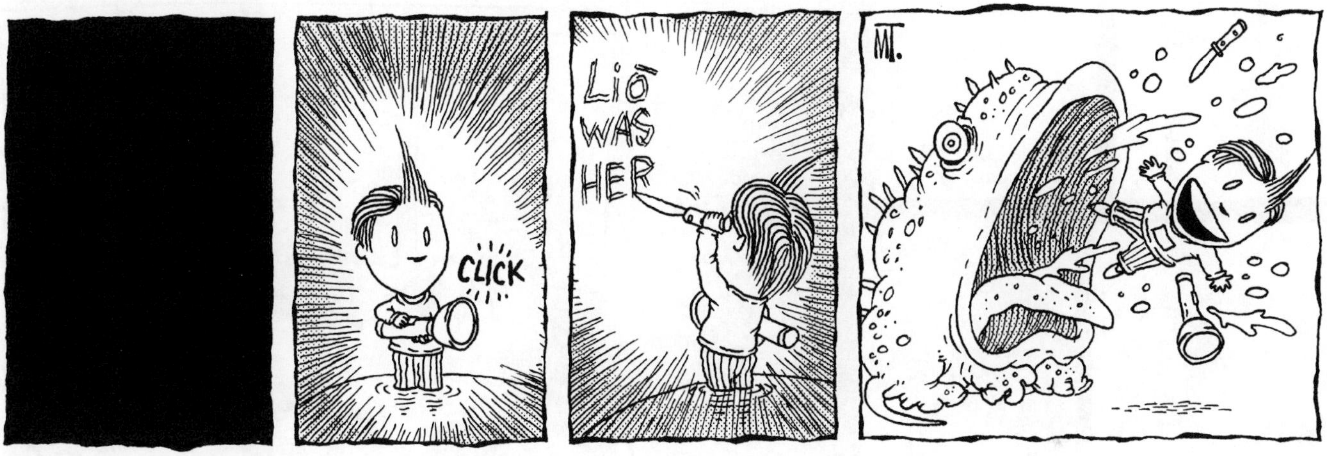
CLICK
LIŌ WAS HER

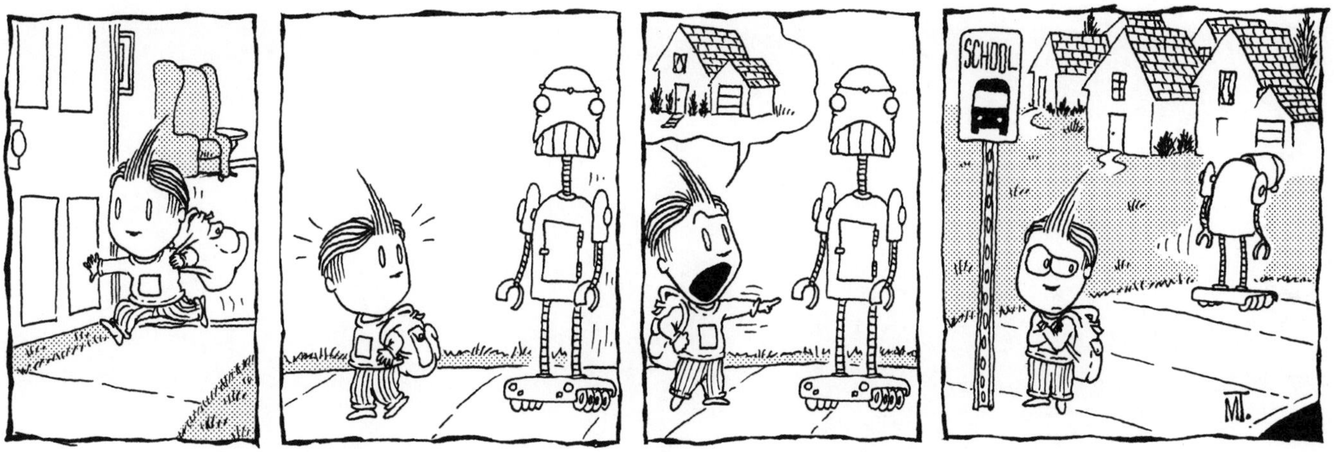
SCHOOL

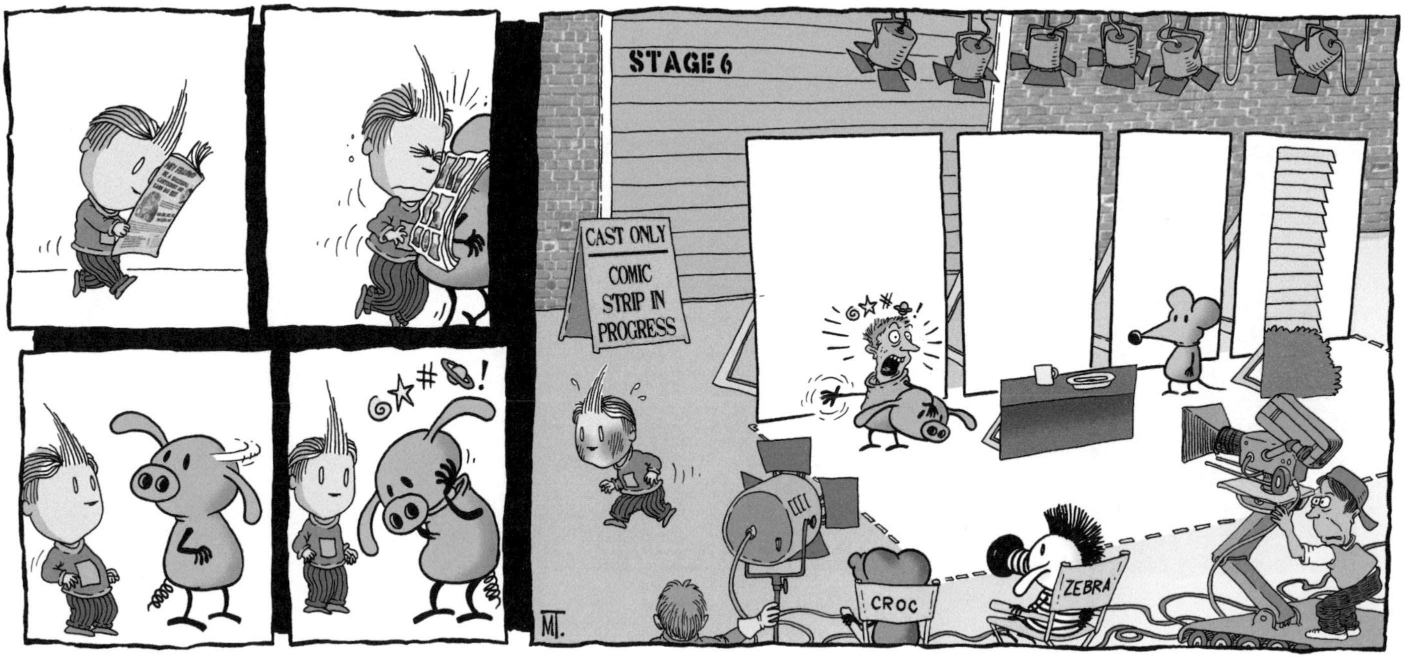
STAGE 6
CAST ONLY
COMIC STRIP IN PROGRESS
CROC
ZEBRA
MT.

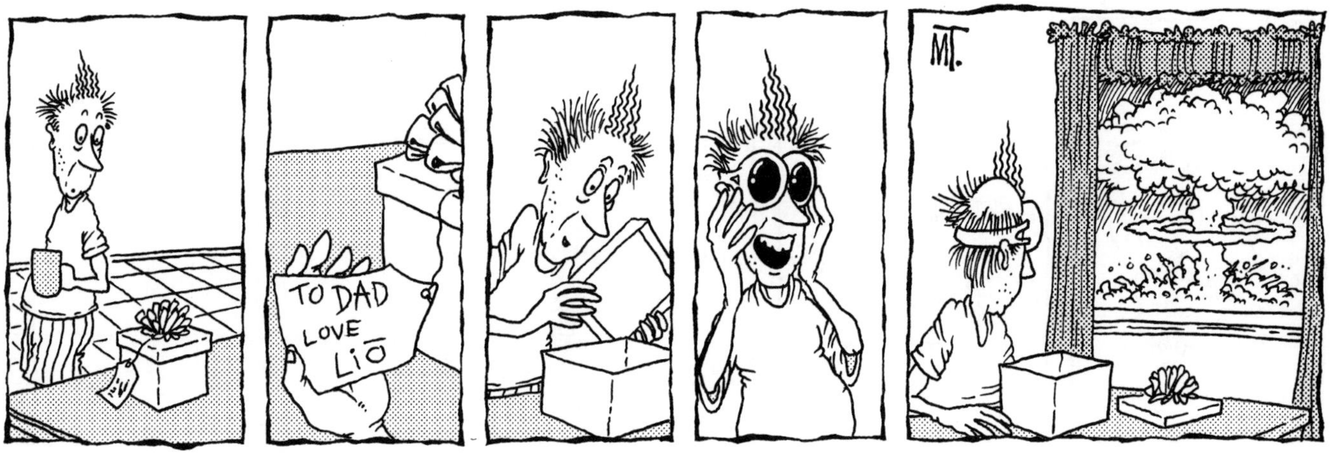
TO DAD
LOVE
LIŌ
MT.

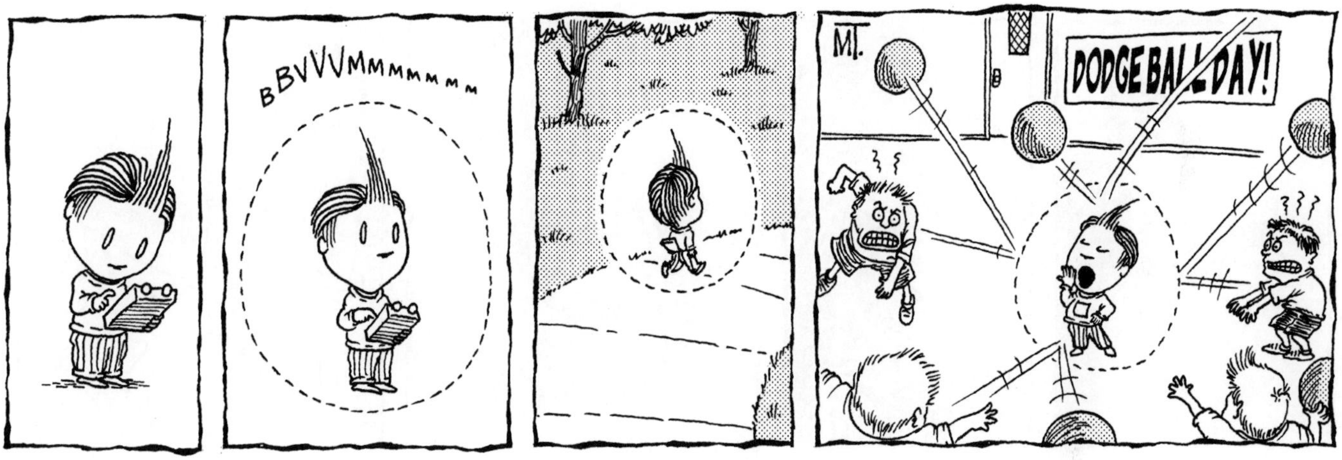
BBVVVMMMMMMM
MT.
DODGEBALL DAY!

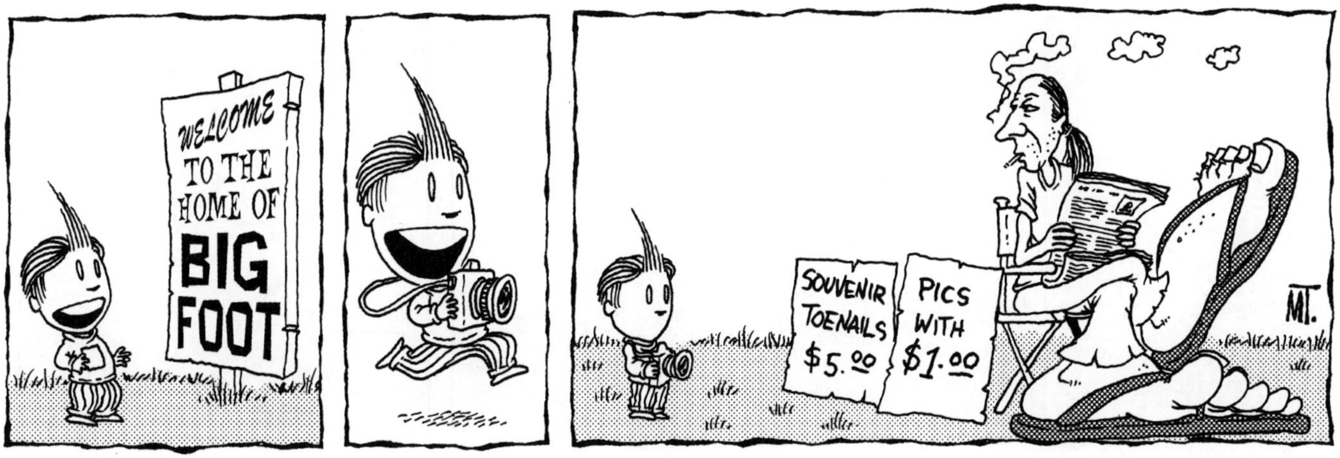
WELCOME TO THE HOME OF BIG FOOT
SOUVENIR TOENAILS $5.00
PICS WITH $1.00
MT.

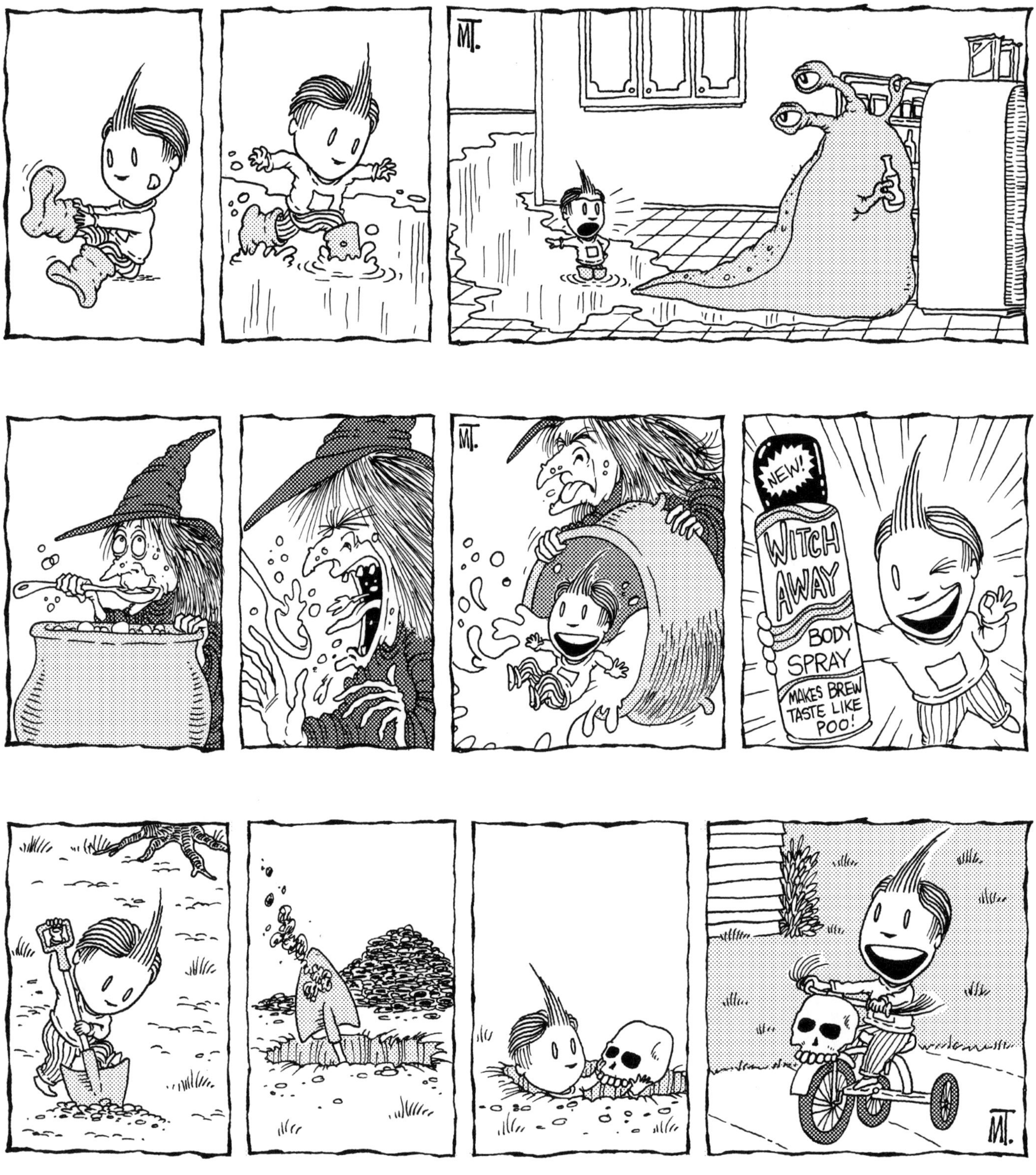
MT.
MT.
NEW!
WITCH AWAY
BODY SPRAY
MAKES BREW TASTE LIKE POO!
MT.

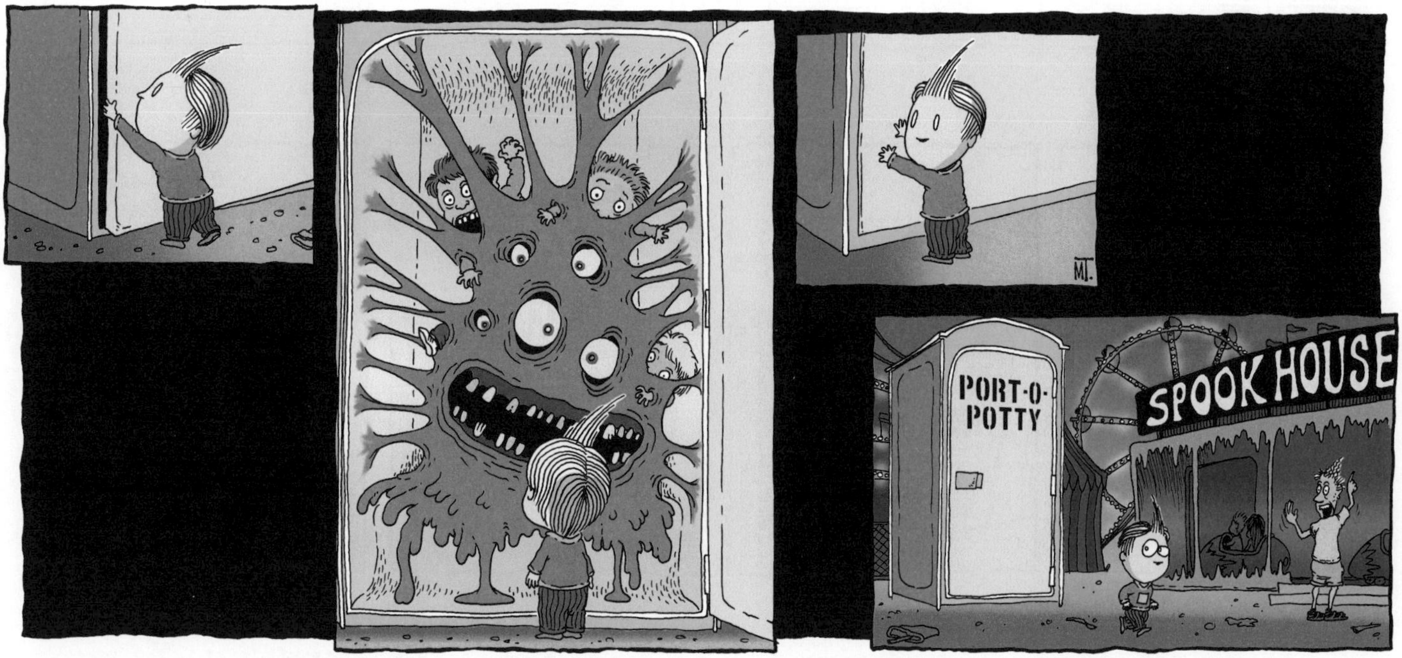
PORT-O-
POTTY
SPOOK HOUSE

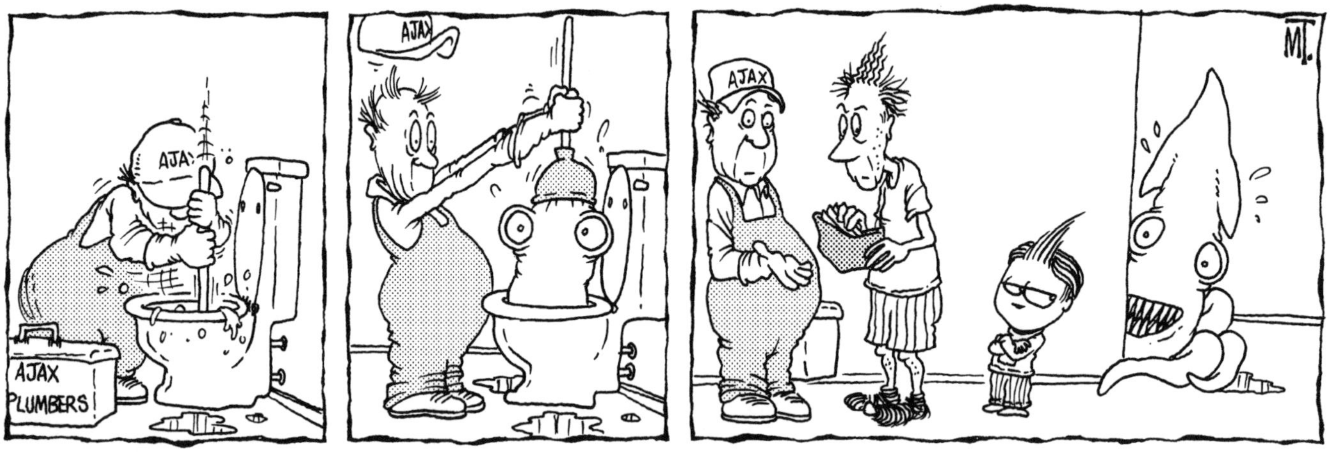
AJAX
AJAX
AJAX
AJAX PLUMBERS
MT.

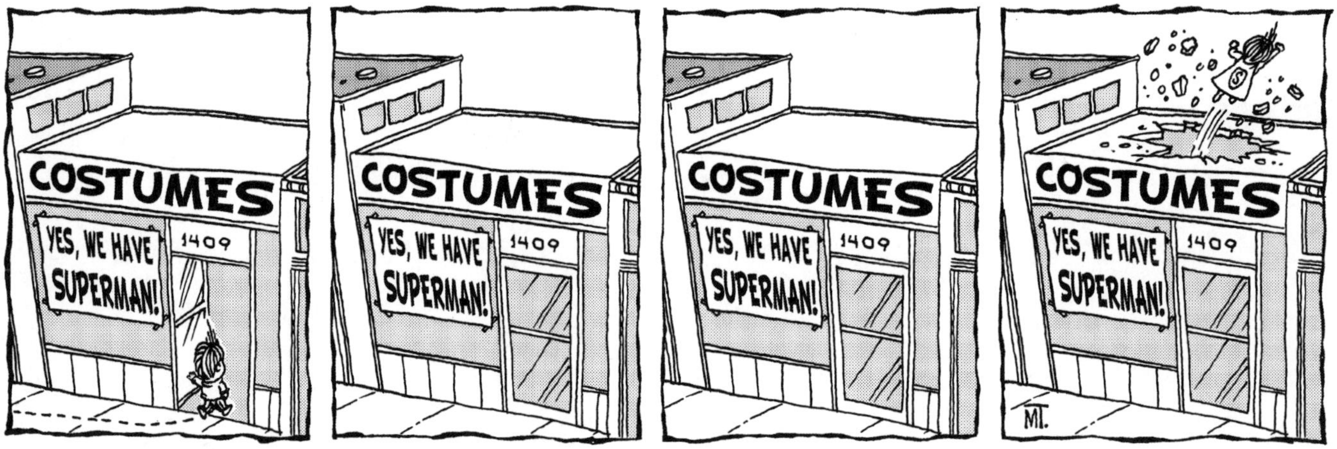
COSTUMES
YES, WE HAVE SUPERMAN!
1409
MT.

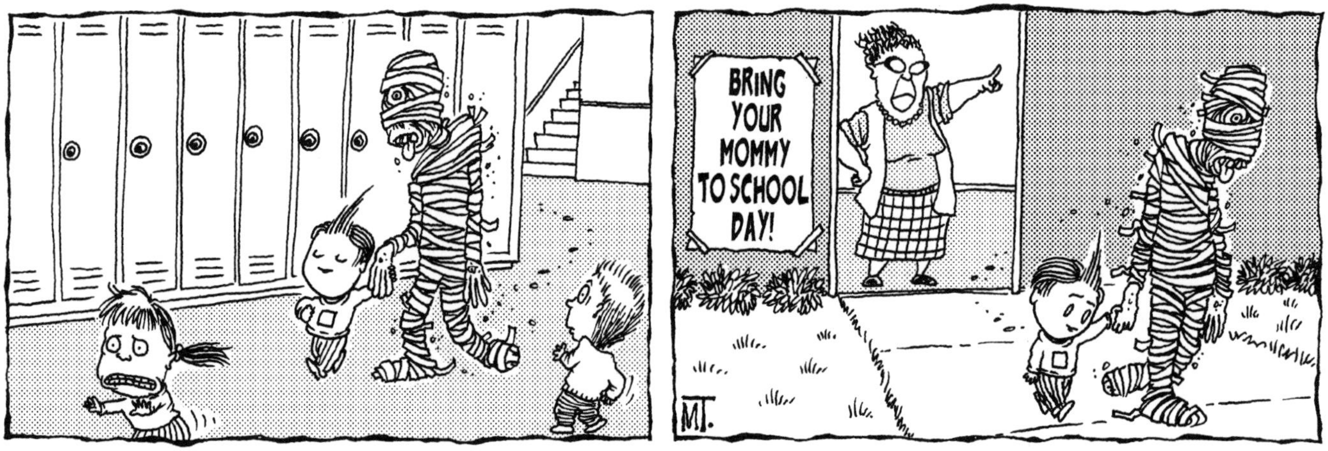
BRING YOUR MOMMY TO SCHOOL DAY!
MT.

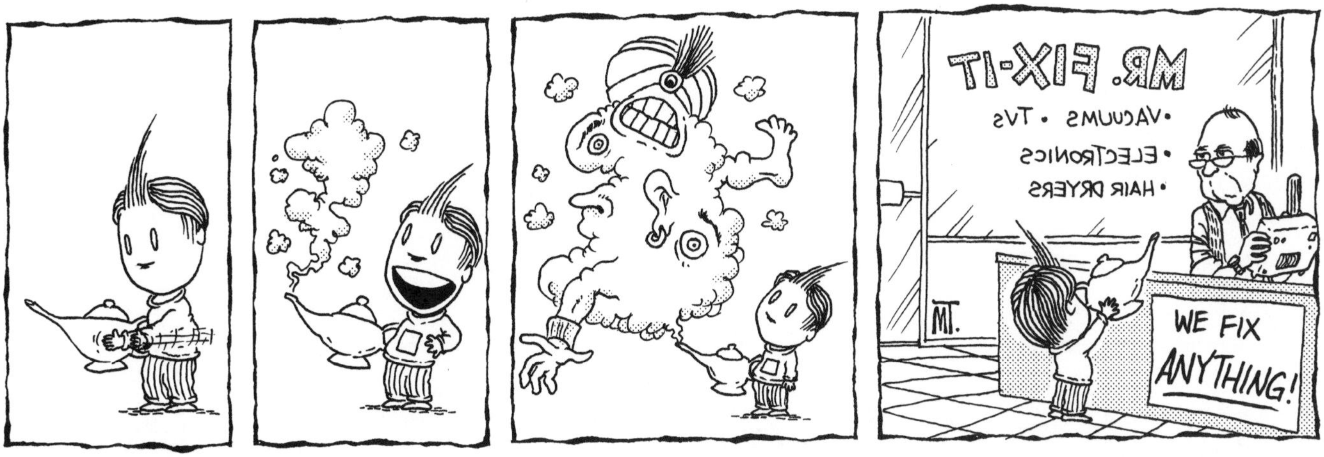
MR. FIX-IT
•VACUUMS • TVs
• ELECTRONICS
• HAIR DRYERS
MT.
WE FIX ANYTHING!

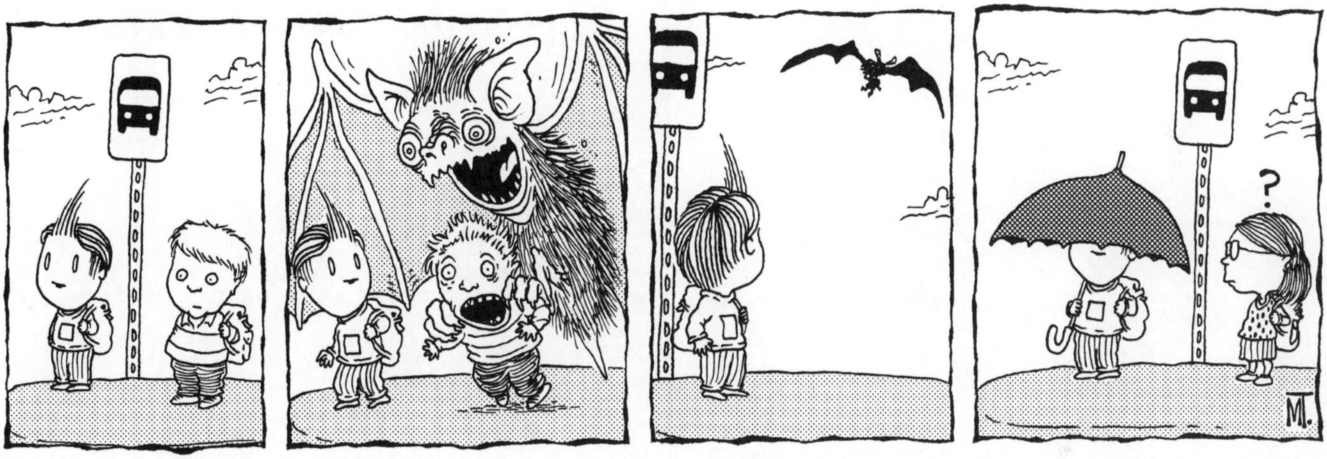
?
MT.

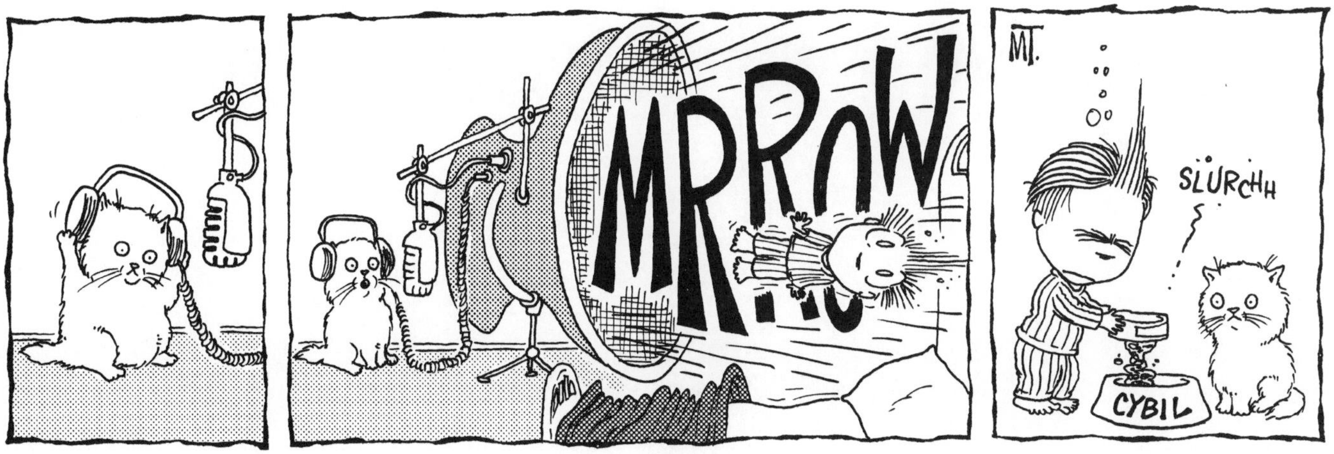
MRROW
MT.
SLURCHH
CYBIL

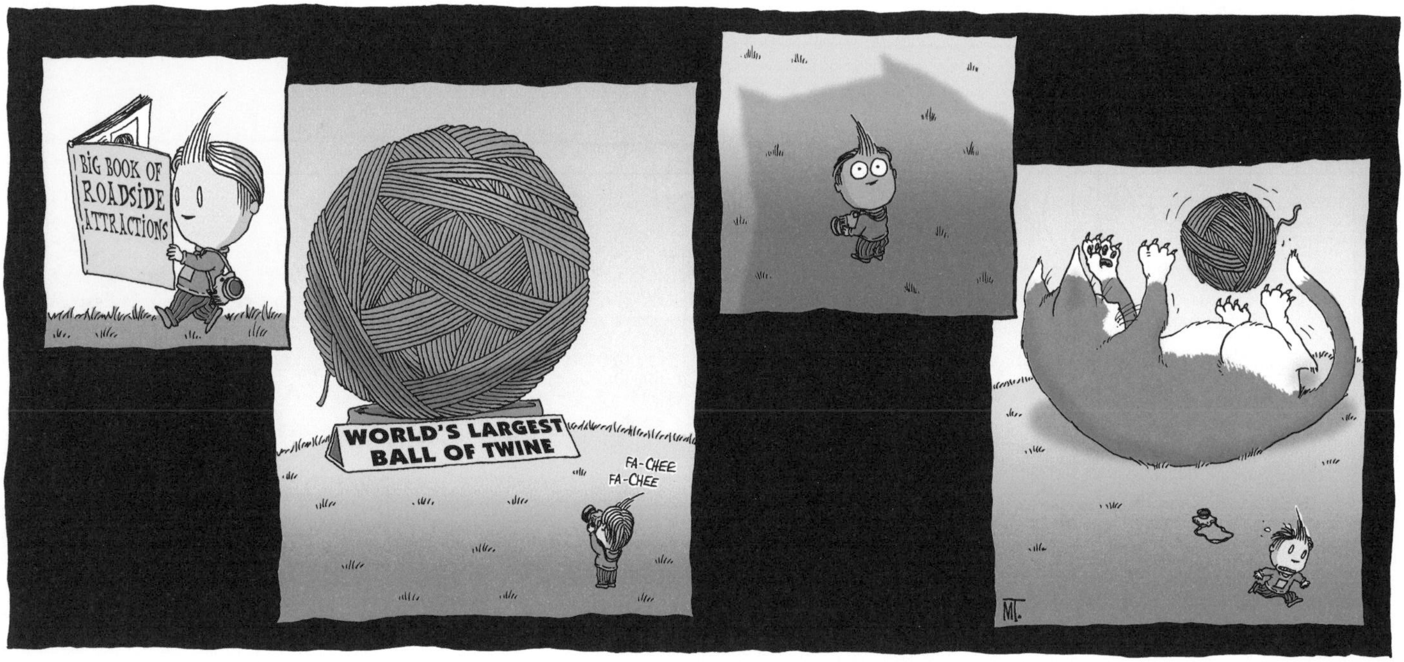
BIG BOOK OF
ROADSIDE
ATTRACTIONS
WORLD'S LARGEST
BALL OF TWINE
FA-CHEE
FA-CHEE
MT.

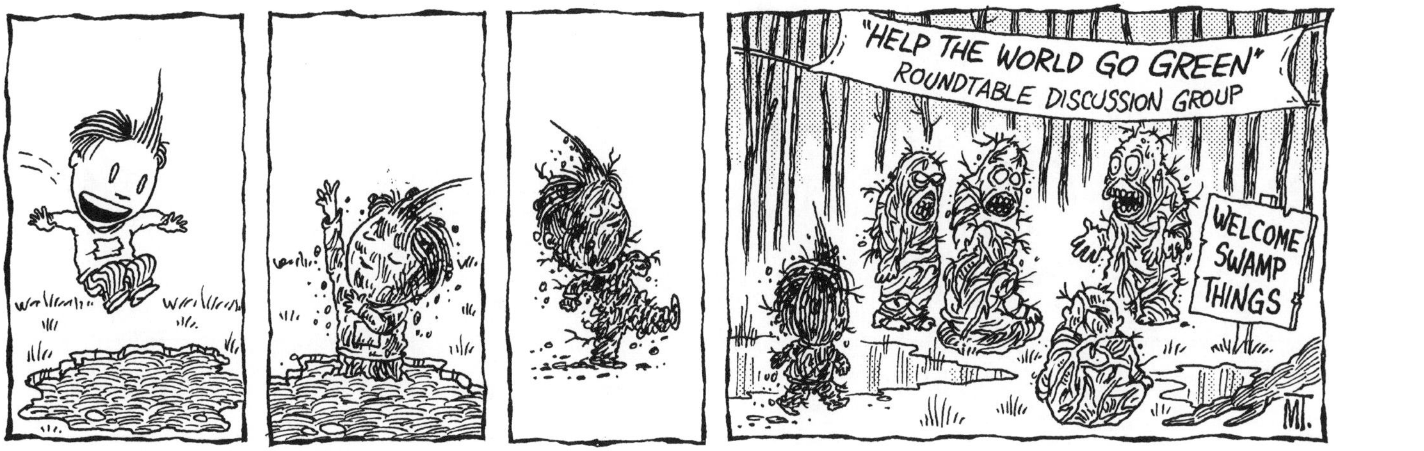
"HELP THE WORLD GO GREEN"
ROUNDTABLE DISCUSSION GROUP
WELCOME SWAMP THINGS
MT.

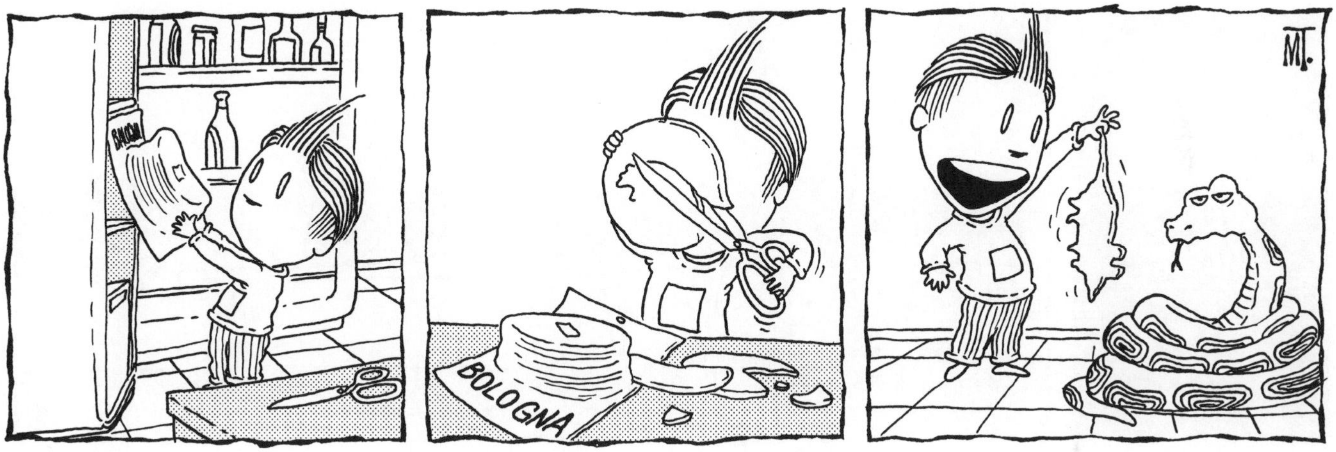
BOLOGNA
MT.

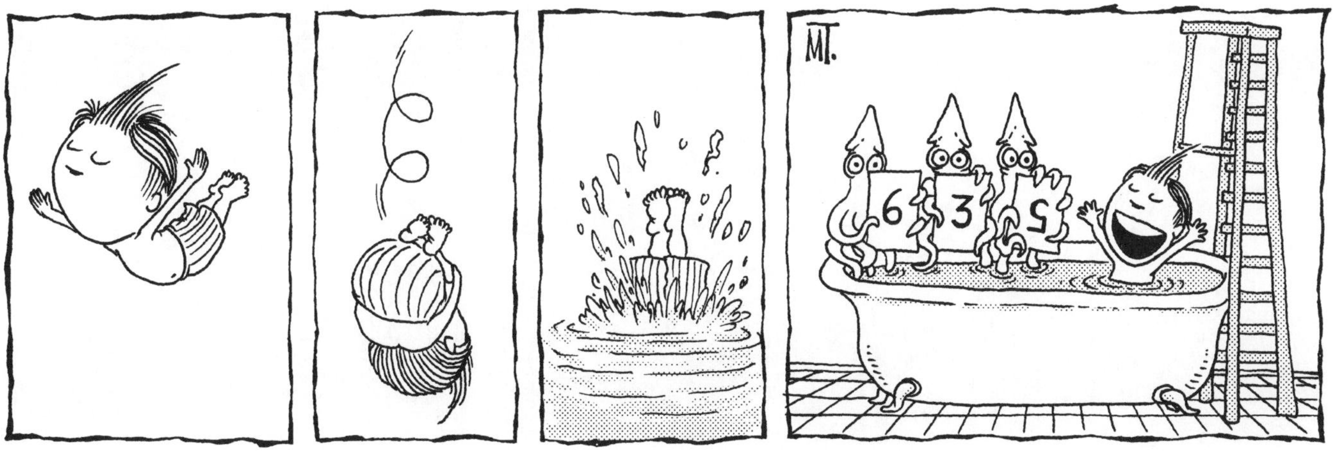
MT.
6
3
5

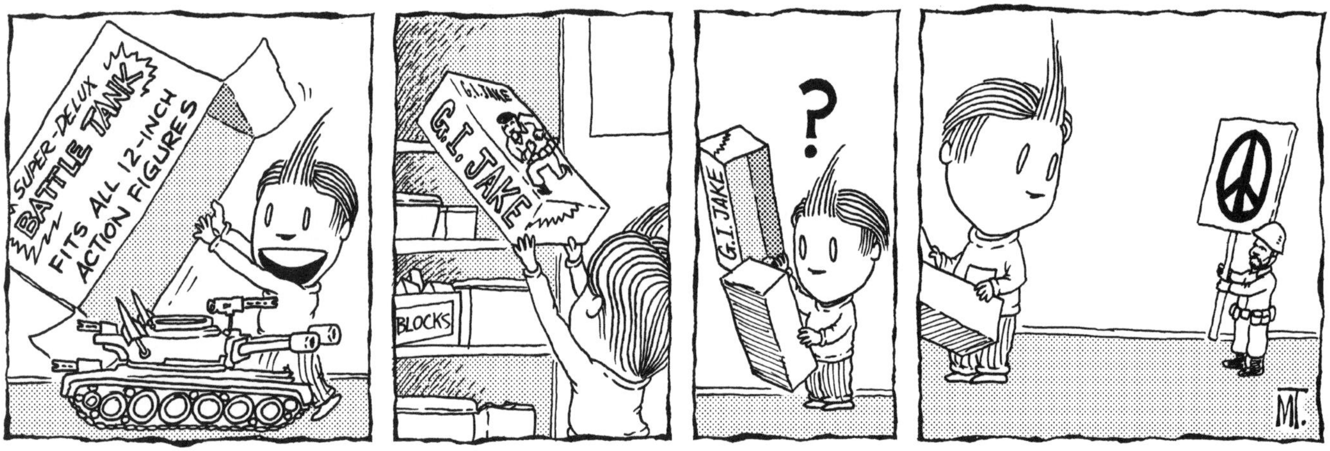
SUPER-DELUX
BATTLE TANK
FITS ALL 12-INCH
ACTION FIGURES
G.I. JAKE
BLOCKS
?
G.I. JAKE

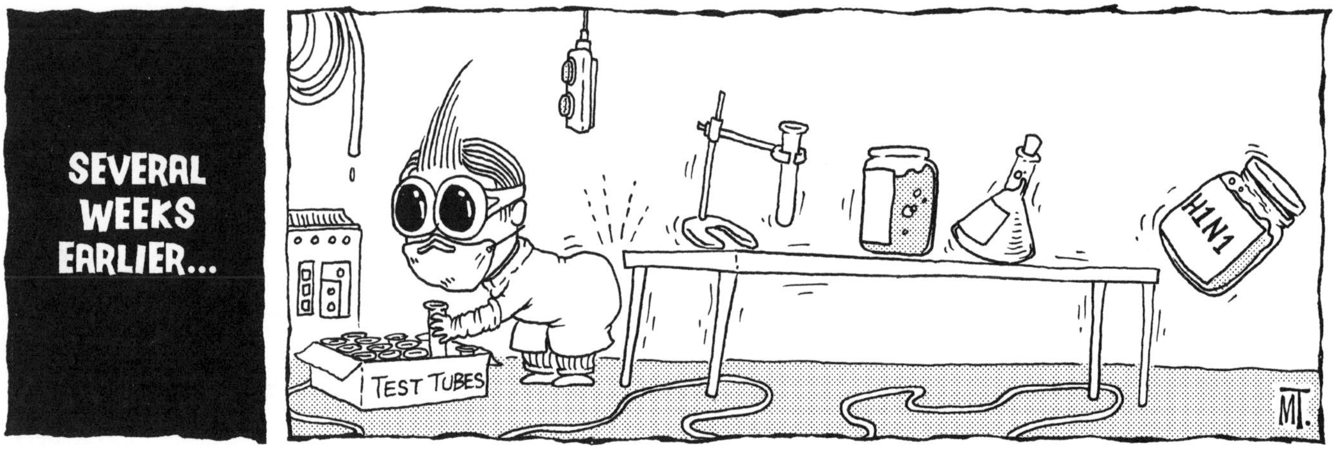
SEVERAL
WEEKS
EARLIER...
H1N1
TEST TUBES

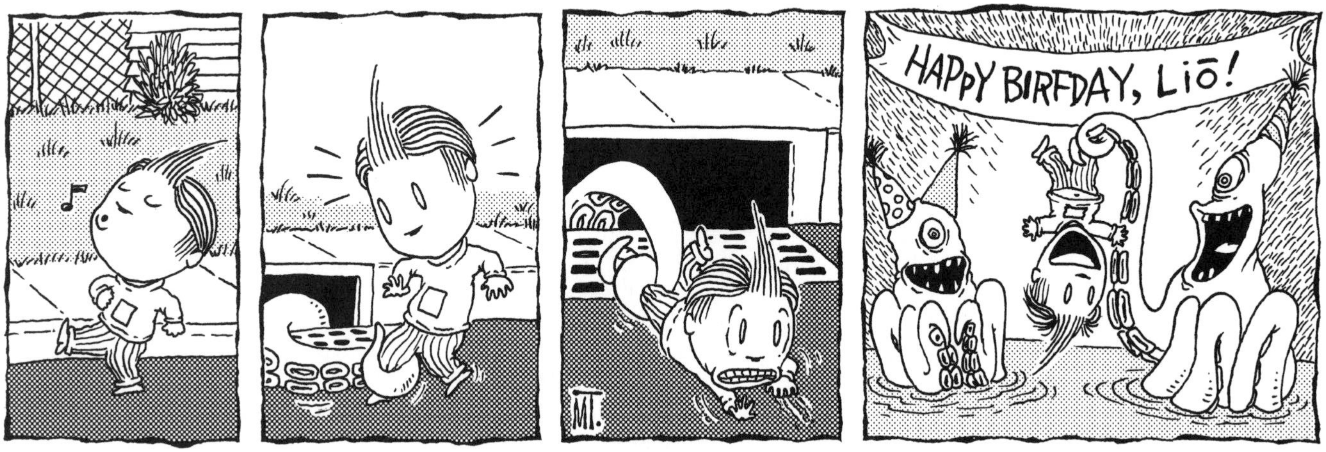
HAPPY BIRFDAY, LIŌ!

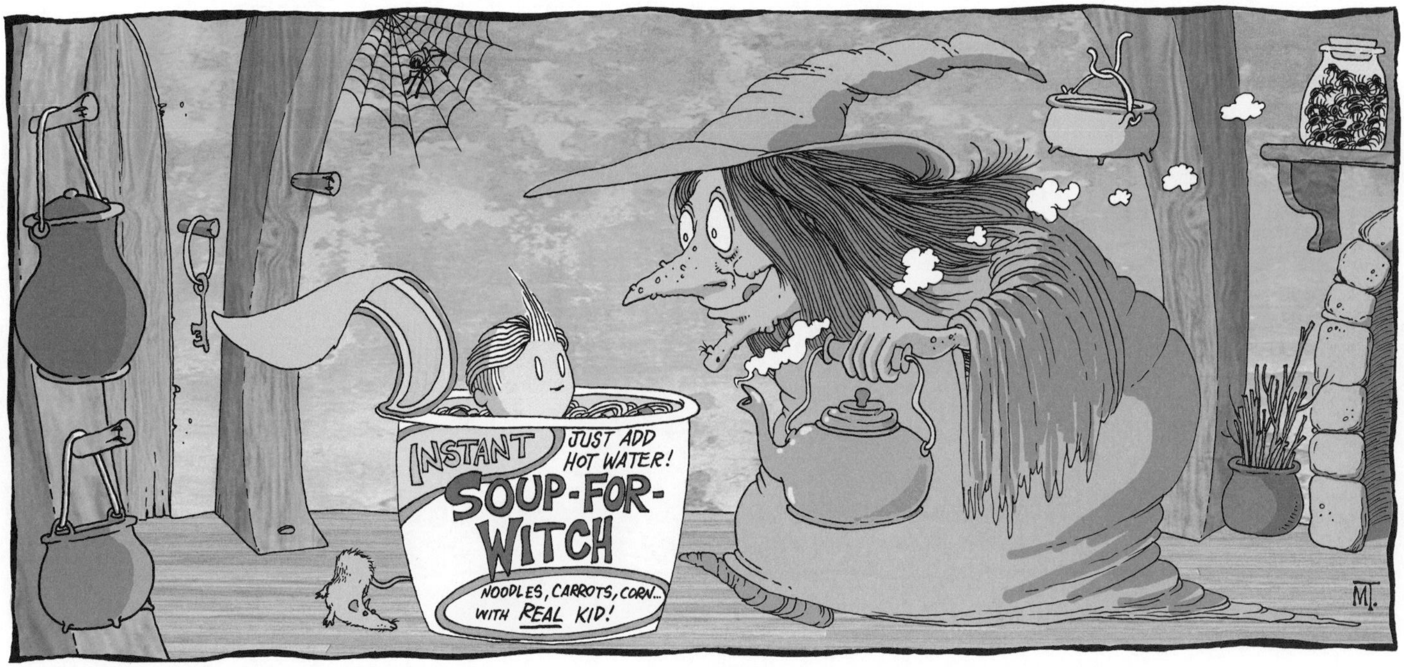
INSTANT
JUST ADD HOT WATER!
SOUP-FOR-WITCH
NOODLES, CARROTS, CORN... WITH REAL KID!
MT.

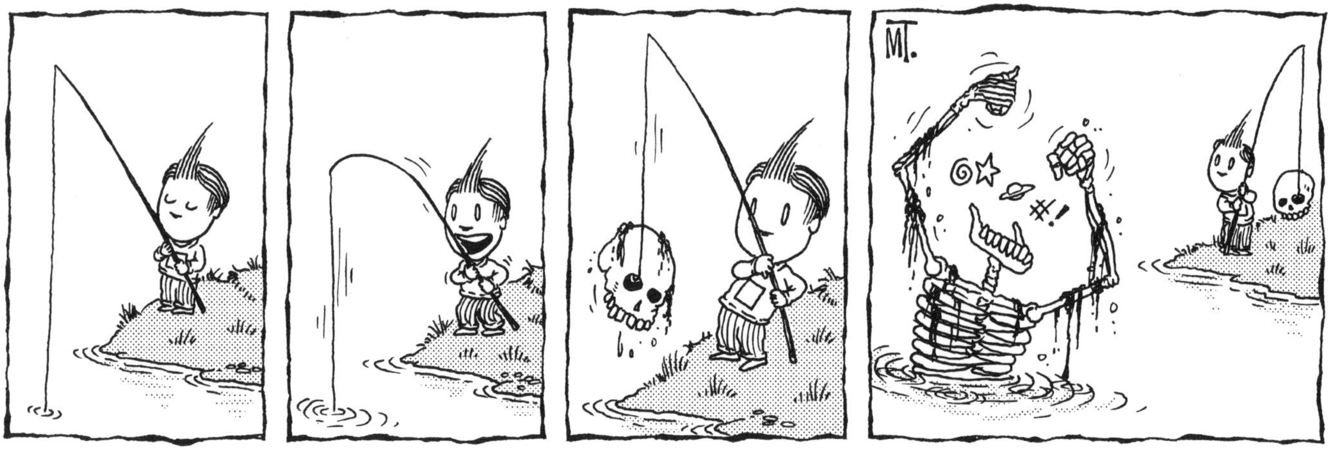

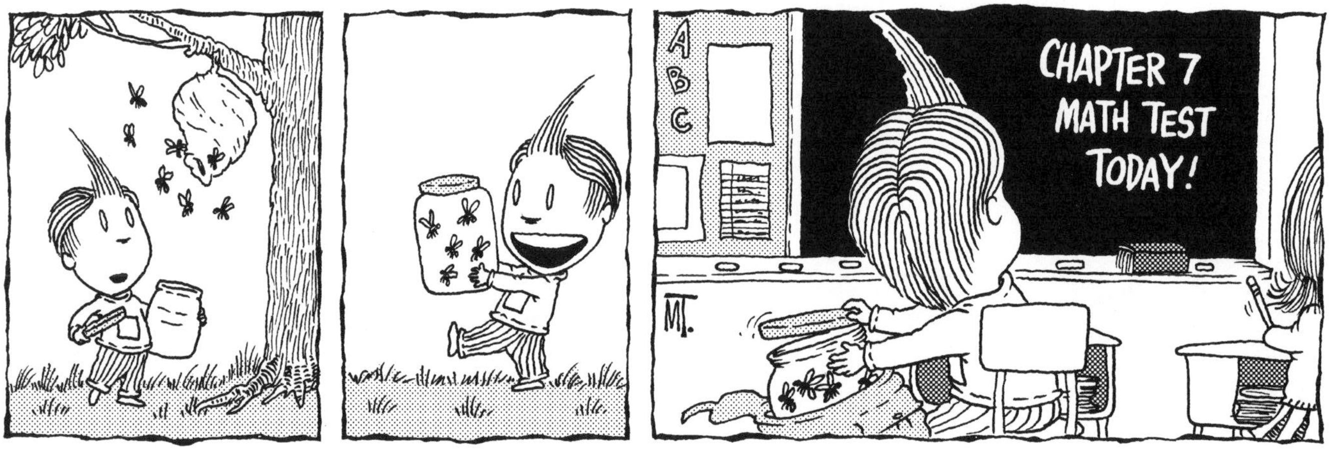

A B C
CHAPTER 7
MATH TEST
TODAY!

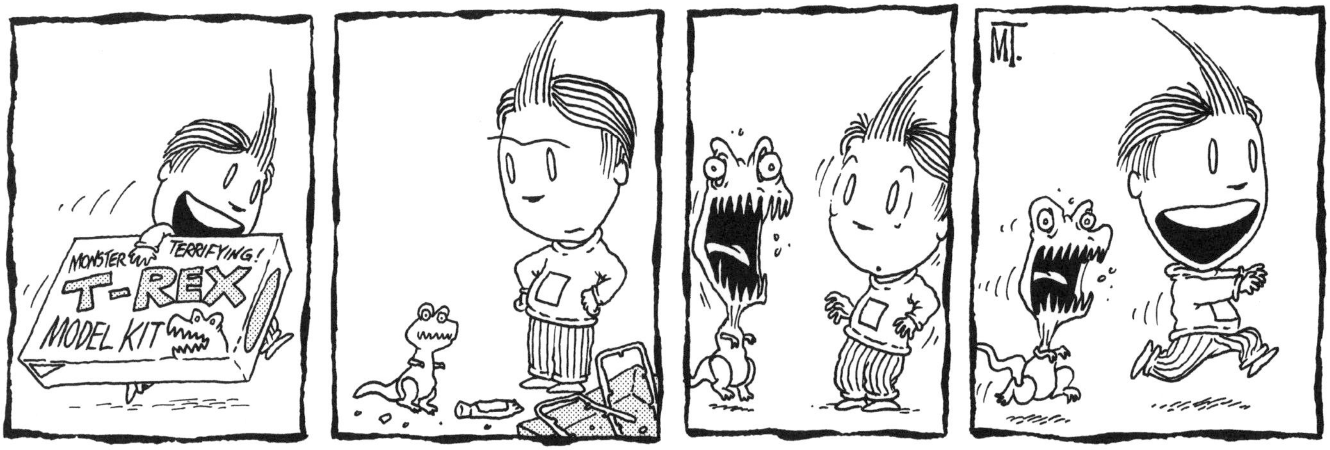

MONSTER
TERRIFYING!
T-REX
MODEL KIT

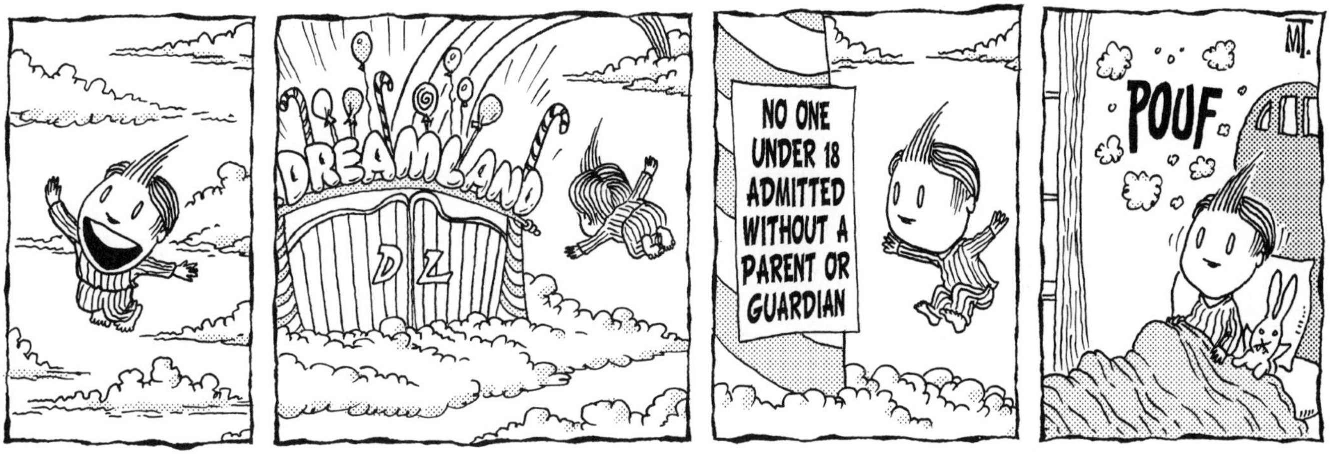
DREAMLAND
DZ
NO ONE UNDER 18 ADMITTED WITHOUT A PARENT OR GUARDIAN
POUF
MT.

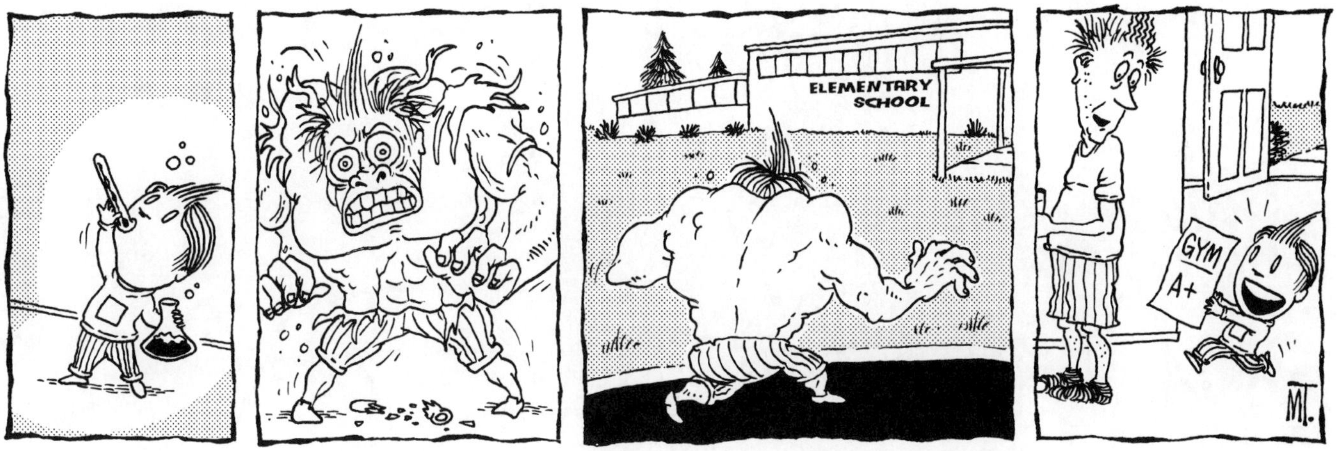
ELEMENTARY SCHOOL
GYM
A+
MT.

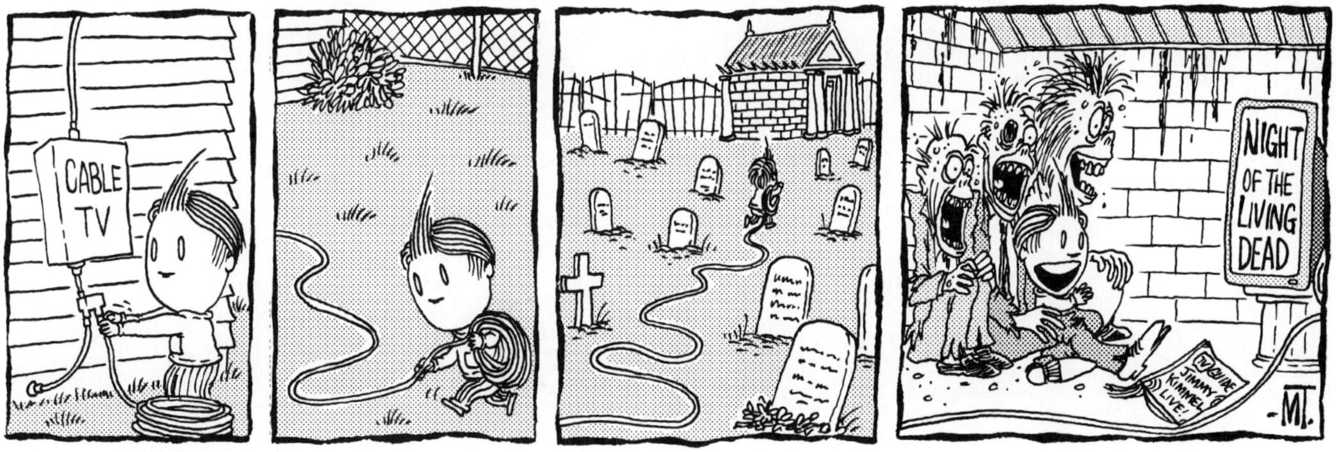
CABLE TV
NIGHT OF THE LIVING DEAD
TV GUIDE
JIMMY KIMMEL LIVE!
MT.

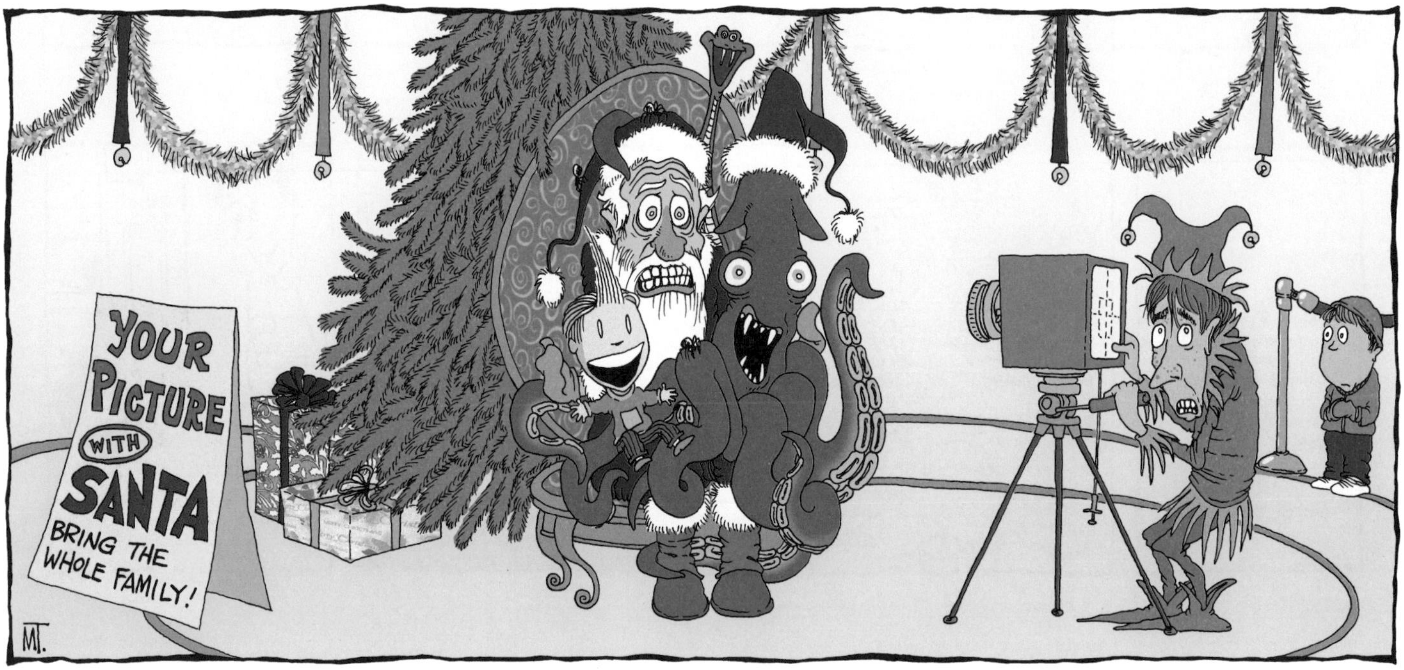
YOUR PICTURE WITH SANTA
BRING THE WHOLE FAMILY!
MT.

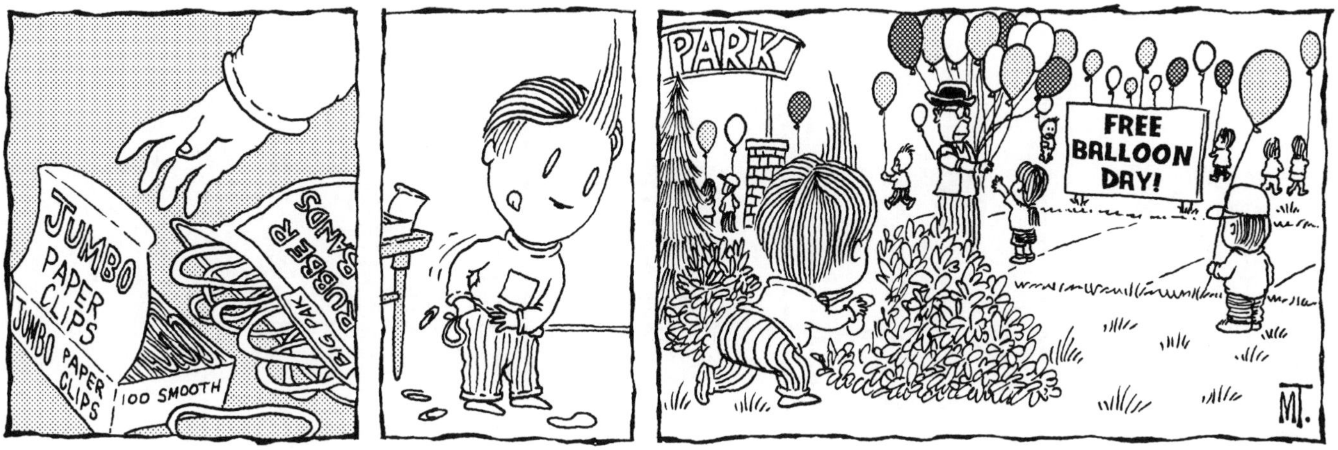
JUMBO PAPER CLIPS
JUMBO PAPER CLIPS
100 SMOOTH
BIG PAK RUBBER BANDS
PARK
FREE BALLOON DAY!
MT.

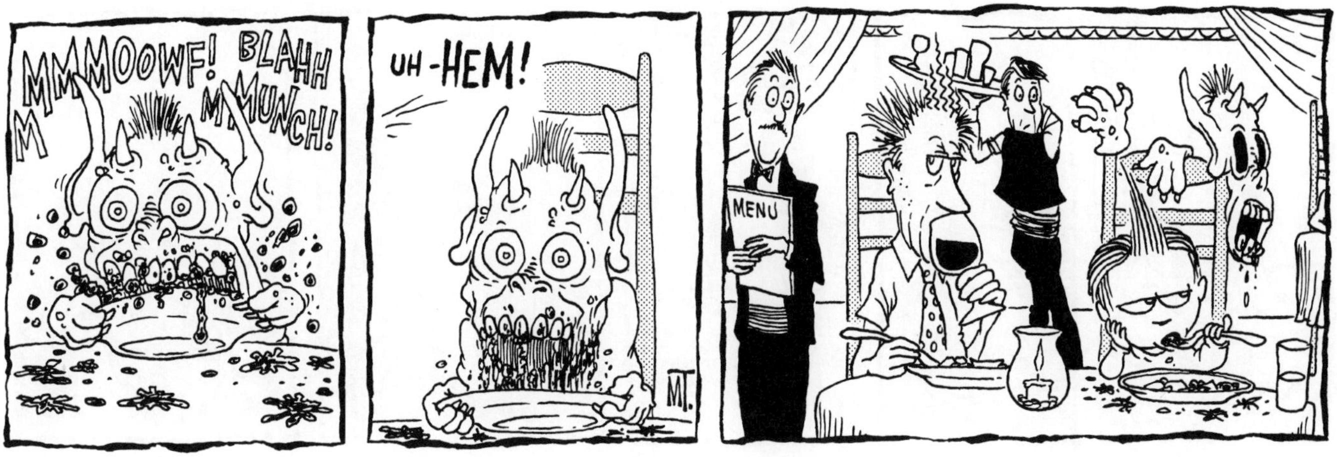
MMMMOOWF!
BLAHH
MMUNCH!
UH-HEM!
MT.
MENU

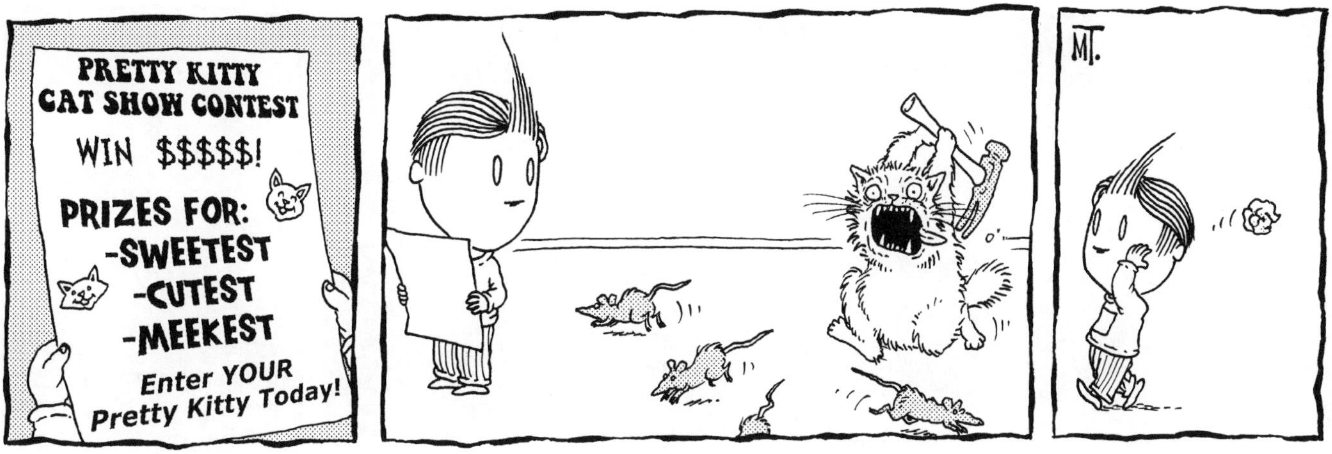
PRETTY KITTY CAT SHOW CONTEST
WIN $$$$$!
PRIZES FOR:
-SWEETEST
-CUTEST
-MEEKEST
Enter YOUR Pretty Kitty Today!
MT.

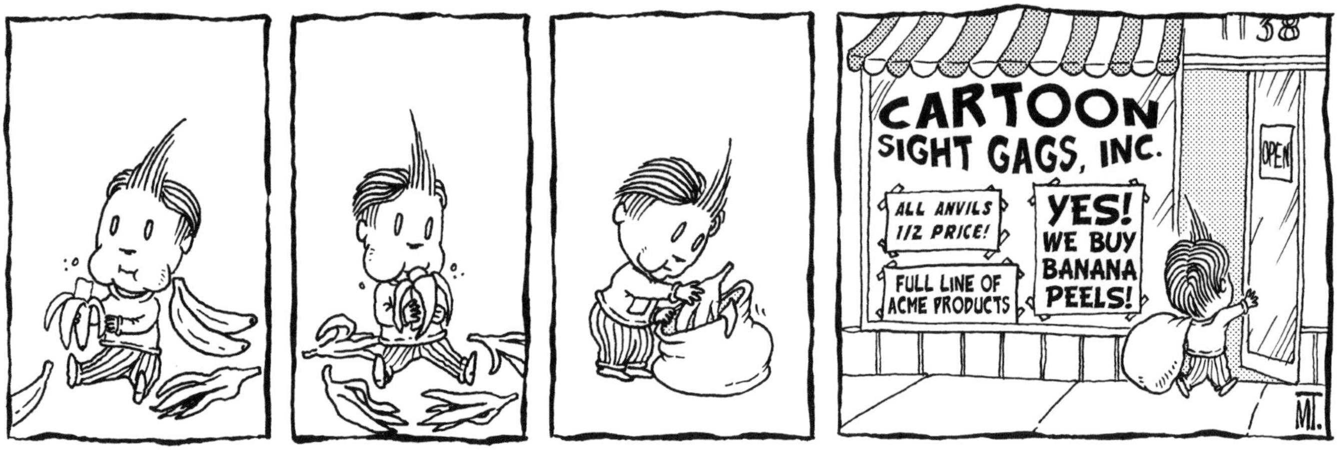
38
CARTOON SIGHT GAGS, INC.
ALL ANVILS 1/2 PRICE!
YES! WE BUY BANANA PEELS!
FULL LINE OF ACME PRODUCTS
OPEN
MT.

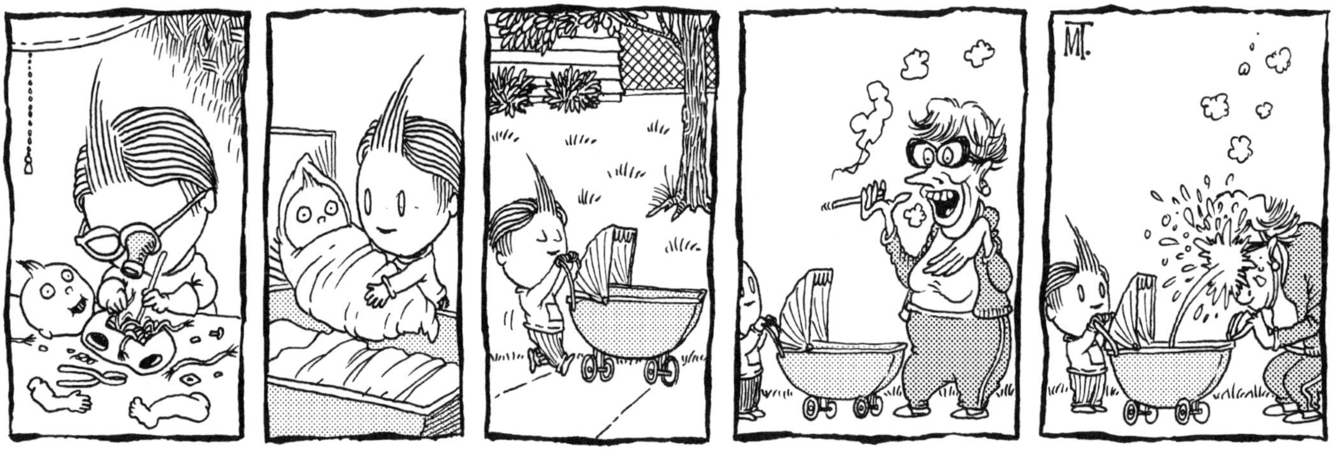
MT.

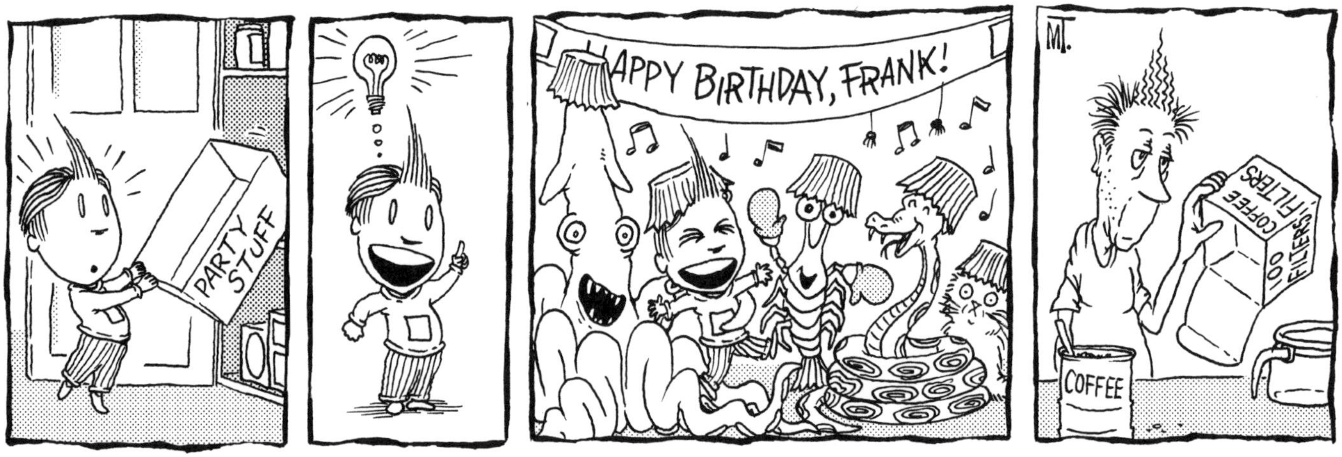
PARTY STUFF
APPY BIRTHDAY, FRANK!
MT.
COFFEE FILTERS
100 FILTERS
COFFEE

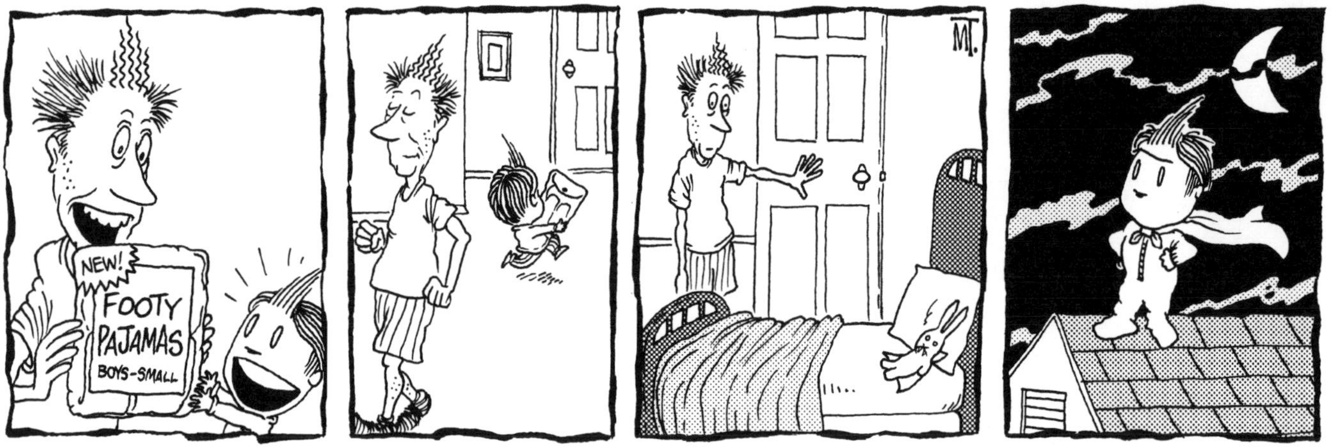
NEW!
FOOTY PAJAMAS
BOYS-SMALL
MT.

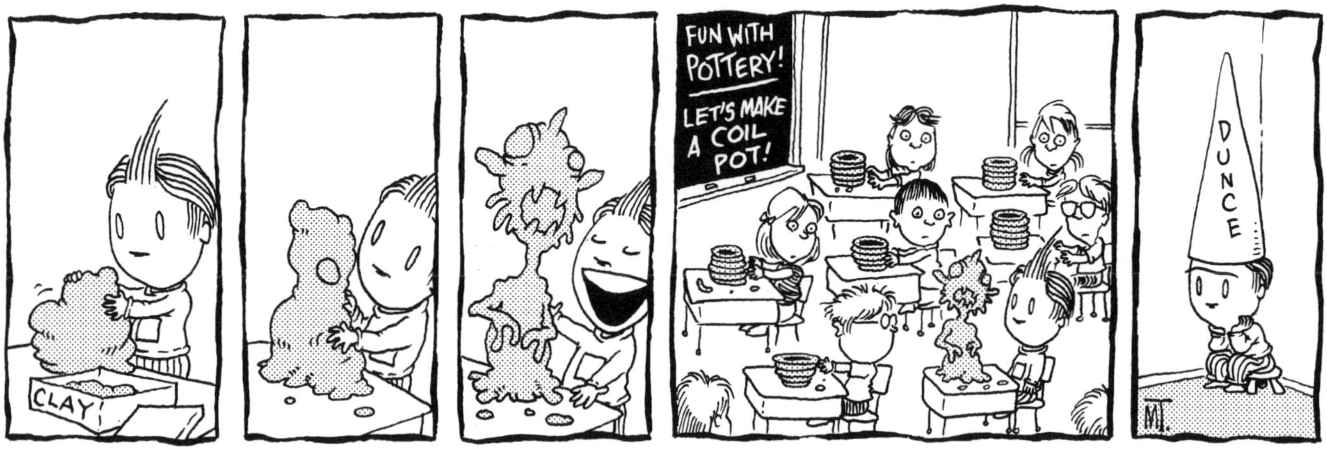
CLAY
FUN WITH POTTERY!
LET'S MAKE A COIL POT!
DUNCE
MT.

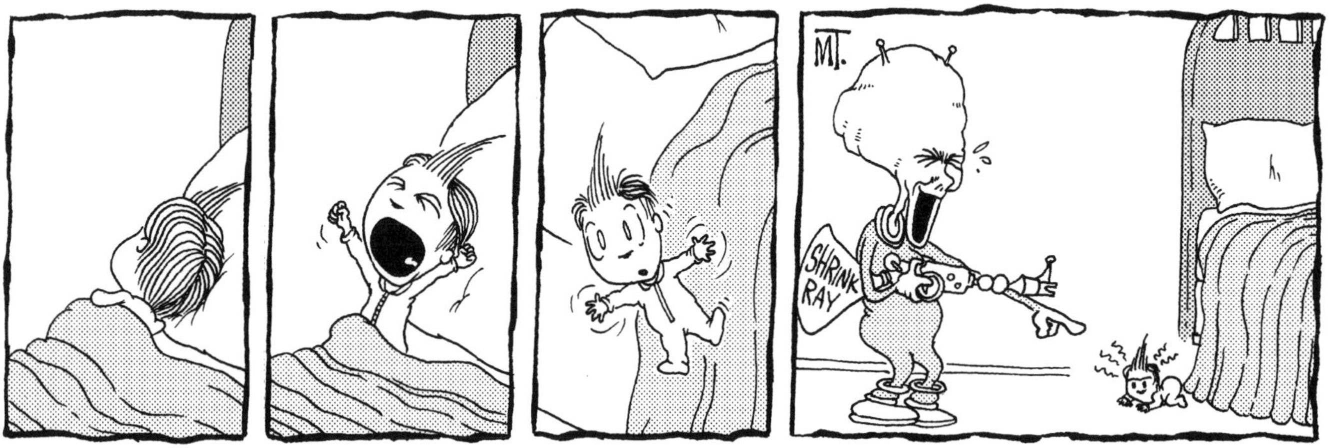
MT.
SHRINK RAY

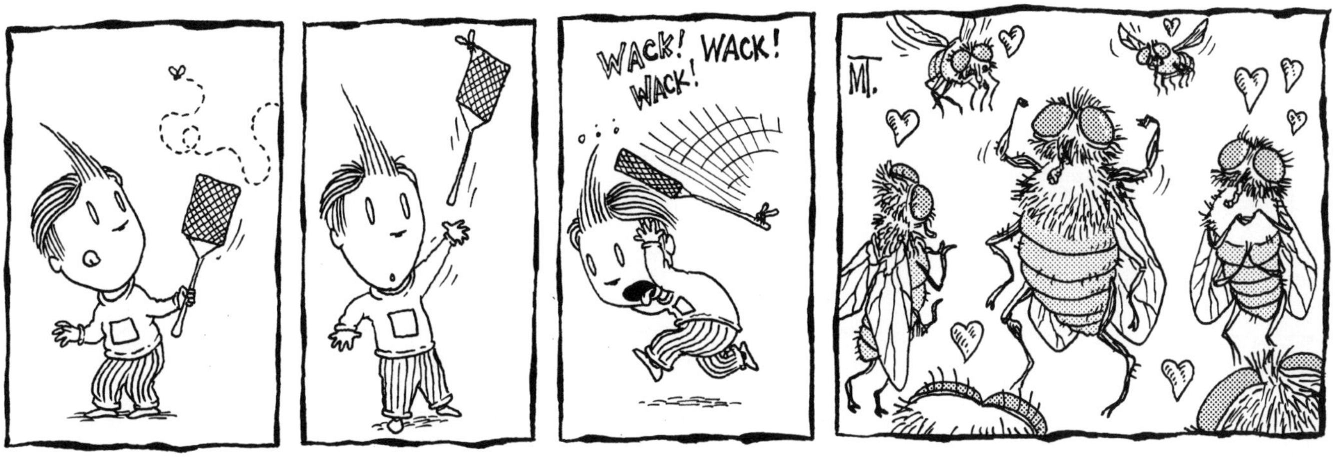
WACK! WACK!
WACK!

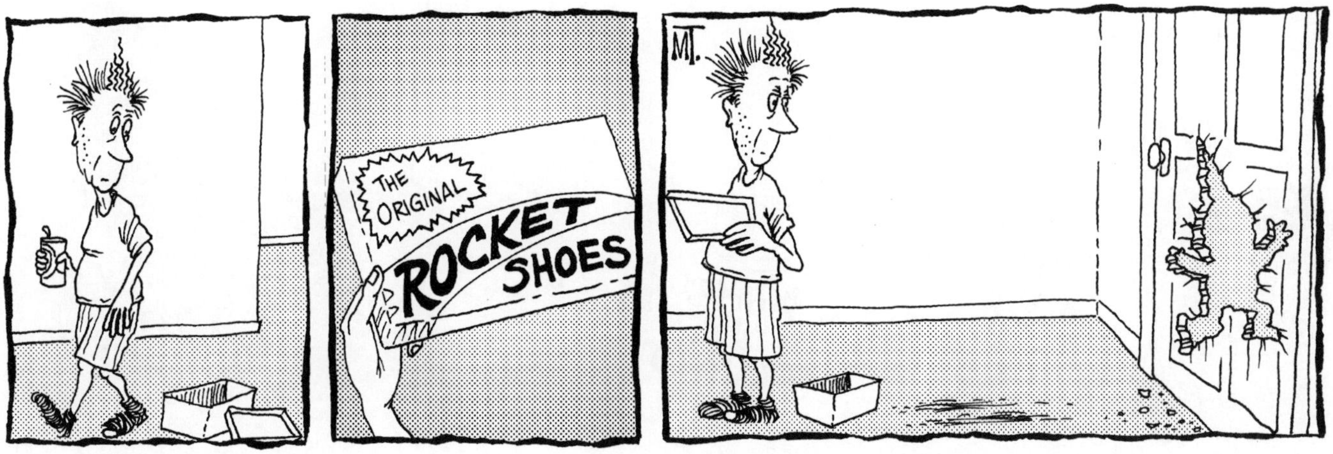
THE ORIGINAL
ROCKET SHOES

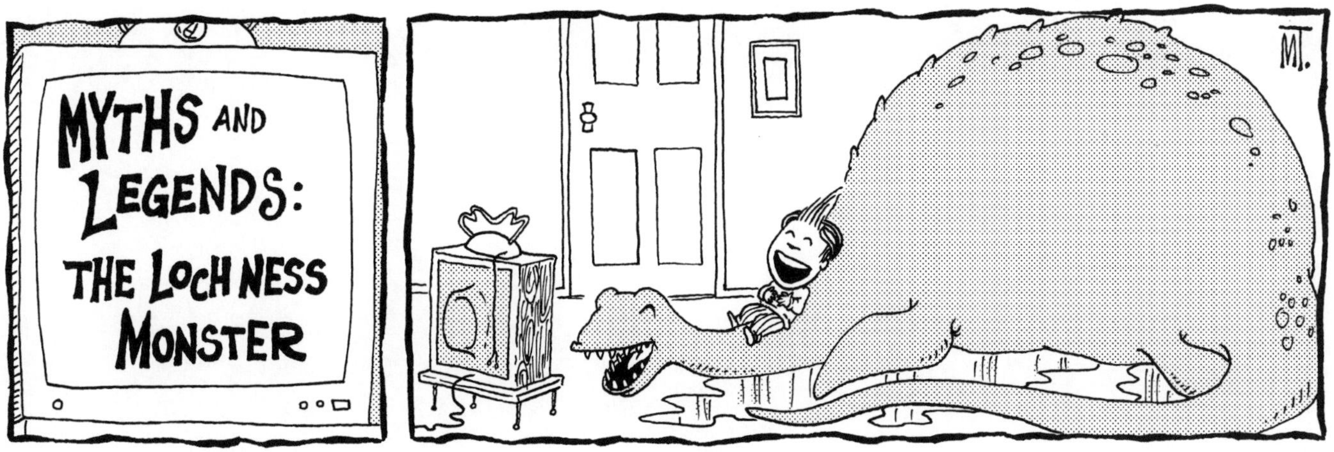
MYTHS AND LEGENDS: THE LOCH NESS MONSTER

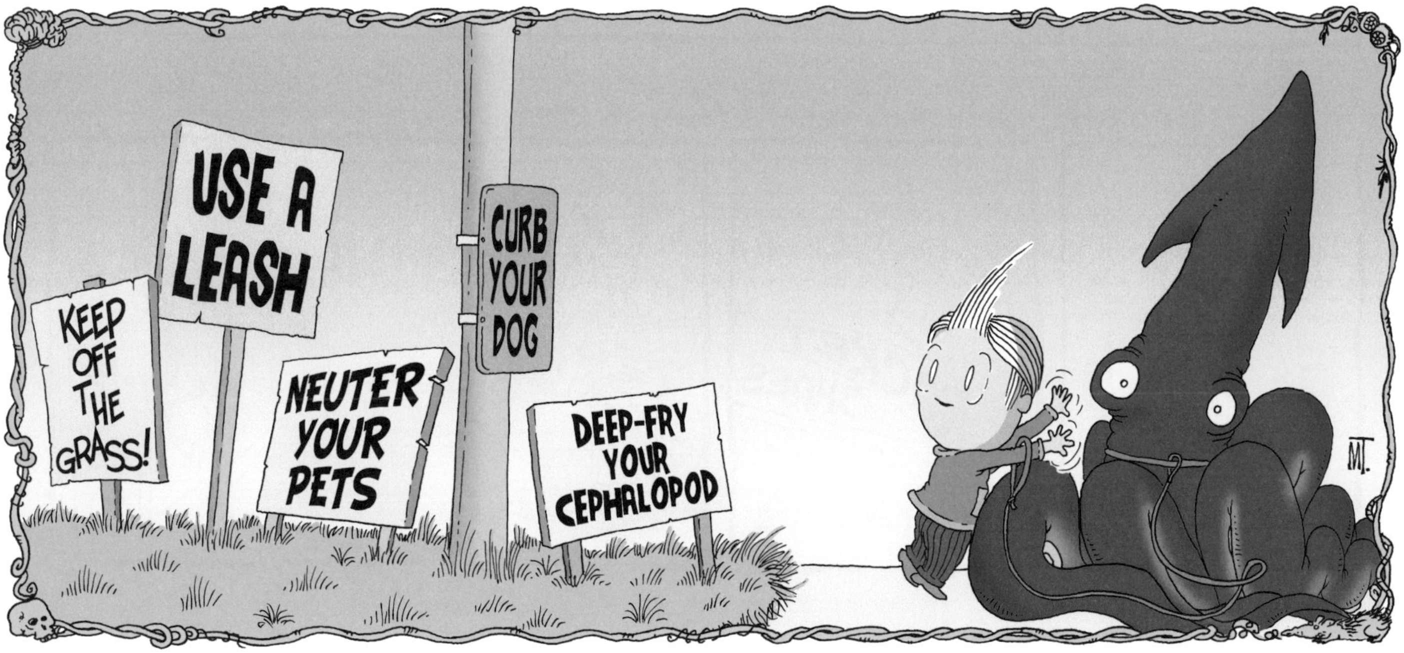
KEEP OFF THE GRASS!
USE A LEASH
NEUTER YOUR PETS
CURB YOUR DOG
DEEP-FRY YOUR CEPHALOPOD
MT.

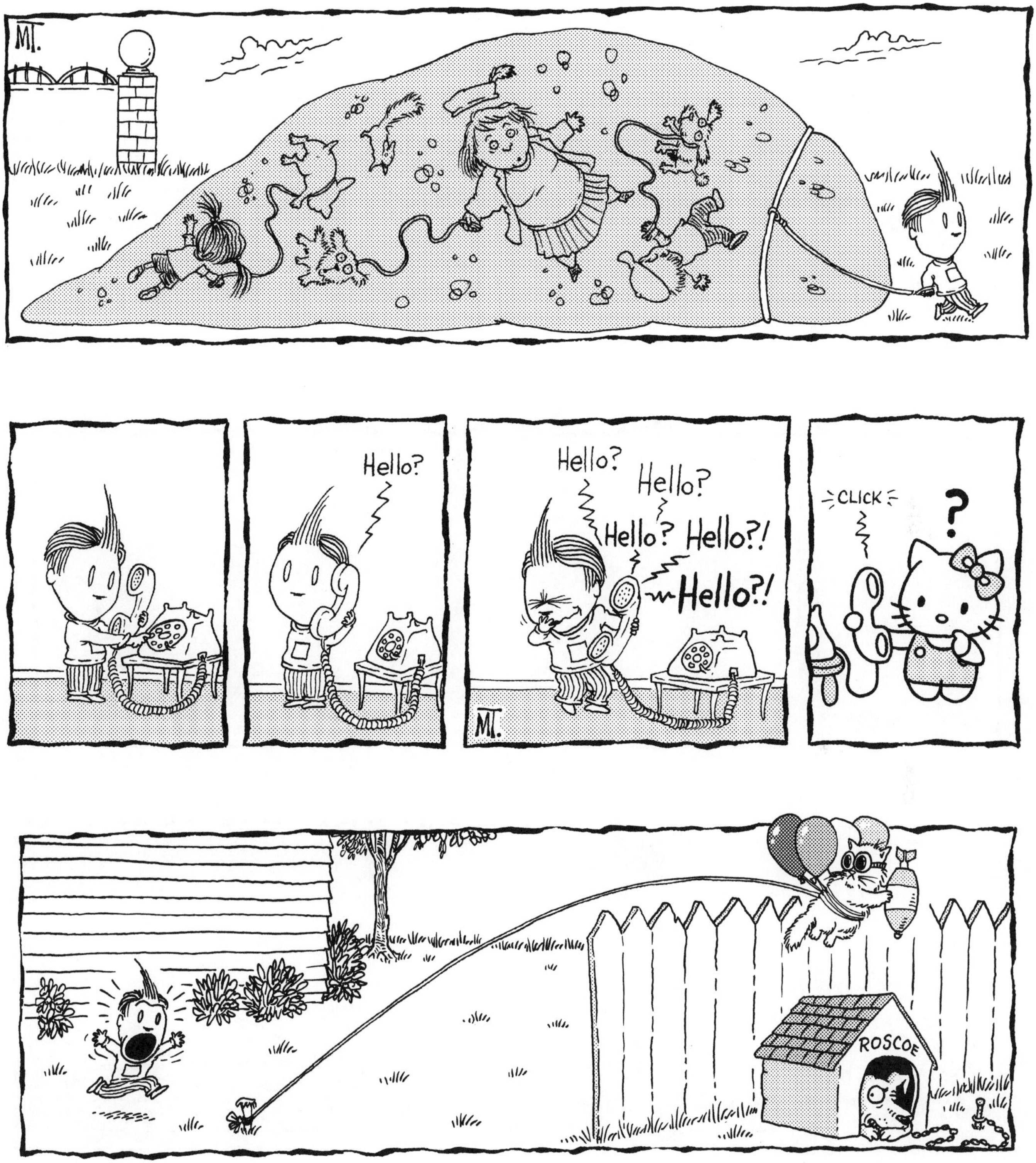
MT.
Hello?
Hello?
Hello?
Hello?
Hello?!
Hello?!
MT.
CLICK
?
ROSCOE

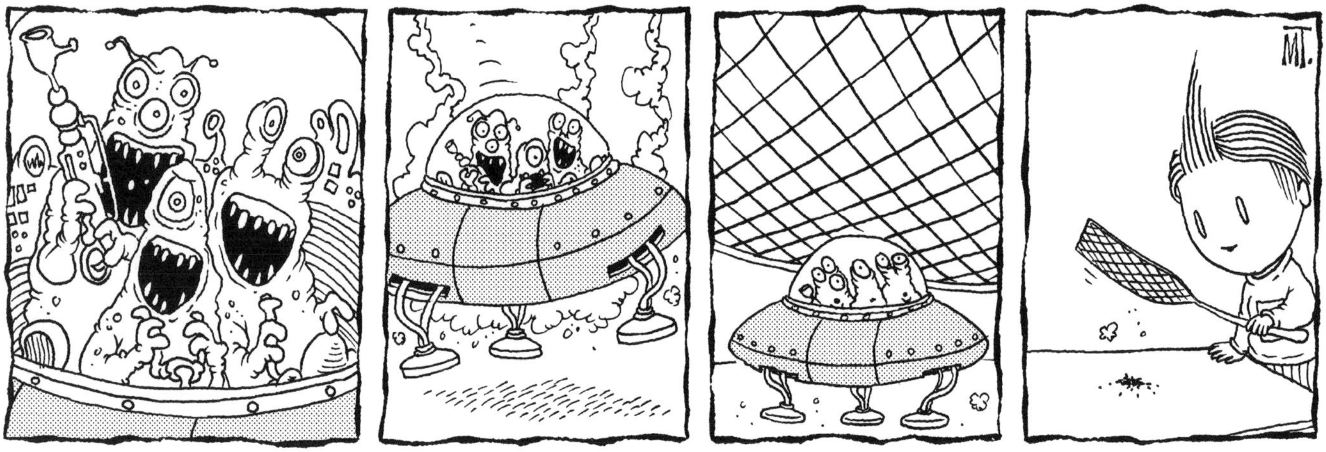

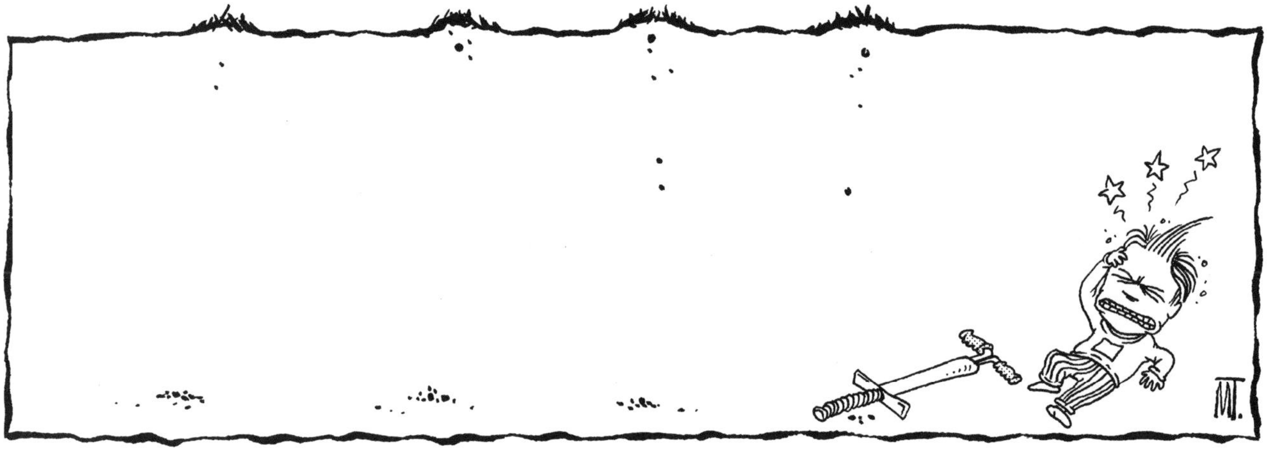

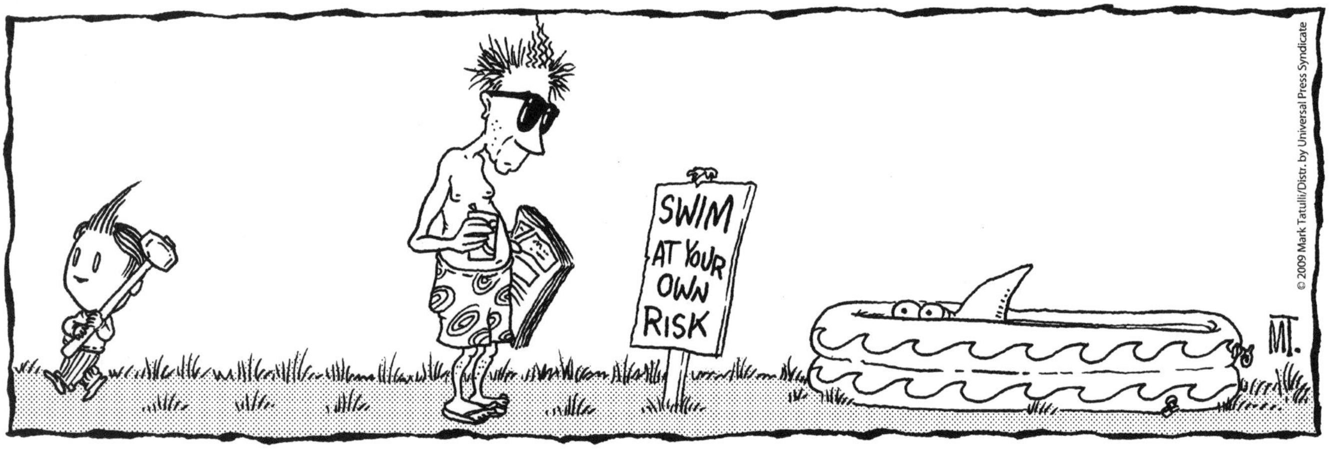
SWIM AT YOUR OWN RISK
© 2009 Mark Tatuli/Distr. by Universal Press Syndicate

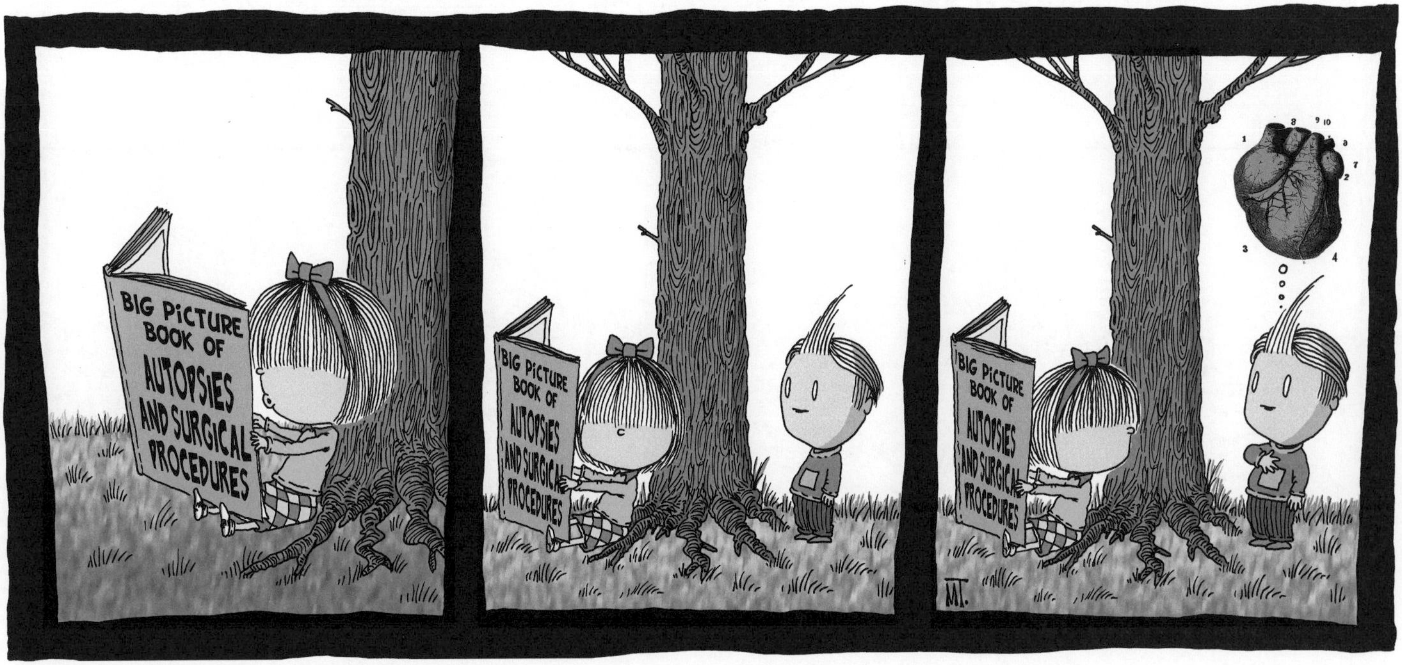
BIG PICTURE BOOK OF AUTOPSIES AND SURGICAL PROCEDURES
BIG PICTURE BOOK OF AUTOPSIES AND SURGICAL PROCEDURES
BIG PICTURE BOOK OF AUTOPSIES AND SURGICAL PROCEDURES
MT.

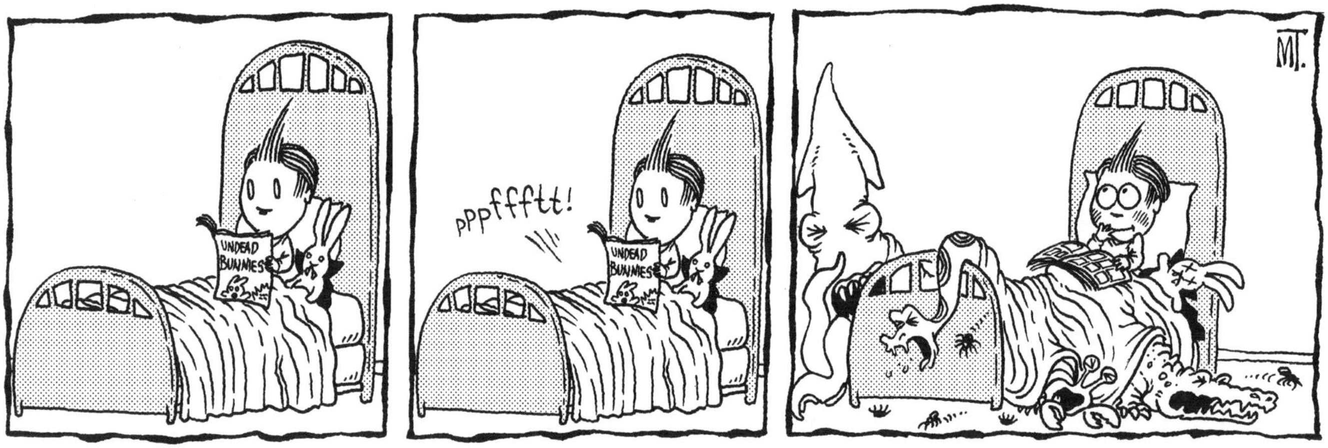
UNDEAD BUNNIES
pppffftt!
UNDEAD BUNNIES

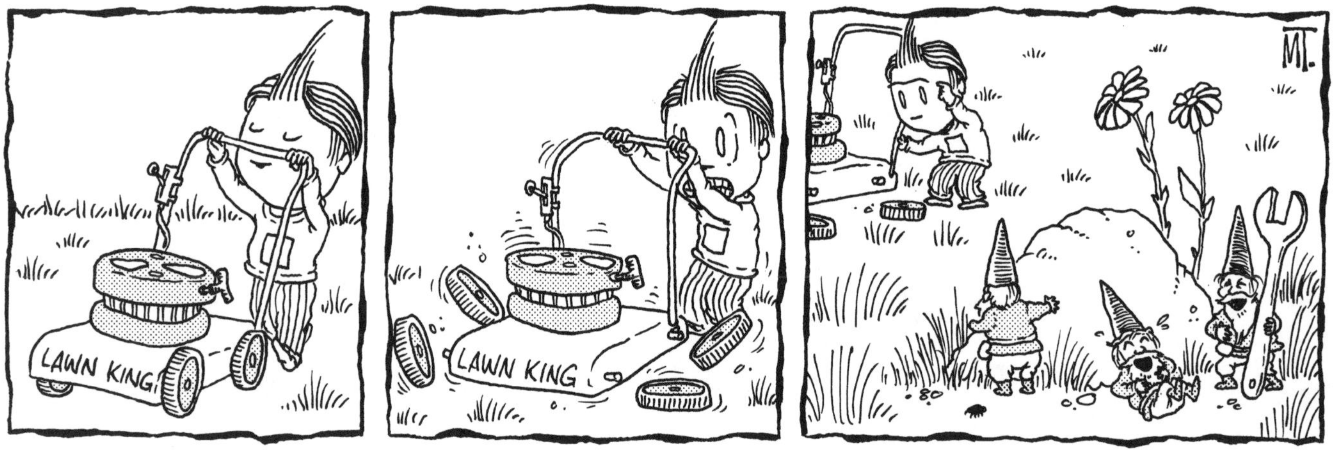
LAWN KING
LAWN KING

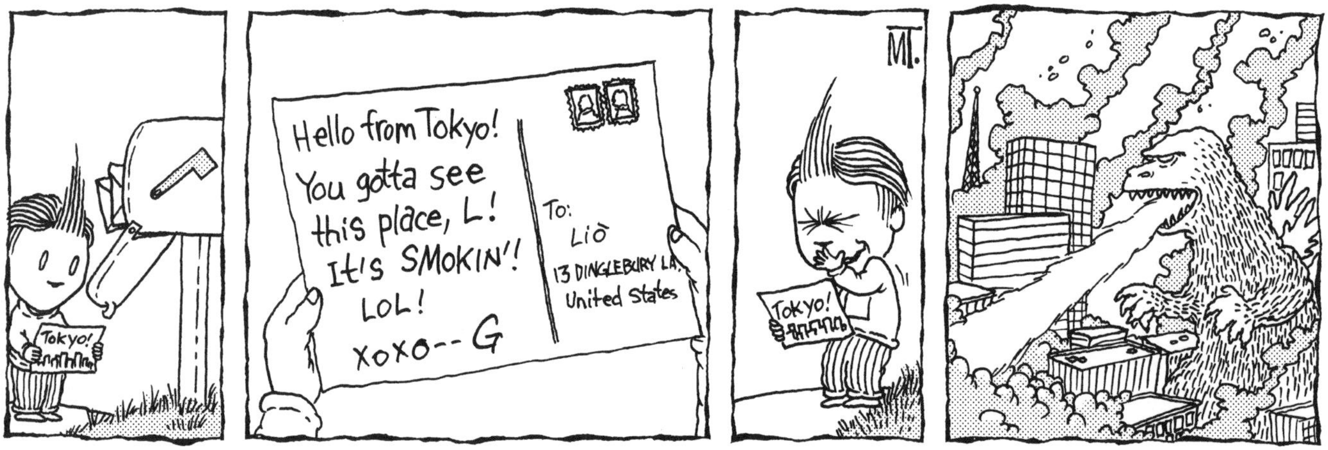
Tokyo!
Hello from Tokyo!
You gotta see this place, L!
It's SMOKIN'!
LOL!
XOXO--G
To:
Liò
13 DINGLEBURY LA.
United States
Tokyo!

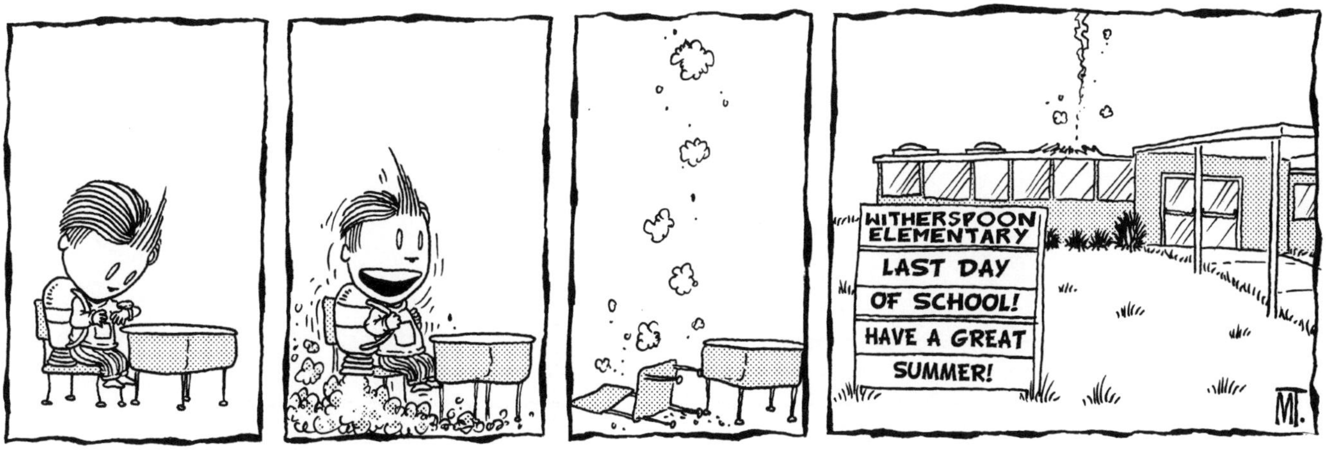
WITHERSPOON ELEMENTARY
LAST DAY
OF SCHOOL!
HAVE A GREAT
SUMMER!

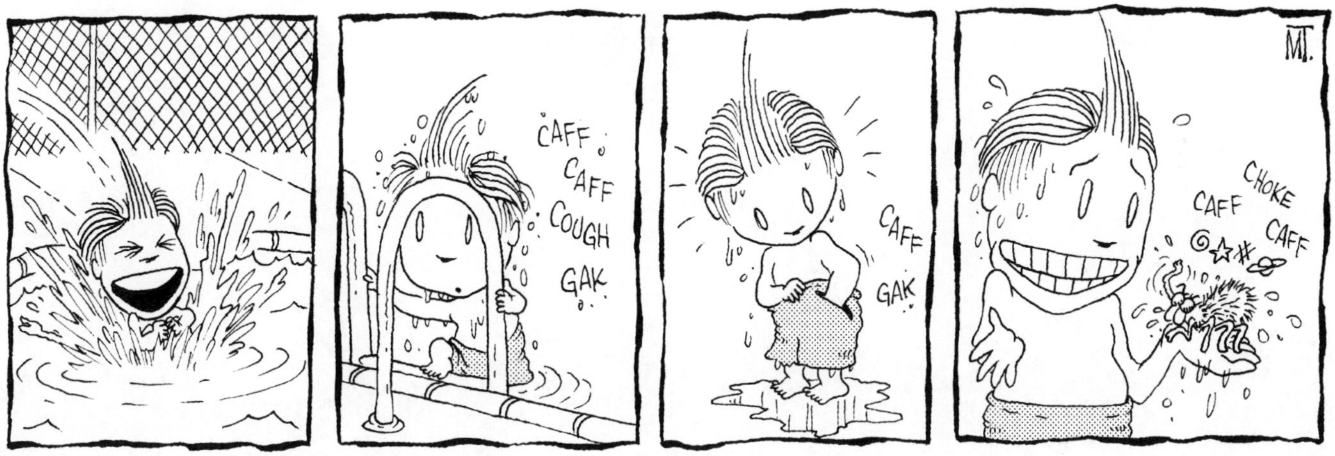
CAFF
CAFF
COUGH
GAK
CAFF
GAK
CHOKE
CAFF
CAFF

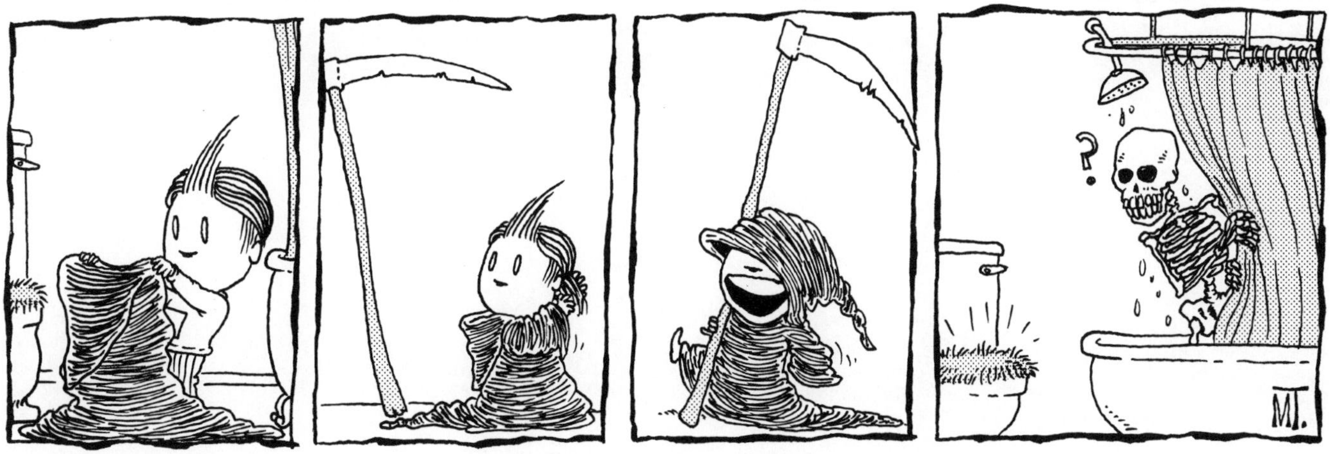

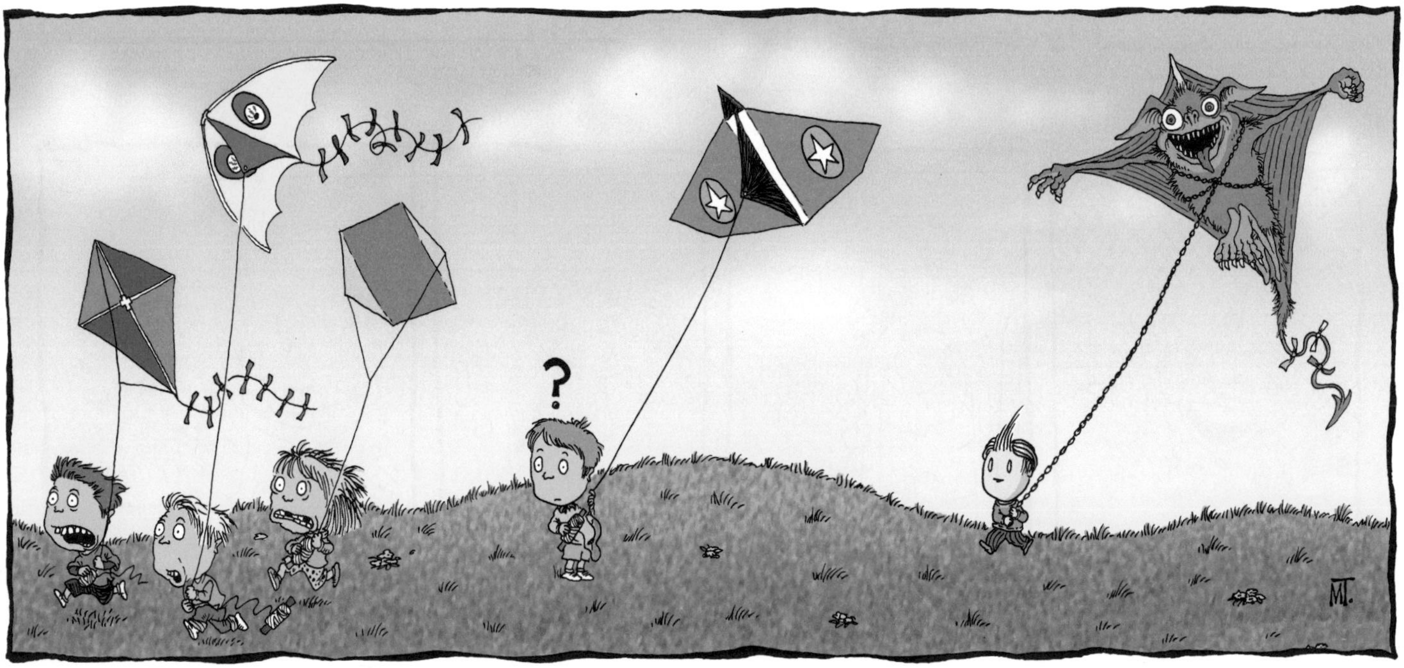
?
MT.

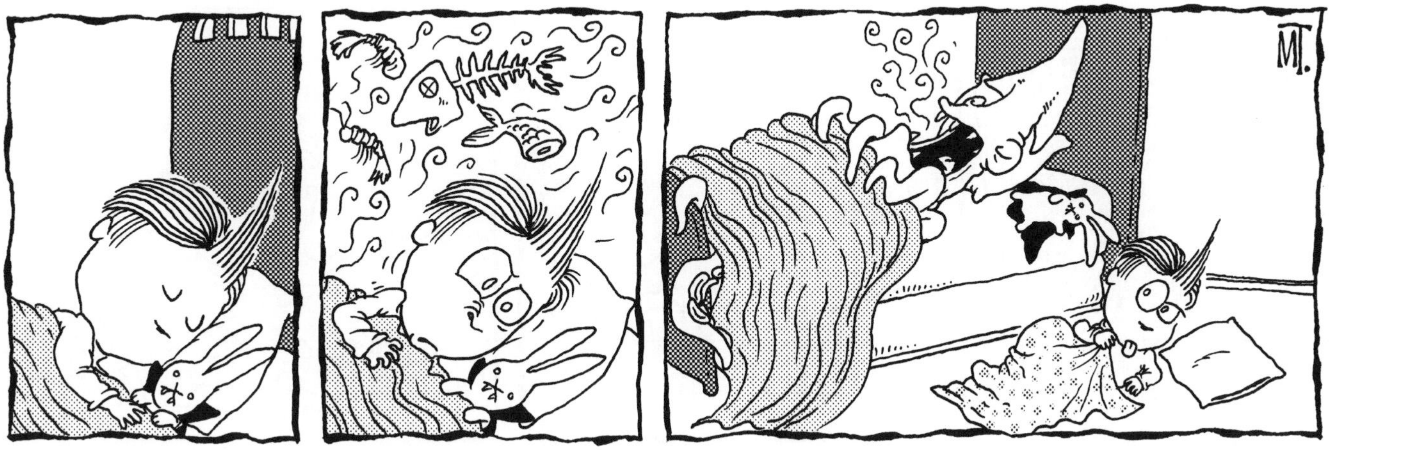
MT.

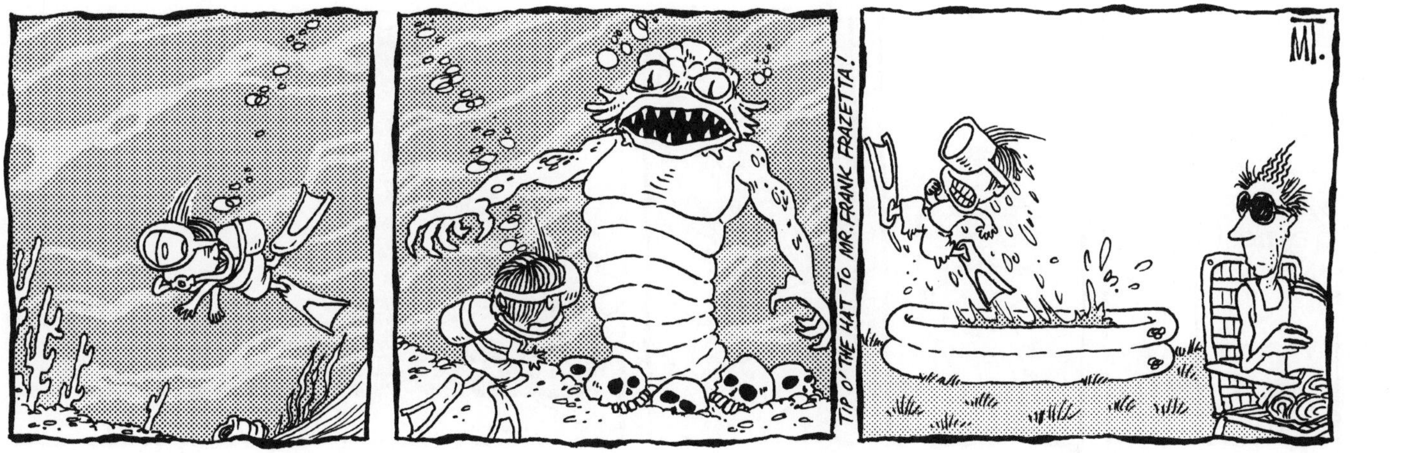
TIP O' THE HAT TO MR. FRANK FRAZETTA!
MT.

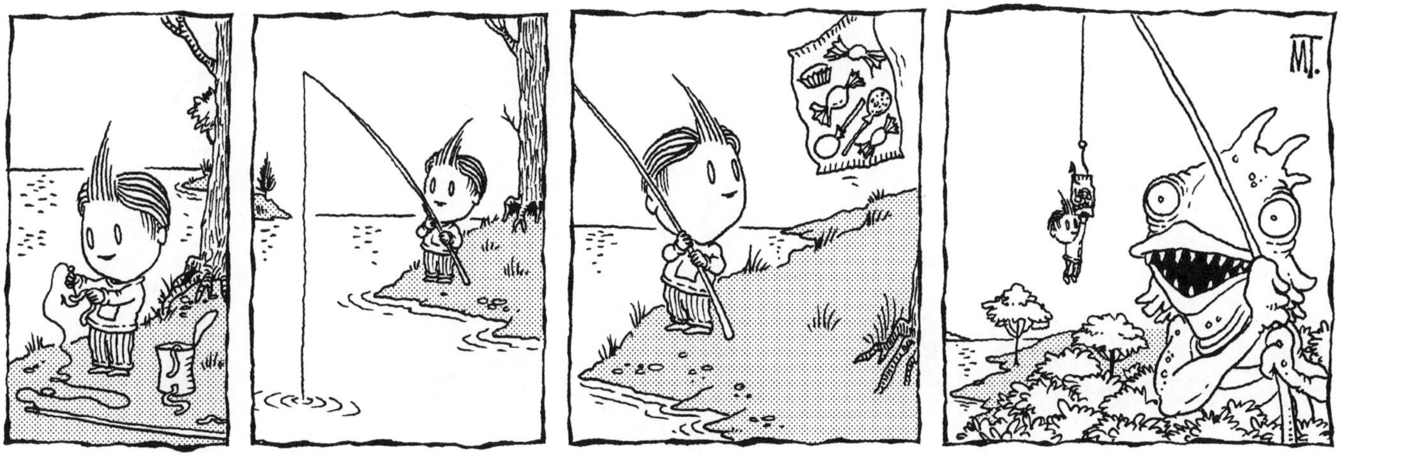
MT.

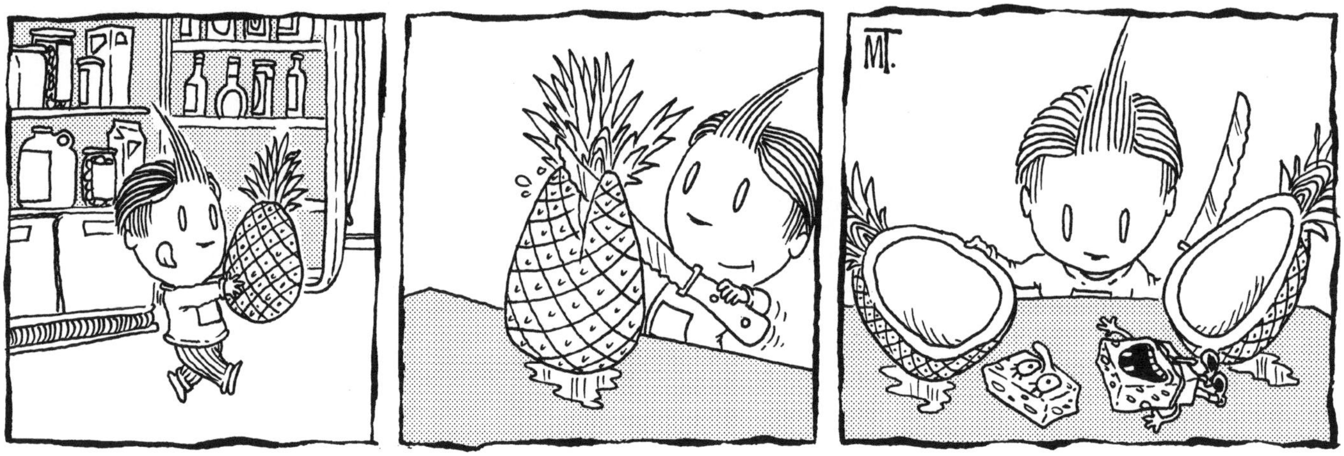

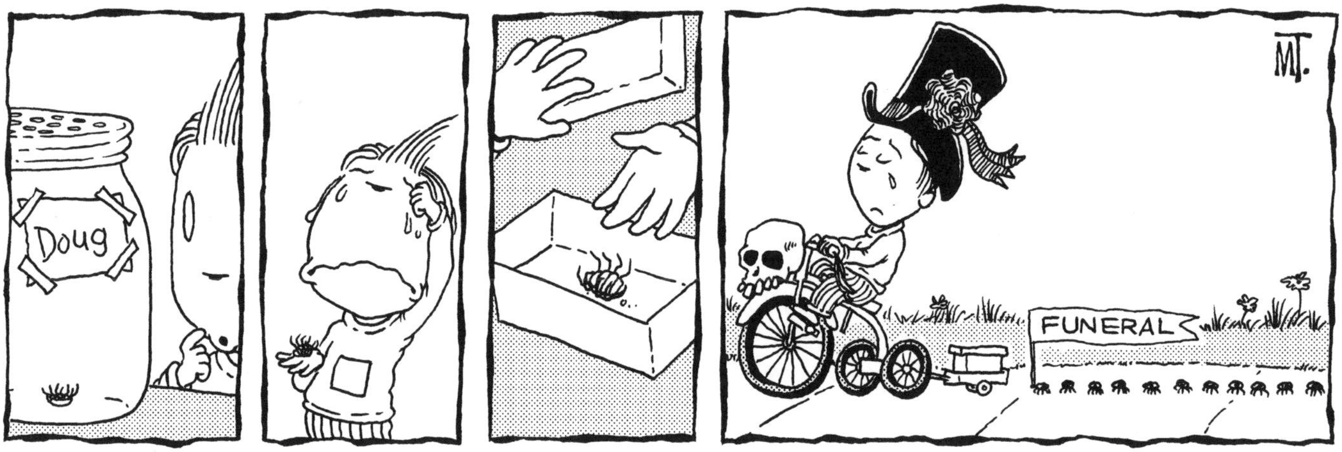
Doug
FUNERAL

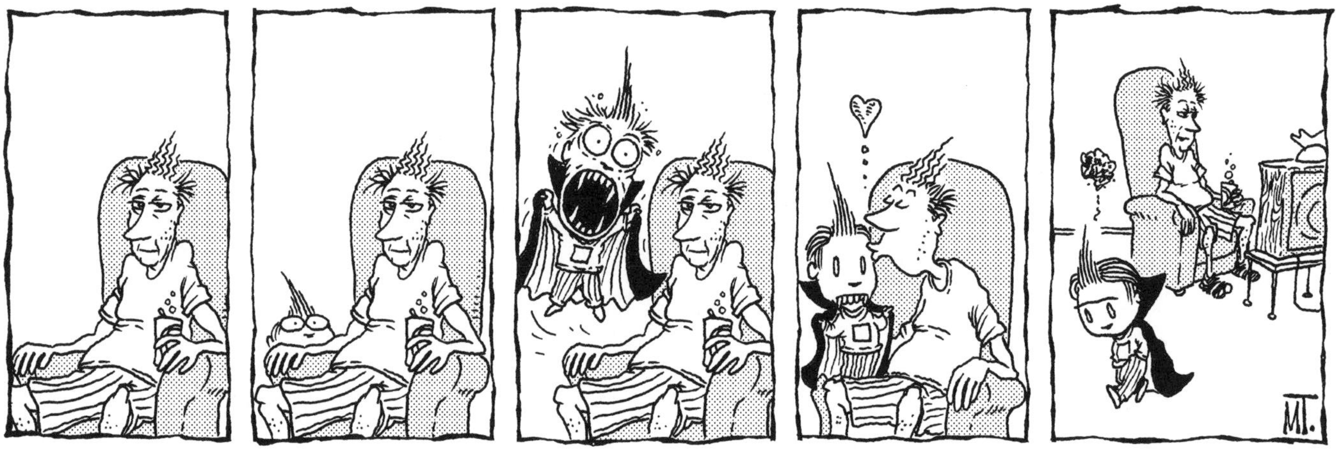

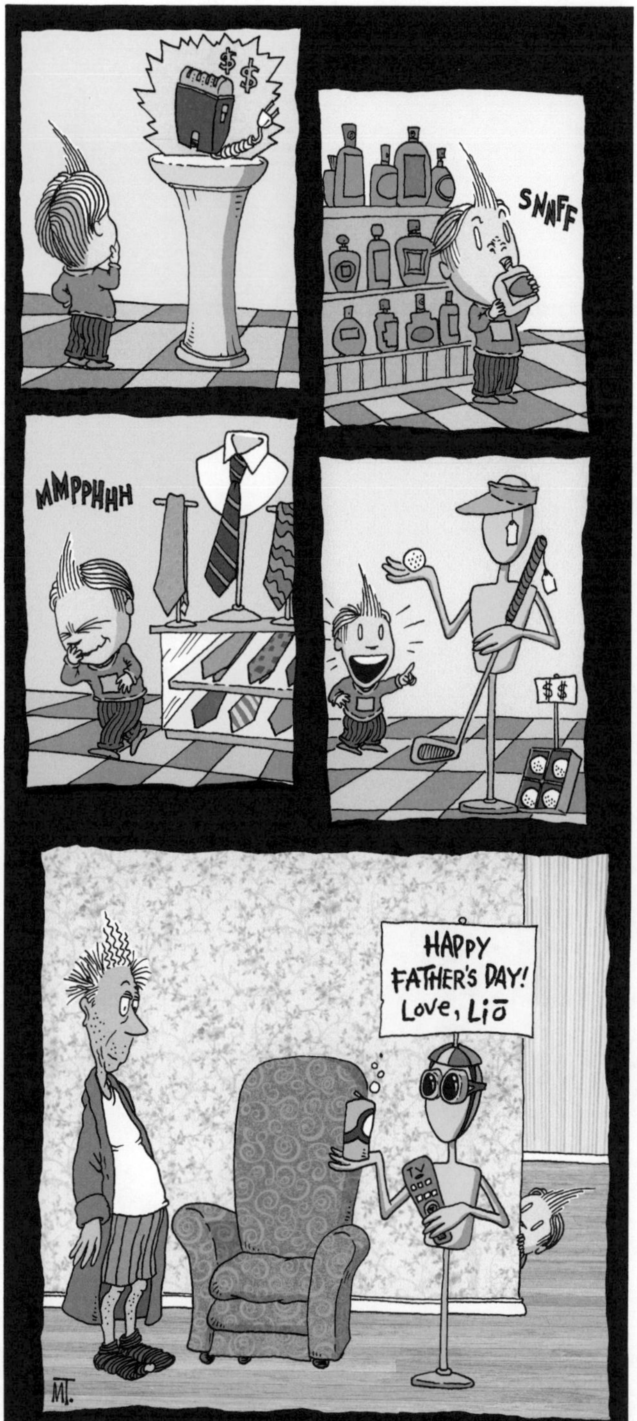
SNAFF
MMPPHHH
HAPPY
FATHER'S DAY!
Love, Liō
MT.